MARRIAGE OF INCONVENIENCE

Terry Bushell

MARRIAGE OF INCONVENIENCE
An Anglo-Soviet Alliance

 ANDRE DEUTSCH

First published 1985 by
André Deutsch Limited
105 Great Russell Street London W1

Copyright © 1985 by Terry Bushell
All rights reserved

Phototypeset by Falcon Graphic Art Ltd
Wallington, Surrey
Printed in Great Britain by
Ebenezer Baylis & Son Ltd, Worcester

ISBN 0-233-977-28 7

Ларе

CONTENTS

Chapter One
A SORDID SCENE

Autumn is beautiful in Moscow. The city is full of trees: some are evergreen while others become red, gold or yellow. The golden onion-topped churches still reflect the sun even if it has lost its warmth; the pastel-coloured buildings still shine; and the girls bravely continue to wear mini-skirts even though they now have to wear thick tights, which rather spoils the effect.

And there I was, the new *Morning Star* Moscow correspondent. Pig-ignorant, I was. I knew very little about the Soviet Union and spoke only a bit of Russian learnt at the last minute. On the way from the airport as we crossed the bridge over the Moskva river I asked if it was the river Volga, which at its nearest point is about five hundred miles away.

At one of the first Moscow receptions I attended a Siberian blonde, flirting mildly with me, said 'You're very young for such a big job.' 'I'm old enough and big enough,' I boldly replied. The world was my oyster, I felt. I was a golden boy, a rising star of labour movement journalism, respected and valued, not the slightest bit anxious about the job. Nor was I worried by the prospect of loneliness, for I'd already made some friends and, what is more, at a party held by one of them – a translator at the Novosti Press Agency publishing house named Igor Borodin – I'd already come very close to having my end away.

Igor's flat being small, with one room doubling as a living room and bedroom, some of us had had to sit on the edge of the bed while eating. Reclining on the bed behind us was a dark-eyed Jewish girl from the Ukraine named Sula, who, alas,

though the night was young, was pissed out of her mind. Tall
and beautiful Sula was, with slender, manicured hands. I was
getting stuck into my *zakuski* when one of these hands alighted
on my thigh. I considered the most appropriate reaction. Should
I shove the hand away? Caress it? I moved to another place.

Three vodkas later, I thought maybe I had been a bit hasty.
Sula no longer being in the room, I went in search of her. I found
her in the bathrom, whither she had repaired for a lie down in
the bath. She looked lovely, the top of her blouse unbuttoned,
her skirt rumpled up to above her knees, her long legs stretched
to the plughole.

She said '*Privyet*' invitingly – 'Greetings.'

'*Privyet*,' I said. Having thus well-nigh exhausted my Russian,
I added lamely, '*Kak dela?*' – 'How are things?'

'*Nichivo*,' she said.

Nichivo literally means 'nothing' but is used all the time to
convey all sorts of meanings, the most common being 'all right'
or 'doesn't matter'.

Locking the door, I joined Sula in the bath. It was very
uncomfortable. Still, she was lovely, 'dark but lovely' like the
bride of the Song of Songs she was named after. Her lips did
indeed seem to drop sweetness like the honeycomb, and her
parted lips exactly put me in mind of a pomegranate cut open.
Unfortunately I never did discover if the curves of Sula's thighs
resembled the work of a skilled jeweller, as did those of the
Shulamite bride, for I was suddenly assailed by the thought:
'What if we're being filmed?' What, I thought, if there was a
camera peeping through the shower nozzle? From there the
scene would appear sordid and absurd. Not only does one read
about these things, but I had actually been warned about it by
my foreign editor. In Russia one should be careful about who
one goes to bath with. Maybe Sula was not as drunk as she
seemed? Suddenly I no longer had the slightest desire to continue
our relationship. Sula said '*Nichivo*' and turned on her side for a
good kip. I went home.

I had a marvellous flat, spacious and bright, two floors up,
across a wide quadrangular courtyard from the main road,
Leninsky Prospect. The only trouble was the noise. The ground
floor of the building facing the road was given over to shops, the

delivery points of which were round the back, in the courtyard. At all hours of the day, lorries thundered in, crashed open their doors, smashed the deliveries onto the pavement, slammed shut their doors, revved up and thundered off, shaking the building and rattling the windows. As if this was not noise enough, the job was done with peculiarly Russian loud acrimony. Sidling their lorries up as close as they could to the walls, the drivers and their assistants jumped from the cabins shouting harshly at the shop assistants who had come out to take the goods. The shop assistants yelled back. Always there was an argument. Sometimes it was about where to stack the goods, sometimes about what had been ordered, sometimes about the timing. All involved seemed, if not actually to enjoy the tumult, at least to welcome the opportunity to let off steam and to define the borders of their small pieces of responsibility.

The inner courtyard, typically, was surrounded by one huge block, with high arches linking the yard to the outside roads. It was like a small, unkempt park. It had a shrubbery in the centre. Children's swings and slides and a flat wooden platform shaped like a boat were always in use (the children playing in fur hats), clothes fluttered on lines, rubbish overflowed from skips, *dyedushkas* – old men – bent over games of chess, dominoes or cards at trestle tables left permanently out in the open, while *babushkas* – beshawled old women – sat on benches chatting and observing comings and goings; and usually there would be at least one young mother rocking a pram while she read or held her face up to the watery sun. The ground was wet and spongy and dotted with puddles that increasingly in the mornings were rimmed with ice. Other correspondents lived in blocks reserved for foreigners. I, as a Communist, was allowed to live in an ordinary flat surrounded by Russians.

The flat had parquet flooring, freshly papered walls, and floor-to-ceiling shelves in the main room and hallway for my books and piles of newspapers. There was a wall unit incorporating a bar and a bureau, both of which smelt of new wood when opened. A table by the window served as a desk with a phone, because the living room was also my office. I did not mind living with my work. On the contrary, I welcomed it. I was a foreign correspondent! I had come a long way.

Chapter Two
A PROLE IS BORN

My old man's old man was a dustman. He lived in the Deptford slums, where he sired twelve children, last of whom was my father – the seventh son of a seventh son. This did not bring my old man as much luck as it is supposed to except that, much later, he was allowed to buy his two up, two down terraced house as a sitting tenant for the give-away price of £1,000.

He married my mother during the war when they were both in their early twenties, with no fear of being called up as he was in a reserved occupation – blacksmith down the gasworks: 'slinging a sledge-'ammer', as he put it.

His interests were cars, boxing and drinking. Now he is only interested in drinking, and he said to me once he does not even really enjoy that. He is so scared of forms that he had a nervous breakdown when buying the house and once asked me to confirm that he had spelt his own name correctly. Lacking the Consolation of Philosophy, he started to bemoan the onset of old age at about forty. 'I've only got a few more years of good living in me,' he would say. A man of narrow intellect and blunted sensibilities, he is by nature what you might call a miserable git. As I grew older my irritation with him became almost incessant. He had a nervous sniff that used to drive me mad. A course of electric shock treatment during his breakdown destroyed his memory so he could not remember the simplest message nor recall of his past any more than a mechanical repertoire of anecdotes. Scared of the slightest responsibility, he would sit with his *Daily Mirror* for ages without turning a page, not reading it but hiding behind it. Crude and obscene when drunk, he would be absurdly puritanical when sober.

I dwell on him rather than on my mother because it was he who fouled me up. I do not know how he did it exactly for it goes deeper than memory, but I was a pathologically shy child, timid and inhibited and a tremendous blusher. In consequence, I avoided people as much as possible and if trapped never spoke. As I had a lively mind and read a lot there developed in me an urge to see the world at the same time as a disinclination to leave my room. In my childhood and adolescence I did little else but play football and read books and by the age of seven I already had two future professions in mind. I wanted to be a footballer and a writer of books.

As a player I was very fast and very skilful. If success in football depended on speed and skill alone I would easily have made it as a professional. But courage and confidence are also needed and I was a coward. My imagination, stimulated by reading, ran riot at the thought of what could happen when unstoppable forward met immovable defender in a clash for the ball. And knocks did seem to hurt me more than other players. It is possible they actually did, for when my son was born doctors said he had unusually sensitive, soft skin, which is hereditary. Possibly I am thin-skinned. So there was that physical problem. And then I had my old man saying regularly in a voice full of anxiety and doubt, 'You won't make the grade, will you.'

At secondary school, composition and English language remained subjects of deep interest: but not one teacher showed the slightest concern to help me develop in them. The teachers were frightfully middle-class, and I remember one actually rebuking us for speaking the way we all did, i.e. Cockney, like our fathers before us. David Holloway notes in his review of Philip Oakes's autobiography how Oakes's brightness is recognised and he is sent to a grammar school where the 'inevitable' sympathetic schoolmaster encourages him. 'Some day,' writes Holloway, 'there is a research thesis to be written about the importance of eccentric schoolmasters in the nurturing of our writers'; while I read somewhere else recently, 'I suppose all English teachers live for the day they catch a budding writer.' I suppose my English teachers lived for something else, not giving a toss about nurturing budding writers.

I got only one GCE, in English of course, which was as good as useless as qualification for any decent job, and began my working life as an office boy at Crosse and Blackwell, famed purveyors of baked beans. I soon gave this up however and spent the next five years drifting from job to job, helping to run an amateur football club and travelling abroad. I worked as a *garçon de cuisine* at a hotel in a Swiss Alpine village called Leukerbad overlooking the Rhône valley, hitch-hiked round Scandinavia, travelled round India and, in the summer of 1968, spent a fortnight watching some East European football in Czechoslovakia and Hungary – where (apart from the football) I liked all that I saw. Left wing and right wing still meant to me only the opposite sides of a football pitch however, so why one Saturday afternoon I got talking to a group of young people conducting a political rant on the pavement, I do not know. But I did. They were members of the Young Communist League. The speaker, when he descended from his platform, came and spoke to me. He was interested in local football and had heard of me. I suppose I was flattered. And there were girls. I joined the YCL.

Chapter Three
SOFTLINERS AND TANKIES

I became engrossed in political and social activities with my new friends. They were, like me, mostly well-read and self-educated and their language was a mixture of colloquial Cockney and 'big' words not ordinarily used by Cockneys, a mixture that echoed my own way with words. We also shared a vulgar jibing humour. I felt relaxed with them in a way I never had with my footballing team-mates. That winter I went on all the weekend rants (at which I did my bit by selling copies of the YCL's monthly magazine, *Challenge*) and to all the Saturday night parties and weekday evening meetings.

Like every group of young people, my new comrades had clear and self-assured ideas about what was good and what was bad. I already agreed with their fundamental ideas, so I went along with their secondary views. When it came to sectarian discussion, however, I stopped even pretending to understand or be interested. The split between hardline tankies and liberal Euro-Communists was very pronounced in the YCL. (Tankies were named after the tanks that had recently rolled into Czechoslovakia, an action they supported. One shy and nervous newcomer, asked to define his position at a meeting, replied hesitantly, 'Well . . . as long as they are small tanks. . . .'). The two groups formed almost two separate organisations. Hardliners, softliners, bin liners, it was all the same to me, but simply because I had enjoyed my week in Czechoslovakia when Dubček had been in power, and had spoken first to Euro-Communists, it was assumed I was a softliner. I went along with it. Softliners' discussions among themselves were not as long and earnest as those of the tankies. I have never had the slightest urge to make points, influence people or convert them, which makes me apathetic in serious discussion. With the softliners I could more easily get away with a little trick I had developed, that of wantonly interrupting a serious discussion with an irreverent witticism or facetious judgment. Not caring to make an impression with my profundity, if I cared at all it was to impress with my wit. This went down well with the Euro-Communists, for it demonstrated their tolerant liberalism, but it did not make me popular with the tankies. If tankies were making their presence felt at a party or meeting I sank without trace. I could think of nothing to say and my friends would keep asking me, 'What's wrong?' If I did attempt conversation it was unnatural. Like someone speaking an imperfectly known foreign language, I said not what I thought but what came to hand. Demos also held no attraction for me. I had no inclination to march or chant or shout with the others. Still, I did attend meetings and go on demos, and do not regret for one minute doing so. Morally and intellectually I was quickened into life by my new friends. I had been prim, nervous, dejected, hunched up. Now, in the warmth of my friends' respect, I unfolded. I expanded and developed. I had had a life outside politics, which was rare in the YCL, most of whose members had political parents. They respected this.

As might be expected, I became especially close to one girl. She was at the very first YCL meeting I attended. On the way to the meeting I had bumped into my Best Friend, and took him along. In the pub after the meeting my Best Friend and I fell to talking with the Girl. She was unhappily married and we were both unhappily celibate. You can imagine what, in the fullness of time, happened.

The Girl fancied me at first. As for me ... you would not believe the number of excuses an inhibited person can find for avoiding intimacy. I tested the water when I should have either stood back or taken the plunge. And she, desperate for total commitment, turned to my Best Friend – without, you understand, wanting to lose me as a Good Pal. Towards the end of it all, the words of the most banal pop song acquired significance, I could not utter her name, food lost its taste, I took to chewing gum like mad (the only time I've ever been able to stand the stuff) and I lost my memory. Life went on: no one suspected my anguish. I even had a couple of affairs; I founded a YCL football team, called Red Star, which gained promotion in its first league season; and – vastly important for me – I had an article on football published in *Challenge*, the first article I ever had published; but I was in a terrible state.

I sought psychiatric help. Having heard of a psychotherapist based near Marble Arch, I saved some money and phoned him. I was very lucky, for he turned out to be extremely helpful. In his late sixties, Dr Gregory had the gift of wisdom as well as that of detachment and compassion combined. A lot of what he said was simply the practical advice of a wise old man who had been around. Nothing I write about those sessions can convey his soft, calm professional manner, his solid immediate answer to my every self-doubt. 'Don't be harsh with yourself,' he would say. He even introduced me to another of his 'friends', an attractive, sensitive girl with whom I hit it off delightfully. And all for £3 per session. He knew I earned little.

It all took time, of course, and you may say that time would have healed me on its own. Maybe, but he took the sting out of my shame almost immediately, and I do believe that without his help I might have been blundering around to this day like a confused adolescent. Life for the unstable introvert is a bed of neuroses. Experience, from which we are supposed to learn, has no effect upon us except to push in ever deeper the sharp anxieties, the inferiority feelings, for whenever we tentatively poke our heads out we get hammered. Sooner or later we are going to think 'Sod this for a game' and withdraw permanently.

Meanwhile – and this also helped my recovery – I was getting very involved with *Challenge*. My writing interests broadened. I wrote first little pieces about football; then about other sports. Then I became features editor. As features comprised half the magazine, it was a responsible job. Some articles I commissioned, some I nicked from other journals such as the American *Daily World*, and some I wrote myself. I wrote headlines and chose pictures. It was all great fun. The work entailed going once or twice a week to the magazine's office on the top floor of the party's headquarters at King Street, near Covent Garden, and attending the monthly editorial meetings where everyone argued over what to include in the next issue.

The serious business of putting the magazine together was

done in a lighthearted manner, for we were a playful bunch. Not only were we out to change the world, we also desired to shock the staid older party members and the tankies. The tankies and softliners differed as to what sort of magazine *Challenge* should be. The former believed it should contain only straight undiluted politics, while the latter thought it should reflect all the interests of the young working class (which was why my articles on football were acceptable). The editor went too far once by putting in a picture of a nude woman, enraging feminists, tankies, nearly everyone. Unrepentant, he published in the next issue some of the complaining letters under the heading, 'No Nudes is Good Nudes?' Another memorable debate followed a front cover of prime minister Ted Heath with fangs. It was poorly done and made *Challenge* look like a joke horror comic, and of course the idea was juvenile anyway.

By now I was also writing football reports for the sports page of the *Morning Star*, covering First Division and FA Cup matches. At this point I conceived an idea for a football novel: what would happen if a professional footballer, at a critical period in his career — say just when a top club is thinking of signing him — goes all to pieces over a girl? It could easily happen, and seemed like a good idea for a novel. Encouraged by Dr Gregory, I began.

He recommended I keep a record of the number of hours worked on it each day and to set a target of so many hours a week. This I did. I wrote ten hours a week in two-hour evening stretches, which was not much; but the book grew. I could now go behind the scenes at professional clubs, thanks to my *Morning Star* press ticket, which helped.

I did not neglect my *Challenge* duties. My enthusiasm in fact led me to a scoop. In the news at that time was a young black athlete named Marilyn Neufville who had been born in Jamaica. She, to the indignation of many, chose to represent Jamaica in the Commonwealth Games at Edinburgh rather than to run for England. She refused to give interviews or talk to journalists. I travelled up to Edinburgh, passed in a message to her in the athletes' village that there was someone at the gate to see her, and when she came, simply said I was from a small left-wing magazine and had come all the way from London solely to see her: surely she could not turn me away? She could easily have turned me away of course; but she did not. She invited me in and, over a cup of tea in the canteen, gave me an interview in which for the first time she made public the detailed reasons for her unprecedented decision. She emphasised that I must not give or sell the interview to any other journal. It was a national scoop, a big story, and it appeared only in *Challenge*, which had a circulation of a few hundred.

Because of this initiative and the quality of my match reports I got a job on the *Morning Star* sports desk, replacing Trevor Hyett, now a television personality. Settling in, I was soon as happy as anyone has ever been on earth. The job seemed made for my talents. The sports editor, Stan Levenson, had trained a whole succession of young journalists, and had done it with such a light hand they did not realise they were being trained. So it was with me. Years later I tried to express my gratitude and appreciation but only succeeded in embarrassing both of us.

I felt very comfortable seated at a typewriter. Soon came the chance to do freelance work for other journals, with the added satisfaction of being paid. I loved every stage of this work too – gathering the material, putting it together into an article, seeing my name in print, and receiving the cheque. (All this still applies: in particular I have never become deadened to the glamour of seeing my name in print.) Somerset Maugham and Dr Johnson were not correct when they wrote that people never appreciate happiness until it is past. For the moment ambition was sated. Having found my niche, I stopped blushing. I felt secure. The low circulation of the *Morning Star* bothered me not at all. *Times*' readers in the last century, when that paper was at the height of its influence, formed no bigger a percentage of the population than did the *Morning Star*'s readers in the 1970s. It was said, by enemies as well as friends, that the *Morning Star*'s influence was out of all proportion to its tiny circulation. But I was not even concerned with influence or lack of it. I was simply content to see my name in print over an article. I felt nothing else: not vain because 20,000 readers were now seeing it as against the few hundred who read *Challenge*, nor humble before the circulation figures of the other national dailies. (The human mind cannot appropriate to its imagination any number larger than a few hundreds anyway; twenty thousand seems to it the same as twenty million.)

When I had finished my novel (which remained unpublished) Dr Gregory informed me I did not really have a novelist's mind. It was not a question of talent. Like Carlyle, I had a powerful imagination but no invention. I had no power to see what was not there. The only fiction that would come naturally to me would be drama, for I could write dialogue. I had noticed these strengths and weaknesses while writing the novel. Dr Gregory had not drawn my attention to them at the time so as not to discourage me, but now he confirmed them. This took some accepting, for I had always wanted to write a novel. Accept it I did, however, for his observation so precisely corroborated my experience. I was not to be a novelist.

Now I had to decide what to do with my time, which meant what to write. In order to lead a satisfying life I had to give pride of place to writing. I did not believe, however, that I would ever write a book again, even a non-fiction work. I knew now the immensity of the job. I would write only articles instead. News articles were written on the spot and were in print the next day, while the longest *Morning Star* features could be done in two or three days. I found I was good – very good indeed – at invective. Attacking people in print was my forte. I delighted in argument and invective on paper, where I could express my feelings without personal confrontation. I really let the insults fly, whereas if I had met any of my victims face to face I would have slunk timidly from their presence. This is only to say I am a coward, not that I was not correct.

Then I was asked to join the party's youth committee with a view to discussing the possibility of my writing a pamphlet on leisure and recreation. The committee met only once every two months. By the time it next met I had finished the pamphlet. I handed out copies of the manuscript to committee members at the same time as being introduced to them. I explained that as I'd had no brief I might have gone beyond the brief I would have been given. Within a few days I was told that the chairman of the committee, national organiser Gordon McLennan, had described it as 'fucking brilliant'.

By the time it was published McLennan had been promoted to general secretary of the party. I received a letter from him written on his first day in his new post regarding some technicalities of producing the pamphlet. The pamphlet received favourable reviews in the *Sunday Times* and *New Society*, but as usual I was not bothered about how many or how few readers I had.

The next thing was, I received a phone call from James Klugmann, editor of the party's monthly theoretical magazine *Marxism Today*: maybe, he suggested, I could write something for him? I wrote two fine articles, devoid of jargon.

It had been a good, productive year. I was well satisfied. Then one day I arrived at work and Stan said, 'Colin Williams is giving up the Moscow job. Why don't you apply for it?'

Dr Gregory thought it was a good idea. I had felt for some time the 'treatment' was over. Dr Gregory continued to see me simply because he liked talking to young people. So there was nothing to hold me in England. I had been at the sports desk for nearly five years and though it was still the best job in the world I could develop no further in it.

The Moscow job would certainly be a challenge, given that I knew little about the Soviet Union and did not speak Russian. I had a couple of points in my favour: the only other serious applicant, who spoke Russian, stipulated he would go for only two years; and I was not a dreaded tankie. After a wait of several months, I was given the job.

I was to stay on at the sports desk for the Montreal Olympics, so that there would be someone experienced at the desk while Stan was covering the event, and depart for Moscow shortly after. I gave an assurance that I would remain there until after the Moscow Games: an Olympiad (an Olympiad is the four-year interval between the Olympics, not the Games themselves). The assistant editor, Chris Myant, said, 'We would like a steady flow of short features.' The foreign editor, Sam Russell, said he would like something that had not been provided for a long time, a picture of how ordinary Russians lived. 'It's the most difficult job in the world,' he said. 'Never forget you're a representative of this paper and the British working class.' Then he warned me about Russian spies. 'Be very careful with the girls,' he said. 'I know an horrific story of an East German who got involved with a Russian girl . . . I won't bore you with it now but . . . it was awful . . . Be careful.'

I did not feel happy about working under Sam. He had once

been Moscow correspondent himself and had made life difficult for all who succeeded him – perhaps he wanted to go down in history as having done the job better than anyone else. He had wanted my rival to get the job, and his opinion would probably have prevailed under the old general secretary and the former editor, who had been confidants of his. The new ones were not. He was an aggressive man, and aggressive people make me nervous, so I had always avoided him and had never spoken to him voluntarily, while he – I think – despised my shyness and naïvety. Having him as my boss bothered me a bit, but not so much as it should have done. Those who do not respect me diminish me. Dealing with Sam I became a fumbling fool. This was going to be a problem.

Chapter Four
YURIAH HEEP AND OTHER PROBLEMS

I inherited from Colin an interpreter/secretary, a Russian teacher and a cleaning woman, all of whom were on holiday when I arrived in Moscow. I did not mind. I had no teletype machine or telex yet so could not be expected to send many articles. I got to know some of the British inhabitants.

Len Wincott had lived in Russia since before the war. He had been in Leningrad during the nine hundred days' siege, when nearly a million died. As an able-seaman he had become famous in 1931 for his part in the Invergordon mutiny, in which men of the Royal Navy refused to take the Home Fleet to sea after the sudden announcement of a cut in basic pay. Upon being released from jail for his part in it he was sent to Leningrad by the Party to spread propaganda among British sailors. Then, after the war, he got a factory job in Leningrad making precision instruments.

One day Len was on a train travelling from Leningrad to Moscow when two men asked him to get off with them. They were security officials and they wanted to ask him a couple of questions. It was night-time.

'There's no station,' said Len.

'That's no problem,' one of the men said, and pulled the communication cord. 'It'll only take a minute.'

Len returned ten years later. He was never told what his crime had been. Most of his stretch was served in the coal mines of Inta, in the Vorkuta region north of the Arctic circle. He was a very bitter man. Harry Pollitt, then general secretary of the

British party, had advised him before he left Britain to adopt Soviet citizenship. He had accepted the advice and regretted it ever since. Though he was married to his third Russian wife and had lived all those years in Russia he still spoke with a Staffordshire accent. He delighted in telling stories of the post-war period in Russia, some of them distinctly tall. Once, he said, he had been sitting in his flat when he heard someone trying his front door. Going out into the passage, he saw a man's hand reaching through the letterbox, searching for a key on a string, or the lock, so he grabbed the hand and tied it so its owner could not withdraw it. Then he called the police. While waiting for them to arrive he heard horrible screams from the outside corridor. When the police arrived they found a headless corpse, its hand still stuck in the letterbox. The thieves had been a professional gang: their trapped colleague would have been recognised by the police. So they cut off his head. Len told me this blood-chilling story in order to impress upon me the importance of having a strong chain on the door, and a peep-hole: a sensible message, although I never had reason to be grateful for it.

Another Briton who had been in Russia since before the war was Bill Campbell, stepson of former *Daily Worker* editor Johnny Campbell. Bill had drifted into show business. Strangely, while Len Wincott, a Communist, was put away for a decade, Bill, who was never in the Party, spent the war entertaining Red Army troops with his song-and-dance act, sometimes at the front. He also had adopted Soviet citizenship (a move he also came to regard as a mistake) so that when, a few months after my arrival, he and his Russian wife Elena wanted to move to Britain, he had to 'defect' while on holiday. He has written an autobiography, *Villi the Clown*.

Colin Williams's predecessor, Peter Tempest, remained in Moscow to work as a translator after giving up the *Morning Star* job. Married to a Bulgarian journalist named Brigita, with two grown-up bilingual children, he kept up all his old contacts and remained informed of what was going on, had a unique collection of ikons and samovars and had snuggled down into a very comfortable expatriate life. A specialist in poetry translation, he was completing an anthology of Bulgarian poetry, a labour of love he had been engaged in for twenty years. When I was introduced to him he said he had meant to write to me to congratulate me on my *Marxism Today* articles.

Campbell Creighton also made a point of keeping himself informed of what was going on but he was not as well placed as Peter, nor was he as comfortable. A Canadian who had worked at the *Daily Worker* in London for several years before going to Moscow, he was now approaching retiring age only to find that he had lived in such a way that no country was obliged to pay him a pension. He was a style editor at a publishing house that specialised in science books.

Diana Miller was another style editor. She worked at *Moscow News*, a weekly paper published for tourists in several languages. She used to have endless loud arguments with the editor of the English edition, Boris Kreshin, over her habit of altering the text of anything she disagreed with. She would for example simply delete the word 'not' from a passage to give it the opposite meaning to what the author intended. Boris would go berserk. 'That is not your job!' he would scream. Diana would continue to argue, giving the reasons why the author, in her opinion, was wrong. 'That is not the point!' Boris would yell. He was right, of course. Diana would call me sometimes in order to conduct a monologue that usually went on till I made some excuse to terminate it. Once, out of curiosity, I did not interrupt, to see how long she could keep it up. It was well over half an hour before she stopped.

One expatriate who became a good friend was Donald Maclean, who had gone to Russia as an idealist in May 1951, on the eve of Stalin's last purge, and had remained an idealist in spite of all he had learnt and experienced since. Not naïve, he yet retained balance and optimism. One cause for optimism, he said, was that no one in the Soviet Union believed the official ideology any more. 'They are relating to the world realistically,' he said. Eleven years after he had fled to Russia, when it was believed in Britain that he was contemplating leaving Soviet territory, a warrant for his arrest was issued 'for offences under Section One of the Official Secrets Act, 1911'. Section One of the Act carries a maximum penalty of fourteen years. He often did leave Soviet territory however, spending holidays in other East European countries.

As a journalist I had known several famous people. The

trouble with being with such people is they are never sure if you really like them for themselves, while you can never forget they are VIPs. Donald was the only VIP I have ever known whom I could talk to and relax with as if he were not a VIP. I admired, liked and respected him. Books and articles in which he is mentioned invariably describe him as having a very unpleasant character, with arrogance as his most conspicuous trait, but he did not strike me as arrogant. After having lived in Russia for thirty years; after being for most of that time an adviser to the Soviet government on foreign affairs; after having written a book published in England, *British Foreign Policy Since Suez*; after all this, when discussing the Soviet Union or world affairs with me, he would often say 'Maybe you're right', or would admit ignorance on some point.

When speaking of Russians or the Soviet Union, he would say 'we' or 'our'. He was not at all interested in emulating Kim Philby and writing his memoirs: he had an 'emotional block' when thinking of that time thirty years ago. It was, he said, a different life, a long time ago, and a painful time, when everybody was looked at 'through frosted glass': he had no wish to recall it. He had begun then the heavy drinking that was to lead to a total crack-up. I saw no sign of his alcoholism. He would sip a glass of wine at dinner but would not even finish it.

Silver-haired and stooping (he was very tall), he was made heavy and slow-moving by drugs that he was taking to keep in check cancer of the prostate. He had a check-up at a clinic every month and entered hospital once a year. The drugs, containing female hormones, made his breasts swell. He also had permanent bronchitis, aggravated by the Russian winter and heavy smoking. He reckoned that some of Graham Greene's spy stories 'get close to the truth imaginatively', as does Le Carré's novel *Tinker Tailor Soldier Spy*.

Donald was facing a lonely retirement. His wife Melinda and his two sons had already chosen to live in the West and now his divorced daughter, also named Melinda but called Mimsy, was talking of remarrying and taking her family to Britain. Donald loved her child of the first marriage, his granddaughter. He once said to me, 'Children are a comfort in your old age.' (Melinda married her fiancé, artist Sasha Druchin, two years later and two years after that went with him and her daughter to live with her mother in New York, leaving Donald absolutely alone.) Donald, already semi-retired, spent a lot of time at his *dacha*, writing a second book on foreign affairs. Bob Evans, head of the Reuters' Moscow bureau, used to phone him occasionally for his assessment of some international development. Reuters had been in contact with him ever since their correspondent John Miller (now of the *Daily Telegraph*) found out in 1962 where he lived. At that time the whole British press wanted to know Donald's plans and his reaction to the issuing of the warrant for his arrest, but no one knew where he lived. Then as now, the Moscow telephone directory was published in such ludicrously limited numbers that from the ordinary person's point of view it did not exist – phone booths never contain it, to this day. But Miller happened to have a directory, and Donald's name, number and address were in it. While everyone else was searching desperately for this famous spy whom the Russians had hidden away, Miller found him by looking in the phone book.

Another expatriate I met was a girl called Jan, who went to one of Britain's most exclusive girls' public schools, whose father was Master of the Wilton Hunt, and who was about to marry the Russian poet Yevgeni Yevtushenko. I met her through him after I had covered a poetry festival in which he had starred. This poetry festival was the first big story I covered in Moscow. It was supposed to be the revival of an annual event that had ceased to be held in 1966. (Although packed out and successful, it was in fact not held again.) Yevtushenko gave me some quotes, in English, which enabled me to write a reasonable story. Otherwise, although I attended the festival, I could not have written more than two paragraphs because my Russian was not yet good enough and, I had discovered with dismay, I had been lumbered with an interpreter who did not speak English.

Yuri Tikhaze came from Tallinn to study at the Moscow Institute of International Relations (MIMO). There seem to be cases when one of the qualifications for MIMO is a Very Important Parent. Yuri's father was head of the graphics department at Tallinn polytechnic, a doctor of art criticism, a professor, and a painter in water-colours who got his work exhibited at Moscow's central art salons. In one Moscow joke two men meet in New York. 'How much watch?' asks one.

'Six watch.'

'Such much!'

And they embrace, recognising each other as MIMO English graduates.

When a MIMO graduate becomes your interpreter it ceases to be funny.

Colin had described Yuri as a 'nice lad'. As Colin had already been in Moscow five years when he acquired Yuri he had no need of an interpreter and by the time I arrived Yuri had become used to an eleven o'clock start and a four-hour lunch break with the rest of the day off. We first met a month after I arrived. When I got to know him better I realised he had taken his holidays at that time to avoid helping me settle in. At first I thought we could be friends. But there were two barriers to this: his English was not good enough and I did not like him. Slippery, obsequious, thin and round-shouldered, he only needed to start rubbing his hands together to be a dead ringer for Uriah Heep. I needed a lot of things done, and he was never around.

At a Leningrad factory I interviewed a worker whose mother tongue was not Russian. 'Does he speak with an accent?' I asked and Yuriah Heep turned to him and dully repeated, 'Do you speak with an accent?'

When interpreting he would lose the thread early on and simply stop, saying it was not interesting, or he would translate half the words as 'Thing'.

On one occasion his inability to interpret possibly cost me a good story. We had gone by car to the science town of Dubna. We were very late. Yuriah had looked at a map of the Soviet Union, seen that Dubna was only a quarter of an inch from Moscow and reckoned the journey would take just a couple of hours. We arrived in the late afternoon of a one-day trip. We had missed most of my appointments and what with that and science being almost another language in itself, Yuriah was having a miserable time. He did not understand half of what the scientists were saying even in Russian. We visited an experimental nuclear reactor. As we peered into a particle accelerator, the physicist was rabbiting away about colliding electrons and positrons and how the energy generated there was several times greater than that of the H-bomb, and then he said with a wry chuckle something about how once they had 'nearly lost one'.

'What?!' I said. 'What did they lose? Uh? Yura, what did they lose?'

But my sudden animated interest had alerted the physicist to the possibility that he should not have said it, so he would not repeat it.

Yuriah Heep would never translate articles for me. Once I insisted I wanted a written translation of an article and he prevaricated for weeks and then finally said he had lost it. I gave him another copy, again saying I wanted a written translation, and he said he would give an oral translation. No, I said, I did not have time. When I next mentioned it some days later he said he would speak it into a tape recorder. Then I realised he could not write in English. And I never did get the article. Not one translation did I ever receive from him.

Eventually, after a sleepless weekend thinking about it, I reported him. His superior knew all about him, sympathised with me and said nothing could be done immediately because such a serious thing as a sacking had to be decided higher up. Meanwhile, did I think a good talking-to would help? No, I did not. But Yuriah obviously was spoken to for a few days later he said to me, monotonely, 'Terry, are you satisfied with my work?' I replied weakly, 'Well, I would like you to look through the papers with me sometimes,' which was not even true because the last thing I wanted was Yuriah Heep in my flat first thing in the morning.

A TASS teletype machine was finally installed, an ungainly, old-fashioned noisy contraption that stood in my hallway banging out all the news fit to print. I, who had always loved silence, now had to live with this monster. I must have picked up some Russian by then because I remember talking to the mechanic who installed it. 'A world war could have broken out and I would not have known,' I joked.

'Don't say it,' he replied.

Another monster, the telex machine, for articles and personal messages to and from London, stood in my living room. Every now and then it would light up and clatter and spew a few words from Sam, and I soon found that I was dreading these occasions. His favourite expression in those days was, 'I'm surprised you didn't do so-and-so.' He would never discuss anything, and would not even tell me how long an article should be. Because of the pressure of space at the *Morning Star* it was customary for reporters to ask how long each story should be. Sam always did before he wrote an article. Many stories can be dealt with in anything from two paragraphs to twenty. Sam would answer, 'As long as a piece of string' or 'Whatever you think it's worth.' On the 25th anniversary of Stalin's death he came on in the evening and said, 'The *Telegraph* man went to the grave and saw the flowers laid on it. I'm surprised you didn't go.' Later it was the centenary of Stalin's birth and I asked, 'Shall I go to the grave?' 'If you want to be morbid,' Sam replied. I felt that I could never get any sense out of him.

Incidents such as this used to leave me with a feeling of scalding hatred. No doubt someone whose self-confidence was more robust could have taken them in his stride, but they knocked me off balance and gave me real pain, and I couldn't help feeling that Sam knew this. I would sit there thinking that the greatest sin of all is hurting another person without cause, and Sam liked doing that to me.

And then came the Russian winter. The fizzy drink machines were removed from the pavements, a second set of doors was added to the metro stations, and life was shaped by snow and ice. The cold did not bother me but I hated the permanent snow and ice. I began to feel I had made a mistake. There were many different sorts of journalism and I had gained proficiency in only one. Being a sports reporter was very different to being a foreign correspondent. I was confused; I had no judgment. I could not decide which press conferences were worth attending; once there I did not know what was worth noting; and when writing up my notes I could see no angle. My tendency to see the worst in everything led me to write critical articles, which were not really what were required and which the editor put a stop to. I felt isolated and confused and very lonely. The Moscow job involved experiences almost totally irrelevant to the world I knew. My upbringing had not prepared me for the world into which I had so ambitiously won a precarious way. Four years was going to be a long time through which to carry my commitment without refuelling from outside sources. I did not see how I could last out.

I was crossing the very wide Lomonovsky Prospect one afternoon in January: it was only three o'clock but already dark. Filthy dappled grey snow was banked up along both sides of the road, making it narrower. I slipped on a patch of ice and fell. I thought, 'There's a way out of this. I shall have to get myself expelled.' Dispirited though I was, I could not entertain the idea of simply packing my bags and catching a plane to London. I had a very strong feeling that if I did this, *Sam would have won*!

He himself had nearly been expelled, for revealing that General Zhukov had been sacked: and Sam's successor, Dennis Ogden, had also come close to expulsion when in April 1961 he jumped the gun on man's first space flight with a story describing what he believed had been an earlier flight in which the cosmonaut, said to be the son of a leading Soviet aircraft designer, had been injured on landing. The paper's then editor, George Matthews, supported Ogden in his refusal to name his sources for a story which he now believes related to a first aborted launch attempt. And one young Canadian Communist correspondent had had to be recalled because he was a junkie. But I had no contacts from whom to get scoops and no inclination to get hooked on drugs. The only other method – politically unacceptable stories – would not get past the editor. I was stuck. I resolved I would hand in a year's notice while on holiday in the summer. That meant only another eighteen months in the job, which could be faced.

Relief was provided by trips. The Soviet Ministry of Foreign Affairs (MID) organised trips around the country for groups of correspondents. One trip, for Communists only, was to the world's most northerly town, Norilsk, in the Arctic circle. On the plane we were handed out information sheets, on which was stated baldly: '*Klimat – Arktichesky*'. Our pilot told us the temperature at Norilsk stood at minus 45 degrees centigrade.

Arriving in late afternoon, in the dark of the polar night, we scurried across squeaking snow towards the indistinct mass of the airport terminal, our faces stinging. On the bus into town we could see nothing: the windows were opaque with ice. I had read that if you slowly pour out a glass of water here it turns into an icicle before reaching the ground. I asked one of our guides if this was true and he laughed and said, 'Only if you pour it out very slowly.' (I never got round to trying it myself: I forgot.)

We climbed out of our bus onto a square where stucco buildings loomed dark and still. We entered the nearest of them, our hotel, through an airlock of successive doors. Some local officials were in the foyer to meet us, including a very attractive woman. Up in the suite which I was sharing with an Italian – an old Moscow hand – I peered out of a taped-up, triple-glazed window at a typical town scene: traffic, people shopping and waiting for buses and even a man on the pavement with no coat over his shirt hurriedly saying goodbye to a couple departing in a car. The people waiting for buses were stamping their feet and covering cheeks and noses with their hands but you see that on cold days in Moscow. Life here in the Arctic in many ways went on as normal. Later, under my 'envelope' stuffed with blanket, I let my mind get used to where I was.

Norilsk, now asleep in the rigid night, had been founded in 1921 when the expedition of geologist Nikolai Urvantsev set up a wooden hut. The local Dolgani people regarded the area as magical, and believed these geologists were devils. Possibly the geologists did behave like devils at times, for in the same way that British sailors receive a ration of rum they were issued pure alcohol.

Despite this, and despite the fact that they were looking for coal, they found deposits of nickel-copper, the importance of which was not realised until 1935, when a special commission authorised construction of a metallurgical combine. It was believed that only people under thirty could work here, and only for a short time, but the combine's first director insisted on older experts coming, which meant families settling. On July 1, 1935, a ship brought the first group of construction workers. A railway had to be built to the nearby harbour of Dudinka. The first train travelled on this line, still the most northerly in the world, in 1937. People came here to work from all over the country, attracted by the good money and long holidays.

Breakfast the next morning was in the hotel bar, at a long counter, behind which the shapely waitress fried eggs (called *glazunya*, from the Russian word for 'eyes') and paraded with swaying hips in the most brazen manner I have ever seen. She made eyes for us and at us.

After breakfast we set out for the first item on our programme, an interview with a mine director. When the temperature is minus 45 degrees centigrade the slightest movement in the air, too slight even to be called a breeze, hits your face like a bunch of stinging nettles. Fur-hatted citizens hurried along the pavements, protecting faces with gloved hands. Buses, lorries and cars filled the roads with traffic, a reminder that Norilsk was a busy town of 168,000. My glasses kept icing over, becoming white and useless.

In the evening we each visited a separate family. A journalist of the town's daily paper accompanied me to my family. The husband was a tractor driver and his wife a house decorator. They had a thirteen-year-old daughter who remained in her room. It was very hot in the flat, so hot that even though it was Arctic weather outside they had to open the *fortochka*, the little inset double window. They had come here as a young couple from the Black Sea. She told of how she worried when a blizzard prevented him getting home. If his tractor broke down in the tundra he had no choice but to repair it himself for only then could he get in the warmth of the cab. A colleague in that situation had once been unable to repair his tractor and had frozen to death. Their daughter went to school no matter how cold it was, unlike in Moscow where schools close if the mercury touches minus 28. 'If we were to take any notice of the mercury, schools would be closed most of the winter,' he said. After a few vodkas, the journalist entertained us with dirty jokes. Obviously titillated by the proximity of a young girl, he would precede each joke with an ostentatious glance at the door.

It was an interesting trip. I saw lemonade being delivered frozen solid in the bottles. I heard of wine freezing so that the barrels had to be smashed open and the wine sold in lumps. ('Two medium lumps of Riesling, please'.) We ate braised reindeer. And, as a special favour, I was driven out to a reindeer farm where I bought a pair of boots with reindeer fur inside and outside. I had never before experienced anything like that odourless, colourless, unbroken white landscape. The fields around Moscow were dotted with trees and bushes and huts: even the area surrounding Norilsk contained snow barriers, telegraph poles, pipelines, abandoned vehicles. Here there was nothing. It was an ocean of snow.

My visit to the Arctic circle was spoiled by sexual jealousy. My Italian room-mate had hit it off with the attractive official. He would go off with her in the evenings and not return till the early hours of the morning, the dirty rotten lucky git. I lay in my bed, jealous, kept awake by images of swaying hips and inviting eyes and was glad when we left.

Another interesting trip was to Uzbekistan. This was the land of Tamerlaine, the region whose romance, legends and history had attracted such illustrious travellers as Marco Polo, Sven Hedin and Fitzroy Maclean; and now Terry Bushell, with his intrepid interpreter Yuriah Heep.

Tashkent looked neither ancient nor oriental. Modernisation had already begun by 1966, when a third of the city, including the centre, was razed by an earthquake. Thousands of buildings were destroyed. Rebuilt, the old caravan town on the Silk Road to China, the rich oasis along the Jaxartes, was now a concrete industrial city the size of Glasgow. We visited the earthquake memorial, erected near the epicentre, part of which simulated a wide crack in the ground. Seismologists at the Uzbekistan Academy of Sciences told us that the whole of Soviet Central Asia is part of a long seismic zone stretching from the Atlantic to the Pacific, called the Asian Mediterranean. The Soviet part of this zone repeatedly has quakes of nine to ten on the Richter scale. In the Kuizuilkum desert alone there are a thousand underground tremors a year. Leaving the seismologists, we made the usual rounds – a sprawling petro-chemical plant, a cement works, a cotton mill ('the biggest in the world') – before going on to Samarkand, which is more oriental in appearance and which contains the tomb of Tamerlaine. He would turn in his tomb if he could see how some of his heirs carry on – dancing to western music in western clothes procured from western tourists. The Golden Road to Samarkand is an Intourist holiday on which 47,000 foreigners go every year. In the market a tanned young man sitting behind a heap of melons assumed I was Czech and said, 'Joseph Masopust – great footballer.' When I informed him I was English he said, 'Bobby Charlton – even better.' I countered with 'Oleg Blokhin – better still.' My knowledge of football came in handy for we were able to chat for a while, after which he knocked fifty kopecks off a melon.

Intourist holiday towns were not of much interest to my colleagues, most of whom had been enticed onto this trip by the promise of a visit to a desert township called Gazli, which had been flattened by an earthquake a few months before. In Samarkand our MIDman announced this part of the programme had been cancelled: the correspondents made such a fuss it was hurriedly re-instated. We went there by bus from Bukhara one afternoon, with several correspondents worried that we would arrive too late for them to take photographs.

The road was a thread of asphalt in the Kuizuilkum desert, running for 107 kilometres from Bukhara. Soon after leaving Bukhara the air became thicker, hotter, heavier. Camels chewing at the dry grass by the roadside moved away as our bus passed. The roadside was littered with discarded tyres, bottles, boxes. The grey sand, studded with saxaul bushes, stretched to the horizon on both sides of the road, glistening with salt from a prehistoric inland sea. The saxaul had been planted to stop the sand shifting. The winds and sandstorms, we were told, could be ferocious: one man that summer had tried to escape from an *afganets* (a wind from Afghanistan) by diving into a pool of water – but the sand had soaked up the water in seconds, leaving him lying there dry.

Gazli, built as a geologists' settlement after the discovery in 1956 of a large deposit of gas, now had a population of 13,000. It had been torn apart by a quake much stronger than the Tashkent tremor. Heaps of smashed bricks and broken household utensils and bits of furniture were still lying in the sand when we arrived, with areas looking as if they had been cleared for a motorway, and houses gaping to the sky with big cracks in what was left of the walls. We reached it just before dusk. The *Financial Times* correspondent, a young American called David

Satter, was to write melodramatically, 'I was the first foreigner to reach Gazli.' There were twenty of us in the bus, and he was not even sitting in the front. Those with cameras quickly took their pictures. Hundreds of soldiers in the Red Army's light floppy summer tunics and stetsons were helping with the reconstruction. Bulldozers churned up the sand and left their tracks between rows of temporary bungalows. The town was one huge building site. In the playground of a temporary school some Kazakh children told us what they had been doing at the time of the tremor. Some had been in classrooms, others had been playing football. The sand had churned like a sea, they said, and bricks had jumped as if alive. After the quake, because of the danger from partly destroyed buildings, they had been evacuated to other parts of the country, and had seen for the first time lilies-of-the-valley, birches, firs and pines.

We attended a press conference in the 'Headquarters for the Liquidation of the Consequences of the Earthquake'. Gazli, we were informed, had not been regarded as a strong seismic area. The new houses would be able to withstand much stronger tremors, having metal frames and 'seismic belts'.

I had a lot of material on earthquakes. Back in Moscow, I used some of it in an article on Gazli, then set about arranging the rest and gathering more for a full-length general feature.

On the night of March 4, 1977, came the quake that devastated Romania, with its 'echoes' across half of Europe, from Rome to Moscow. In Moscow people rushed out into the dark streets, some scantily clothed, and then did not know what to do. Of those properly dressed some went for a walk while others tried to get the number of the seismology institute from telephone enquiries. After a time the switchboard operators refused to give the number, saying they were sick of such calls. Those that did get through were told, 'Go to bed. There is no danger.'

I was watching the world figure-skating championships on television when it happened, just before ten-thirty, and felt nothing. Perhaps this was because I was living in a very solid brick building, or because I was not high up, or because the building was standing on firm rock. Up the road near the university the tremors were felt strongly. Floors and walls rocked and chandeliers swayed, causing some people to feel giddy and wonder what was wrong with themselves. In the university itself, a towering building on top of the Lenin Hills, two students were sitting together on a sofa and one, seeing the chandelier sway and the wall tilt but not believing her eyes, thought, 'I'm overworking, I'll give up my studies, enough is enough,' and as she thought it the other said it.

Diana Miller phoned me the next morning to tell me she knew a girl who lived on the top floor of a fourteen-storey block of flats who had felt the building sway and had rushed down the street. Not yet knowing that what had happened in Romania would overshadow all other stories of the quake, I was interested in this girl's experience both for my feature and for a possible news story. Diana, after giving me the girl's phone number, went on and on about her latest argument with Boris. Having lived in Africa for a while, she regarded herself as an authority on that continent, and had made wholesale changes to a report on Kenya, translated from the Russian, that she was only meant to be scanning for poor English. She and Boris had had an argument in the corridor, loud and long, of which she proceeded to give a verbatim report. I virtually hung up on her in the end, saying, 'There's someone at the door, I have to go, 'bye,' and then dialled the number she had given me of Lara, the girl who had felt the earthquake.

Chapter Five
A RED LETTER DAY

'*Mozhno govorit po-Angliski?*' I said. 'Can we speak in English?'

'If you like,' Lara said.

I introduced myself. 'I understand you felt the earthquake. I wondered if you could tell me about it.'

'What do you want me to say?'

'Just tell me what it felt like.'

'It wasn't very nice, it was rather frightening. People were rushing out of the buildings all around. Nobody shouted, there was no panic, they were more embarrassed than anything else.'

That was all she could say about the earthquake. She sounded annoyed at being called. Always easily discouraged if I feel that I am intruding, I hung up with no further questions.

Impressed by her English, and remembering that Diana had told me she was a freelance translator, I phoned again the next day to ask if she would translate two articles for me. She did not sound very keen, telling me she already had more work than she could handle, but she agreed to do them. I took the articles to her on the evening of March 8 – International Women's Day, a public holiday, a red letter day in the Soviet calendar. She lived in Vavilov Street, not far from me, and I walked there through the thick, dirty slush of early spring, dressed in my bulky British sheepskin overcoat. There was a smell of mud and dampness. Red-faced women, padded and bescarfed, chopped at the soft ice on the pavements with mattocks and spades. Poplars and bushes were planted all around Lara's block. Snow-water

dripped from the building. Unnatural mounds of snow surrounded it, the snow that had been hurled with shovels down
from the roof. Cylinders of ice as thick as legs lay beneath the
rusty drainpipes, ice which had formed in the pipes throughout
the winter and which now, thawing, had broken and fallen out.
Icicles dripped from the porch. I took the lift up to Lara's floor
and rang the bell. She came to the door. I was confronted by a
beautiful young woman. She had long straight auburn hair
down to her waist, Tatar eyes and was wearing high-heeled
shoes and a mini-skirt. We were exactly the same height but her
shoes made her fractionally taller. She struck me as a vision of
flawless femininity. I believe I gulped. 'I'm the *Morning Star*
correspondent who phoned,' I said. She lowered her Apache
eyes shyly as she said hello, and gave a funny little curtsey
through nervousness. She invited me in. Already in the flat were
two young men and a fourteen-year-old boy. She did not
introduce me. We sat in the small kitchen, me on a low, lumpy
settee. Dirty crockery was piled up in the sink. A bunch of fresh
mimosa was stuck in an empty wine bottle on the formica table.
The windows were sealed with newspaper and cotton wool. The
young men and the boy stayed mostly in the living room but
occasionally came into the kitchen for different things and to
have a butcher's at me. I showed her the articles, which I was
only marginally interested in. They were not important. I was
not looking my best. Even with my bulky winter coat off I still
looked chunky and overweight. I had been eating too much
during the winter (a sensory pleasure over-indulged for an
obvious psychological reason) and was wearing a heavy woollen
pullover that was too warm for Lara's well-heated flat. I was
sweaty. My face was shining and my glasses kept slipping down
my hooter, necessitating an inelegant push back up. Lara told
me later she felt I had looked comical in my shapeless tent-like
coat but had been impressed by my self-possession. There had
been a time when being in a small kitchen with an attractive
female would have made me squirm with anxiety. Although this
was no longer the case I still could not think of anything to say
and was not really at ease. Like many others, she had mistaken
my defensive mask, my dead-pan look, for self-possession. She
saw strength in me where none existed. I stayed a while, saying

little, eating fried spuds she was cooking for everyone in a frying pan without a handle.

That was the first of many such meetings and the detailed memory of it is lost in a palimpsest of all the others. The articles never were translated. She really did have too much work. We attempted for a while to do them together but as neither of us was really interested in them we kept digressing. She asked me if I didn't have a secretary for such work and I told her about Yuriah Heep. The other three were always there, and I discovered who they were: flatmate Valera, neighbour Igor and nephew Sasha. I resented their constant presence. I also discovered it had been a solecism not to have taken Lara some little present on Women's Day. All women receive some gift from all the men in their lives on this day, the most popular presents being chocolates and perfume, usually accompanied by a bunch of flowers. I had noticed men in the streets carrying flowers wrapped in cellophane or decorative paper, and the long queues of fur-hatted men at flower shops. Red flags had been put up on lamp posts and buildings and even buses had jaunty little red flags stuck on their bonnets. March 8 became an official holiday in the Soviet Union in 1965 for the same reason that January 1 did in England – no one was doing any work on it anyway. Ironically, men benefited more than women because women had always been let off at midday, so women gained only half a day while men gained a whole day.

I fell into the habit of going to Lara's flat every evening. She would cook a meal, often fried potatoes and diced garlic sausage. My portion was my supper: hers was usually her breakfast. She worked all night and slept during the day. It is a mistake to work such hours unless you have to, putting you out of step with everyone else. Lara's sleep was constantly interrrupted.

I got the impression she was having a difficult time. Though in our conversations she was alive to every nuance of meaning (and this in English) she had a desperate brightness, as though she was forcing herself to go through the motions of living. I soon discovered that the troubles were overwork and loneliness. She took her work seriously, and it weighed heavily on her. Her bread-and-butter regular work was for *Moscow News*. She took great care over articles and stories that were so bad in the original that no one would have known or minded if she had skipped through them as quickly as possible. But this was not her way. She insisted on thinking carefully about nearly every sentence. Although I argued with her over this I knew that it was this meticulousness in her nature that had enabled her to learn English as well as she had. She always devoted herself totally to the job in hand, no matter what it was. There was nothing shallow or artificial about her. I learnt how much friends meant to her, how friendship was the deepest need of her nature. All experience was meaningless to her if it was not shared – and she told me how her closest friends had all recently left Moscow to live elsewhere, their departure drowning her world in a mist that poisoned and eroded her spirit. Living in Moscow with no residence permit, she felt lonely and vulnerable, leading a semi-homeless existence that could end only in her marrying a Muscovite for the Moscow registration, or being expelled from the city.

She was also very worried about her older sister Anya, who was also footloose in the capital. Lara and I went to a party once where Anya was drunk and with an unpleasant man, and on the way home, on the path among the poplars and bushes, Lara suddenly burst into tears. Bewildered, I could do or say nothing to comfort her. She was embarrassed by it and waved me on, away, and ran into the shrubbery to cry in private. I sat on a bench and waited till she emerged. I had never seen such intense crying. This was not sobbing, but a psychical retching. I could not believe it was just over the plight of Anya. Lara was indeed very close to her sister: but Anya had simply been drunk at the party to which she had been accompanied by an undesirable male – not an ideal state of affairs but not one warranting the paroxysm tearing Lara apart. No, it was not only Anya that Lara was crying for: it was for herself as well.

And Lara too had been drinking. She was drinking a lot at that time. A bottle of wine was always finished off with our fried potatoes. I did not believe her heavy drinking was necessarily permanent and wanted to help her find some sort of peace, even though I knew the impact upon my own life would be consider-

able. Although there was a danger she was naturally a despair-
ing person, I believed I could help. I was sensitive and sincere,
the two prerequisites for helping, and it was worth it, for at her
best she had a joyful spontaneity that infected all who knew her,
an inspiring enthusiasm. She valued sincerity more than any
other virtue. I hoped I might help her to stop wasting so much
psychic energy on barren preoccupations such as guilt or
remorse. I did not doubt her stability. She had achieved too
much. To learn a subject as well as she had learned English was
an achievement beyond an unstable person.

In my mind there was one condition to my hanging around. I
was not going to accept a platonic relationship. I could never
accept simply being a friend. Physical attraction was far too
strong for that. If some obstacle to the consummation of our
relationship appeared I would stop seeing her. This would be
definite if the obstacle was another man in her life.

We went to other parties. One was at the flat of Barry and Joy
Jennings, translators for the Progress publishing house who
were leaving soon after their two-year stint. Lara called him
'Barrichka'. I was jealous, especially as my name also lent itself
to this Russian form of endearment. When they left, Barry and
Joy left her a pile of books, among them the illustrated *A–Z of
Sex*. Kneeling on the floor going through the books, when she
came to this one she quickly went on to the next, and I never saw
it again. She told me later she gave it to a young Russian couple
who after digesting its contents sold it for 100 roubles.

At another party, two policemen in thick, imposing black
winter uniforms knocked on the door and entered, saying
neighbours had complained about the noise. They asked for our
names one by one, and when I gave mine and said I was an
English correspondent they went on to the next person without
a second's hesitation or interest, obviously knowing already I
was there.

No one at the party was the slightest bit scared or intimidated.
Some even took the mickey out of the policemen, standing to
mock attention, and upon their departure used the slang word
menti ('fuzz') and told popular jokes at their expense such as the
one alluding to the peasant upbringing of many Moscow
policemen: 'Why do *menti* have buttons on their sleeves? To
stop them wiping their noses.'

When the policemen left the party continued. Lara was the first girl I felt at ease with while dancing. During one slow dance she put her head on my shoulder in a gesture of deep world-weariness. She said later that physical contact with me was a big comfort, that all tension left her. She trusted me. There was at the party a lovely girl called Ira, who had a beautiful voice. Normally music has no effect on me but the way she sang her sad songs accompanied by a blond boy on a guitar moved me deeply. I was leaning back on a bed settee against a wall, Lara beside me. The lights had been switched off and the room lit dimly by candles. Sasha was sitting on the floor and Valera was somewhere else in the room. The company would join in some of the choruses that characterise these old Russian melodies but was otherwise silent, listening. There were five or six girls, all of whom looked stunningly attractive in the candlelight. No one spoke. The atmosphere was cosy and intimate. Ira, her flaxen hair pulled back into a braid and tied with a blue ribbon, sang with ineffable sweetness and tenderness her slow, deep songs of the *taiga*, the tundra, the steppe and the great rivers of the Russian plain and I wondered what there was in English culture to compare with this. At an English party we would all be listening to loud meaningless tinned music. Then the guitarist sang the songs of Vladimir Vysotsky, the Russian Bob Dylan, whose lyrics are so deeply rooted in Russian experience that no foreigner, however fluent in the language, can ever hope to appreciate them fully. At about midnight our host fetched in pancakes, which we ate with *smetana*, soured cream. When we left only one couple remained, dancing dreamily and paying no attention to the music. Valera was asleep on the settee. Getting home was difficult as we had to stop a taxi: no mean feat in Moscow. 'It's all part of the fun,' Lara said. One stopped eventually and about six of us crammed in. We were bunched up together. I put my arm round her and she again rested her head on my shoulder. I had never before felt so close to a girl so quickly, so relaxed.

Leaving my flat with me one morning, she suddenly said, 'I don't like your flat, by the way.' It looked unlived-in, she said. It was true that my few possessions were so neatly placed, and so far from filling the flat, that it resembled a hotel suite. Every object, big or small, had its correct place in the tidy scheme of

my existence. But this was not the real reason she disliked my
flat, which was that it was the spacious home of a privileged
foreigner. In her childhood she had been one of five in one
room; at university one of four in a cramped dormitory; recently
she had lived alone but in a tiny room. She had to share her
current flat with Valera because she could not afford the rent of
eighty roubles a month. My flat was spacious and high-
ceilinged, with two big rooms, both sparkling thanks to my
cleaning woman Klavdia Stepanovna – to Lara it was like a
palace. The first time she went there I gave her coffee when she
wanted vodka or wine (I did not have any) and, fed up, she
thought as she sipped her unwanted coffee and eyed the place,
'Oh no, I don't want to have anything to do with yet another
superior bloody foreigner showing off his privileges.' And
though it soon became clear that I was not even aware of being
privileged, let alone showing off, her initial feelings about the
place never left her.

To me it had been luxurious only in being a place of my own.
I did indeed at first appreciate this (though a dog kennel would
have sufficed, as long as it contained a writing desk). When I
first got to Moscow I had wanted nothing more than to be alone
in a place of my own, had regarded it as a wonderful piece of
luck that I was freed of other people's rules and objectives, that
it was up to me to decide my own way of spending the time
(even, to a large extent, regarding work), that I could cultivate
my own habits and pleasures. Now these feelings seemed to have
occurred to another person an aeon ago. So much had happened
to me that I recalled my first impressions of Moscow as though I
had read them in a book written by someone else.

I recalled early days, alone, cut off from the past and
everything known, wandering about the wide, tree-lined streets
like a gawping child. Many things had reminded me of India: the
old-fashioned wooden film advertisements, the spitting in the
street and resultant dappled pavements, the free-for-all at bus
stops – the whole *ambience* of a peasant country. I was
fascinated by the rough stencilled lettering on vans that simply
said BREAD or POST or some portmanteau word such as MOS-
TRANS, and by the black glass fascia boards that said things like
'23rd Bakery' and 'Food Shop No. 15.' I recalled my first tasks,
and the enthusiasm with which I had done them: opening an

account in a bank that seemed medieval in its lack of sophistication; starting files on many subjects (the files made of coarse brown cardboard that you bought flat and folded yourself); joining the local library and ordering *The Grapes of Wrath* even though I could not read it, simply for the pleasure of seeing my favourite novel in Russian; glueing a huge map of the Soviet Union on my wall, the map so big it was printed and sold in four separate sheets.

Russians had seemed to me then the least alien of all the foreigners I had known. (I believed anyway that people were basically the same all over the world.) Facially most Russians could be taken for Anglo-Saxons; they spoke without the accompanying head or hand movements of Indians or Latins; their mannerisms were often the same as British mannerisms; and, in the autumn at least, clothes in Moscow were not markedly different from clothes worn in Britain. Then came the shocks. Instead of fitting smoothly into the neat and tidy society anticipated in my imagination, I was knocked around and battered in a harsh, unexpected rough and tumble that by nature and upbringing I was not equipped to deal with. I discovered with surprise and bewilderment that life in Russia was hard. Everything, even daily necessities, had to be fought for. Russians seemed to have a way of complicating the simplest of transactions. The person in control always seemed to want to cause trouble. Stroppiness was the norm, not the exception, so that you braced yourself for unpleasantness every time you walked through a public door. The arguments civil servants used for withholding service seemed to me devoid of logic. Although I was a much-travelled young man, every country I had been in before had either a European or a Commonwealth background. In Russia for the first time I encountered ways of thinking and doing things that were utterly alien. Now I believed that Russians were the most foreign of all foreigners: yet here I was, paradoxically, in love with one. I had expected to get married during my stay in Moscow: it was inevitable, easily predictable, given my age and situation. But when I was anticipating that, I had not known that Russians would seem so alien. Nor had I expected to fall in love with a girl of such strong personality. It was all a bit much.

Lara had a clear-cut presence. She would do nothing com-

monplace. She was unusual. Without ever faking her emotions,
she never ceased to surprise me. I could never take her moods or
reactions for granted. Extrovert enjoyment would be replaced
abruptly by self-indulgent soul-searching. It seemed she had a
nature that in its demands for excitement, diversion and interest
was insatiable. Restless and bored, she could manufacture a
crisis that could ruin a day out with her. Once we went on a
picnic with a mutual acquaintance. Bored with the chatter of the
acquaintance, and feeling quite desperate that a day of her life
was being wasted on trivialities, she went off and climbed a tree
that could not be descended without assistance. A bizarre scene
ensued: Lara stuck up the tree and us at the foot devising a
means of getting her down. As we stood there helplessly she
dared me to climb the tree as well. I declined the dare.

'Can't you climb a tree?' she said scornfully.

Slightly drunk, I replied that I could but that I didn't feel like
it. And, after a while, resenting the pointless challenge and the
whole absurd situation, I wandered off. Lara said to herself, 'To
hell with him.'

Such incidents, as well as relieving boredom, also served the
purpose of testing friendship. If you became irritable or angry,
that was proof you did not love her. None of her admirers had
found it easy to please her. Analytic and sceptical, she would
question or reject what I had too easily accepted, often with a
vehemence I took as derision. She could be scornful. Still, she
needed me. Even though my strange mixture of diffidence,
shyness and brutal honesty still confused her, so that she
regarded me as an enigma, she trusted me absolutely. She
relaxed totally and immediately in my arms as if I were a faith
healer relieving pain by touch. We were increasingly aware that
we were already, after such a stupidly short time, bound to each
other, committed: and it confused us. Neither of us could
healthily accept what each moment had to offer. Instead we felt
an unrest. My reserve bothered her, I believe, even then. I was
unable to convey my feelings, unable to convey anything but a
defensive approach born of years of self-deprecation. Thoughts I
could express, but not emotions. I concealed nothing of my ideas
but was unable to relate spiritual experience. Feeling so disorientated did not help. I was in love with a Russian girl in Russia:
that was a lot to take in and come to terms with.

As for Lara, she would have much preferred not to love a foreigner. Lara was the only Russian I had known who related to foreigners completely naturally, as people to be judged purely on their personal merits. To Russians, foreigners are like VIPs. Russians can like individual foreigners, have a genuine affection for them, but always in the back of the mind is the knowledge that the foreigner is not an ordinary person, that benefits can accrue from the connection. Contact is often maintained with foreigners when ordinarily the Russian would not pass the time of day with them. Lara, however, refused to waste time on foreigners she did not like and either refused Western goodies when offered them or accepted them with reluctance. She had no illusions about Westerners, and could have done without the additional problems and complications caused by being in love with one.

So, all in all, we did not have the sort of carefree days traditionally enjoyed by young lovers. But there was a tremendously strong mutual attraction. We spent every available spare minute in each other's company, mostly now at her place, and we laughed a lot together. She loved my laugh. It dispelled her doubts and fears. I had 'nice eyes', she said, an engaging smile, 'like the smile of a happy young child', and a 'beautiful laugh'. These characteristics reassured her.

Nature also relaxed her. We went often to the forest, usually alone and usually taking food for a picnic. From the southern suburbs a short bus or train journey would take us to wild countryside, nothing like the trim fields of London's home counties. The woods surrounding Moscow were so unspoilt they could be thousands of miles from any civilisation. My London upbringing made me ignorant of even the most commonly known facts of natural history, while Lara not only knew the names of all the trees and birds but knew them in English. On these excursions, while sitting on tree trunks in a clearing, the air filled with the fresh smell of pine and warmth and damp earth, and then afterwards while strolling back to bus stop or station along deserted country roads (dirt tracks, really) in the sunset-flushed mist of a spring evening, the trees now melting together into great masses of darkness, Lara would tell me about herself, would tell me about her background, that background which was so frighteningly different from my own.

Chapter Six
LARA

Dmitri Adrianovich Putsello met Raisa Iosifovna Mytnitskaya in 1928. They had one daughter in 1940, another in 1945, a third in 1950 and were married in 1951. In that decade the Soviet government had changed its mind, line and law on such rites. Irregular relationships were the norm in the thirties and forties but an anomaly in the fifties.

The first daughter they called Olga, the second Anya and the third Lara. The three sisters were remarkably unalike. Olga and Anya were both strikingly beautiful in their dark and blond ways respectively, and little Lara grew up believing she did not bear comparison. They say there is a bit of Tatar in every Russian. In Lara it came out. For about two years during her adolescence Lara kept on at her parents for producing two beautiful daughters and her ugly narrow-eyed self, and accused them of not loving her because of her ugliness.

Dmitri Adrianovich was a journalist who came from St Petersburg, of an upper-middle-class family, members of the pre-revolution intelligentsia. His life after the revolution was devoted to surreptitious physical survival and hanging on to his class's cultural standards and traditions.

Raisa Iosifovna was Jewish, from Samara on the Volga, a region which, when she was a child after the civil war, suffered a terrible famine and reverted to semi-barbarism and cannibalism. Typhus raged among the starving peasants, who had not the energy nor the means to keep themselves clean, so were all crawling with lice, the carriers of the disease. To discourage the insects, every night before going to bed Raisa's parents used to sprinkle turpentine round the walls of their wooden house, scrub the floors with it and rub some on the hands and feet of themselves and their children. From this experience Raisa emerged obsessed with hygiene, an obsession she has always retained and passed on to her daughters.

She and Dmitri Adrianovich lived together in Moscow until 1941, when they moved to Ufa, the capital of Bashkiria, to escape the invading Germans. Here they lived in one half of a huge barn. Ufa, by the Ural mountains, has a continental climate, hot in summer, freezing in winter. Others suffered badly from the cold, for fuel was hard to obtain, but Dmitri Adrianovich as a journalist with many contacts could always get a supply of logs to keep the stove burning. In midsummer the unoccupied half of the barn would be stacked right up to the ceiling with fragrant birch and lime logs. The Putsellos ate better than most, too. In spring they bought a piglet from a collective farm, fattened it on potato peel mash and, illegally, on heavily subsidised bread, slaughtered it in the autumn and ate salted pork, smoked pork and pork pies throughout the winter. They also kept chickens and grew vegetables. It was Raisa Iosifovna who attended to the pig, chickens and vegetable patch, fetching water from a pump half a mile away, for Dmitri Adrianovich would have nothing to do with such plebeian tasks.

The barn overlooked a wide lilac-filled courtyard and a big orchard full of Chinese crab apple trees, the smell of which in the season permeated the whole street. Lara and her sisters and friends climbed the trees, of course, to pick the best apples, from which was made jam for the winter. There were also cherries, pears and plums and maple trees. This sprawling orchard was Lara's childhood domain, where she made a dug-out and immensely enjoyed herself. The far side was bordered by a high fence concealing an orphanage, while the near side led into the courtyard, which contained the traditional *besyedka*, or summer-house (literally 'talking place') – a pavilion with flimsy wooden walls about three feet high in which were placed benches and a wooden table for card games and dominoes. In the house opposite lived a large Tatar family with no curtains, so that one could see the women at their ablutions and other intimacies.

During the first year in the Urals one of the parents was always at the side of baby Olga's cot, guarding her against rats. Several babies in the town, as well as much precious food, had been devoured. When Lara was born rats were no longer a problem and their successors, mice, Lara remembers as furry little friends to be talked to when cornered and offered sugar and bits of cheese.

Raisa Iosifovna, after having breast-fed Lara for eighteen months, broke out in huge boils due to undernourishment and exhaustion, so she had to give it up, much to her husband's annoyance. With Lara weaned, she was free to resume her career. Stealing her domestic passport and certificate of higher education from Dmitri Adrianovich's drawer and pretending to go shopping, she went to BASHPROEKT, the Bashkirian Central Bureau for Civil Engineering Designs, where she had been offered a job in her profession of electrical designer. This was in the winter of 1952–53, the last months of the Stalin era, when a campaign against Jews was being launched. She had been turned down at an Ufa electrical plant because its boss thought electric light bulb production too sensitive to have a Jew on senior staff. But the woman in charge of the personnel department handed Raisa Iosifovna a slip of paper with BASHPROEKT's address on it and said the bureau's head was a very nice person. And indeed Raisa Iosifovna was warmly welcomed there and at forty one made a fresh start in her career after a fifteen-year interval. Dmitri Adrianovich, presented with a *fait accompli*, confined himself to occasionally, when drunk, tearing up sheets of technical drawing, his wife's overtime work, so that she had to stay up all night doing it again.

Dmitri Adrianovich was a dominant figure in the town and a disciplinarian in his home. Keeping out of political trouble entailed constant enervating vigilance, especially as he did not believe a word he wrote as a journalist and, though he was an anti-Semite, his wife was Jewish. If circumstances had been slightly easier he could have done very well for himself. Ufa had been growing steadily since before the revolution and now, with the decline of the Baku oilfields, it was becoming an important regional centre, with a population approaching half-a-million that within a decade was to reach over 600,000. In this period,

before the development of the Tyumen oilfield in Siberia and the
offshore Baku rigs, Bashkirian oil was vital to the Soviet
economy. Dmitri Adrianovich could have benefited from this
importance. But his life had been too nerve-wracking for too
long, and by the time the taboos and prejudices against people of
his origins had ended, and official anti-Semitism had eased, he
was an alcoholic. Even in this he maintained his standards,
drinking only cognac and special or flavoured vodka. He would
not touch ordinary vodka.

He was a pessimist whose favourite self-coined aphorism was:
prepare yourself for the worst as you will always be able to take
the best in your stride. He had refused to return to Moscow
when the war was over, forfeiting his state flat by Izmailov Park
and the promising career of a *Trud* journalist because he did not
believe peace would last for twenty years, the time he needed to
put his children on their feet. There were more immediate
reasons for staying in Bashkiria too, such as food. He sent
monthly food parcels to his old mother and unmarried sister in
Moscow, where food was so scarce that Raisa Iosifovna's
mother quietly starved to death through refusing to touch her
husband's daily ration of three hundred grams of bread, which
he was entitled to as a working man. She, as a dependant, was
expected to live on one hundred grams a day. Also, Stalin was
still alive and still kicking and Dmitri Adrianovich, though an
unwavering believer in Russia's need for an iron hand at the top,
felt safer with a cushion of a thousand miles between himself
and the seat of Russian central administration.

He was very strict in his upbringing of the girls. He would not
even let them listen to the radio, calling the programmes
'corrupting rubbish', and when Raisa Iosifovna bought one to
listen to music as her only relaxation in a very hard life, he
smashed it.

His wife and daughters were expected to live by a rigid moral
code: he himself had many extra-marital affairs.

After Anya was conceived he hired a lusty sixteen-year-old
peasant girl called Dasha to look after mother and baby, and
impregnated her too. Dasha gave birth a few weeks after Anya
was born. This child was a boy, one of three illegitimate boys
Raisa Iosifovna knows for sure he sired. She suggested they

adopt the child but he, in the best traditions of his dying caste, had already arranged a morganatic marriage for Dasha with a widowed *khutoryanin*, well-off farmer. Dmitri Adrianovich insisted on Dasha going straight from the hospital to her new home, claiming that if he saw the baby he would not be able to let it go.

All this was very galling to his relatives, who, sticking to the old traditions, regarded boy-children as much more desirable than girls: and he had fathered three girls by his Jewess wife and three boys (at least) by other women. His relatives kept on at him to leave her but, creditably devoted to his daughters, he never did. She left him in the end. She had left him briefly (going to live in Moscow) when she discovered the Dasha affair, but returned when he made clear he was not going to give up Olga. They rarely talked to each other, and when they did converse he always spoke with his back turned. On their way to register Lara's birth they walked on opposite sides of the road.

(Lara often wondered what happened to Dasha's boy, her half-brother. Many years later there was published in the magazine *Yunost* a poem by one Putsillo. It is such an unusual name [possibly Polish] that this may have been he: and she was told in Yalta of a young man of that name living there, but she did not have time to go and see him.)

When Raisa Iosifovna left for good, she took the two eldest daughters, leaving Lara with her husband. Lara remembers the morning she woke up and found them gone. She was seven. She woke up to find herself alone with her father, who was snoring. She gently woke him. 'They've left, you know,' she said. He seemed not to believe it, saying they had simply gone to visit someone, but Lara realised later he was merely putting on a brave face. She never ceased to love him deeply. Although she only stayed with him for one year he remained devoted to her right up until she was thirteen, when he realised with what must have been unbearable pain that his role as a father was over. By then his drinking had cost him his job and his standing in the town and he had nothing.

During that year with him she began school. Postwar shortages affected everyone, and the family fortunes had already deteriorated to such an extent that she entered the infants' class in clothes handed down from her sisters. Because her father was always reluctant to wake her up and always insisted on a big leisurely breakfast, she was often late for school, so had to enter the classroom with everyone's eyes on her, acutely conscious of her uniform pinafore inelegantly long, her hair ridiculously short (father insisting on a shaven head every summer) and the humiliating absence of the usual white collar and cuffs. But she loved school. Having a capacity to retain everything at first grasp with very little effort, she quickly rose to top of her class. She shared a back bench with an older boy, a naughty hooligan named Kolya Starikov, who was repeating every year two or three times. He was supposed to improve under her influence. They did prove to be an efficient team, Lara mercifully sporting no tantalising pigtails and a match for him in fisticuffs. Kolya's academic performance soared through copying her homework and lip-reading while answering questions at the blackboard. One day during a maths lesson he proposed an ultimate test of her toughness. Saying, 'It can't be true you aren't scared of anything,' he produced a *finka*, a knife with a mother-of-pearl handle. 'If you don't move while I cut your arm, the *finka* is yours,' he said. Lara did not move as the shiny blade cut her skin, so won the *finka*. It was confiscated the same day by Dmitri Adrianovich.

Raisa Iosifovna tried for a long time to keep her husband from knowing where she was. While waiting to be given a room in a new block of flats being built for BASHPROEKT employees, she, Anya and Olga lived with a young friend named Rosa in a room measuring ten square yards. A bed, divan, camp bed and small table in the middle of the room left about six inches either side. One of the beds obstructed the door, so the room had to be entered sideways. It was impossible to move in the room, one had to either sit or lie down. When Lara, missing them badly, stayed with them at weekends and on holidays, she slept on a bench by the stove.

Lara remembers Rosa as a typically Russian blond beauty whose smile seemed actually to radiate warmth. Rosa came from a village about sixty kilometres from Ufa where she and her cousin Alya had been brought up by her mother and aunt in a manless household. Aunt Marusya, being the younger of the two old women, did the rough chores on their smallholding, went out to work at the collective farm pig-sty and occasionally, after a hard day's work, would get drunk on *kislushka*, home-brewed apple wine. On these occasions she and her sister would sit on the porch and sing sad songs lamenting women's lot and cheerful ones reviling men. Rosa's mother had once been happily married to a handsome rugged man who had gone off to make other women happy. Aunt Marusya's Alya was the product of an obscure accident.

The Putsello girls had for years spent each summer with them in the village, which was called by the strange Latvian name of Brivais Darps (Red Labour) because it had been filled with refugees from Latvia during the war. Raisa Iosifovna visited the girls most weekends, rushing straight from work to catch the Saturday afternoon train to the small station of Tavtimanovo, from where she walked the remaining twelve kilometres, carrying a bag in each hand and two strapped across her shoulders. The journey, as well as being tiring, was also rumoured to be dangerous, with wolves and robber bands lurking at such places as Monk's Clearing and Wild Wolves' Winter Hole. Her daughters would be waiting anxiously for her on the road far outside the village. At the cottage, down would come the bags on the freshly scrubbed pine floorboards and the hosts would sigh contentedly over the gifts Raisa Iosifovna had fetched – delicacies such as salami and salted herring, sober kerchiefs and, for Alya, whose dream was to become an actress, a copy of the latest *Soviet Screen* magazine or a washed-out photograph of Alain Delon. The next morning Raisa Iosifovna would be woken up by crowing cocks and Marusya swearing at the red-flanked Mashka who had just slapped her in the face with her tail while being milked, and would begin the homeward journey. Lara's heart sank as she watched her poor mother trudge away back down that twelve-kilometre unsafe road.

When Rosa moved to Ufa to study at a medical college Raisa Iosifovna found a rented room for her and helped her as best she could to stick it out on her meagre 25-rouble monthly grant. Then the roles were reversed. Rosa opened her door at three o'clock one dismal October morning to an excited though apologetic trio: could she possibly put them up for just one

night? Dmitri Adrianovich had hit Olga and called her a whore
for being an hour late back from a skating rink. They had had
enough. Rosa kissed and cuddled them and said they had at last
done what they should have done ages ago. They stayed with her
in her tiny room for ten months. Nights were a bit of a jigsaw
puzzle. Rosa occupied the bed, Olga slept on the divan and
Raisa Iosifovna and Anya shared the camp bed.

Once a week, during Lara's visits, Raisa Iosifovna took her
brood to the nearby central *banya*, the bathhouse – a festive
occasion in a different world, with its special micro-climate of
steamy warmth, that Lara always enjoyed and looked forward
to. Nude women of every age, size and shape would be
scrubbing each other's backs, bathing pink babies in zinc bowls
or posed in solemn concentration, officiating at the rite of Hair
Washing. Laughter and screaming and slapping resounded
against the streaming stone walls. Each woman had two bowls
of water. Seated on a marble bench, she rested her feet in one
and washed with the other. Many brought their own herbs to
soak, for the aroma. On the raised platform of the sauna women
thrashed themselves and each other with bundles of leafy birch
twigs to stimulate the cleansing. Lara was not allowed on this
platform, for it was so hot there it burned the nostrils. If she had
ventured up there she would have been shooed away. One
Sunday afternoon a hot water pipe burst and a male plumber
had to be called for. The news spread like wildfire and the
women swiftly regrouped into battle formation: columns of five
or six, each female holding a bowl like a shield, with the
youngest and most innocent in the front line. A hush fell on the
naked ranks as a ruddy-faced overawed male stumbled across
the washroom guided by a white-clad cloakroom *babushka*, his
eyes tightly shut.

Dmitri Adrianovich was surviving for the moment on freelance
work. He was soon to lose even this, as the knowledge spread
among editors that it was his custom to take payment in advance
and then not keep to deadlines. He was a great liar, elevating his
profound belief in the 'salutary lie' to a personal philosophy.
Raisa Iosifovna said that if she had found him in the orchard on
top of a woman, 'he would have insisted with absolute convic-

tion that he had just slipped on a dead leaf'. He tried to pass this
philosophy onto Lara. They played the game of dissimulation,
telling each other cheerful adaptable half-truths, gaining little,
losing nothing. Outside their relationship, however, Lara,
though not averse to the occasional fib, would not accept
deviousness as a mode of thought. She was guided by the shining
example of her mother, who had not once in her life uttered a
deliberately untrue word.

After ten months Raisa Iosifovna, Olga and Anya moved to
the room reserved for them in the BASHPROEKT block in the Street
of the 8th of March, and a month after that Lara went to live
with them permanently. On the bright sunny morning she left
her father what remained of his life must have collapsed, but she
was too young to appreciate this and anyway was missing her
mother and sisters too much.

Dmitri Adrianovich continued for twenty more years to hang
on stubbornly to his dogmatic views, his old barn and estab-
lished routine. Of all the people Lara has known he was the only
one who exercised to the full his existentialist right to free
choice, never conforming, never complaining, never admitting
to any human weakness. Few people even knew that he drank.
He could at any moment have exchanged his barn for a flat with
all modern conveniences; but acquiring mod cons would have
meant becoming like everybody else. Gas he distrusted as
unsafe; and a shared entrance and staircase he abhorred as
lacking in privacy. Rather than submit to all this he turned what
was once a family nest into a solitary's lair. The floor was never
washed, windows were rarely opened and piles of paper, books
and parcels took up all the living space except the tiny study
where he slept and worked, drank endless cups of strong black
tea and cooked on an electric hotplate his favourite dish of
thick-sliced potatoes fried in sunflower seed oil. An intellectual,
bred for the life of the mind, he lived for twenty years like a
peasant. Every morning throughout winter he had to shovel tons
of snow to clear a path to the outer world, to chop wood, light
the stove, fetch water from the pump – these chores, disdained
when he had a wife to do them, he now argued kept him fit and
would prolong his life. He drudged slowly and methodically
through each day towards the hour, never before 7.00 o'clock in

the evening, when he poured himself his first drink (from a bottle labelled 'Medicine' in case his daughters saw it).

The impact this extraordinary man had on Lara's character cannot be overestimated. They still saw a lot of each other, and talked. Pride was the highest virtue, independence the most enviable state: hardship was preferable to obligation, difficulties better than debt. This Lara was taught and, loving and respecting her father, this she learnt well.

Chapter Seven
IN THE STREET OF
THE 8TH OF MARCH

The old squat wooden huts that had made up the bulk of Ufa's living accomodation were being steadily replaced by concrete blocks of flats, changing the nature of the town, as demolition and rebuilding was doing to towns throughout the Soviet Union in the attempt to resolve the housing crisis. The new blocks, of which the BASHPROEKT block in the Street of the 8th of March was a typical example, were interspersed with long wide main roads, broad untidy squares, open-air markets, decrepit fences full of gaps where people had torn out planks to make fires, and thousands of birch trees, in which were built the huge unwieldy nests of the ubiquitous black-hooded crows, ugly scavenging birds as big as seagulls. In the winter many of the irregular, winding streets became sheets of ice, while tramlines on the new broad main thoroughfares ran between deep walls of rock-hard snow. Hummocks of snow grew steadily in the courtyards. The fences of the summer-houses were obliterated. Lara skied and skated.

The summer after their parents separated Lara and her sisters were sent to stay at Lodyrevka, a village on the Belaya river. The village's name, which means Loafers, accurately described its inhabitants. It was no more than half a dozen cottages standing in a whimsical pattern on a brief stretch of land between the river and a steep hill. A path ran down the hill, skirted the cottages and disappeared into a neighbouring wood. The owner of the cottage nearest to the path willingly agreed to lodge the girls and look after them for forty roubles a month, this being nearly as much as her monthly wage as a collective farm peasant. The girls saw her very rarely and she never stayed the night. They soon discovered why. One thundery night there was a rap on the door. When they did not answer, the door was pushed in off its hinges and four young men entered. The men made a quick search of the premises, kicking in the pantry door and checking under the bed. Then they turned their attention to the petrified girls, who were on the sofa hugging their knees. A man with enormous shoulders whom Lara had mistaken for Tarzan gave Anya a light flick on the nose and growled affectionately, 'Don't be scared, little one. It's my mum I'm after. Where's the bitch hiding?' As his mum was obviously not there, the men just sat around for an hour, adding half a litre of vodka to the formidable quantity they had already consumed, spilling some on the floor, and then left, wishing the girls a very good night and bidding them take care. Before going Tarzan beamed admiringly at seventeen-year-old Olga and asked her to tell his mum that he was sure to get her next time, waving his woodcutter's axe for emphasis. A neighbour later explained: during the war the girls' landlady had deposited her three children in an orphanage and never returned to collect them. The eldest of them, Tarzan, about ten at the time, had sworn to find her and kill her as soon as he got out but had been delayed by a prison sentence imposed for lending a hand in a burglary. The only really hazardous moment during the nocturnal visit was when the most drunk of the men lit a match to read a notice on the wall (Dmitri Adrianovich's detailed instructions to the girls as to what they should and should not do in their parents' absence). Had the young man held the match a bit closer to the paper or had he dropped it in the pool of vodka at his feet the hut, built of pine and with an attic full of hay, would have been up in flames in seconds. The girls never saw their visitors again.

That summer was exceptionally hot and they had a gorgeous time sprawled on the sandy river beach from dawn till dusk, crossing the river at sunset in a row-boat with local boys to pick bird cherries, and swimming. Lara often went swimming alone. Indolent cows would pass by, spurred on by girls running from one to the other. Young women would come to fill up old wooden casks with the water, which flowed from the wooded uplands of the Urals. Lara would hear them talking in loud voices and then they would depart, shouldering yokes with the casks swinging in rhythm at each step, beautifully graceful. From Lara's viewpoint in the river the figures formed dark silhouettes against the sky at the top of the bluff for a moment before vanishing down the other side, leaving her feeling poignantly alone, which she had not felt before they came. She would swim until late in the evening, when the meadowlands on the opposite bank would be barely visible except for the winking yellow lights of the villages. In the autumn, when the banks of the Belaya had turned red-brown, the trees golden, and the slanting rays of the sun had paled, the girls returned to their cosy room in the Street of the 8th of March.

It was an agreeable life for a child. Idyllic would probably not be too strong a word. Even the split with their father had not destroyed the customary Russian sense of family unity, with its accompanying feeling of security: Lara had many friends, including Tatar and Bashkir children: she was doing phenomenally well at school: and there had early been inculcated a taste for literature. So when later she looked back on this time with deep nostalgia, it was not solely, if at all, because of the donning of rose-coloured spectacles. Probably it really was as happy and carefree as she ever afterwards recollected. With this solid background, either through education or temperament or a mixture of both, she developed a profound attachment and loyalty to her origins – her family, her home town, her first friends and her country.

The happiness ended when she was twelve. From being a supremely self-confident tomboy she became a gauche girl made utterly miserable by the certainty that she was ugly. She left her primary school, where she had been captain of the girls' basketball team and a star pupil, to enter a school specialising in English, where she found herself among a select bunch of town celebrities' children. Dmitri Adrianovich's knowledge of the way these things were done was instrumental in getting her in after the enrolment list was long closed, but the rest was entirely up to her. For months her dreams at night took her back to the simpler and much closer circle of her former classmates and teachers and to the spacious resin-smelling gymnasium in her old school. Her new life was hard. As academic competitiveness was part of the

Putsello family tradition, simply doing well was not good enough. But being first was not easy in a class to which admittance officially depended on top grades in every subject. A lot of sleep and basketball had to be sacrificed. Also, Anya married a man she hated.

Anya had always given a vividness to life that was tremendously exciting. She overflowed with the enthusiasm she brought to everything she did, so others felt stimulated and uplifted – before the exhaustion set in. She set a hard pace that few could match. Erupting with her excess of energy, her heterogeneous interests and enthusiasms, she inspired others to accompany her on her wild, spontaneous trips – to a friend's flat at three in the morning, to the steppe at midnight for a picnic, to Moscow (at the age of sixteen) for a public poetry reading. If she took a tram ride to an art exhibition, she would want to walk back or take a taxi, just so as not to repeat the journey. Once, Raisa Iosifovna had to go to Moscow for a month to have a look at the way Moscow architects designed their first 'Khrushchev kennels', the under-sized, low-ceilinged flats that for all their faults enabled millions of Soviet families to move from communal to private accommodation. Olga having already married and left, Raisa Iosifovna gave Anya a sum of money that normally was stretched to feed the family for a month. This was not Anya's way, however. Throughout the first week she and Lara ate at a nearby restaurant, relishing the Bashkirian chef's delicious (and expensive) dishes of horse meat, leaving just enough money for the remaining three weeks to buy sugar and tea. They survived on food offerings and dinner invitations from friends. On another occasion, she disappeared for a fortnight. With Raisa Iosifovna in tears every night with worry and remorse at her inability to control Anya, and the Ufa police conducting investigations, she was traced to Moscow. She had run away, having made the decision to do so on the spur of the moment after having decided, equally spontaneously, that provincial life was too constraining. She loved passionately literature, poetry, the theatre, music. Her academic career, which had begun just as brightly as Lara's, foundered as she became more and more engrossed in her non-academic interests. Vivacious and lovely, she was the belle of Ufa. She could have married almost any of the town's eligible bachelors – and she chose Edik, a painter in oils who had already begun to drink. He shared most of her interests and was one of the few who could match her energy. She met him at her school-leaving ball. He had just returned from doing his obligatory two-year military service. He was a promising artist with a flair for modern verse, a talent for boxing and a formidable gift of the gab. They took to sleeping together within a couple of weeks. Soon Anya was expecting his child. This spurred Dmitri Adrianovich into furious activity aimed at scaring Edik into marrying her. An illegitimate child was as much out of the question as an abortion. Edik, caught between his passionate involvement with Anya and a no less ardent aversion to marriage and responsibility, was easy game for such a tough schemer as his prospective father-in-law. Anya was eighteen on February 13 and on March 13 married him.

Olga meanwhile, who was known to everyone by the diminutive of Lyalya, had left Ufa. Lyalya had begun the family tradition of being brilliant at school. Throughout the decade of her school life she received the top mark of five in all subjects. Because of nerves, however, she then failed the vital mathematics section of an entrance examination to the Ufa Aviation Institute. Dmitri Adrianovich, in an unprecedented move, used his contacts and influence to get her admitted anyway. She studied briefly there and then, thanks to Dmitri Adrianovich using his connections again, went to Moscow to train as a computer programmer at the Institute of Electronic Engineering. In Moscow she met a handsome naval officer. At first, before anyone had met him, it seemed like a story-book romance. None of her family loved him when they saw him, however, for he was too prim and proper and straitlaced, and when she announced she was going to marry him they were not overjoyed. Still, he was steady and sober and hardworking and would no doubt make a good husband and father. So Lyalya, who by then had graduated from the electronics institute and had a good job as a computer programmer, abandoned her career and walled herself up in a stultifying marriage. For a few years she followed her husband in his various postings throughout the country, and then settled down with him and their baby daughter in the small town of Obninsk, 100 kilometres south-west of Moscow, the site of the world's first atomic power station, where she stagnated. The contrast between her marriage and Anya's was stark, the difference absolute. Lyalya, the sultry gypsy, gradually lost her sparkle in dull routine, while Anya, the blond bombshell, became even wilder in her pursuit of experience and pleasure, and lost *her* sparkle spectacularly in dissolution.

As no young married couple could hope to get a place of their own, Edik moved in with the Putsello family. The communal flat became like an open house, with Anya and Edik bringing their friends home, often drunk, at all hours of the day and night. Parties were held. (One consequence of being brought up in a cramped, noisy room was that for ever afterwards Lara could sleep through almost anything.) When within a year or two Edik's male friends began ogling Lara, she found that though she was young and inexperienced she could anyway easily put them down, which made her disdainful. She felt superior. At least Edik was a colourful figure who was equal to her intellectually, for which she respected him.

Anya gave birth to a boy, Sasha. Lara loved Sasha as if he was her own. He meant so much to her she took on many of the duties of bringing him up and imagined she would devote her life to him. Anya often expressed appreciation of the help. Edik took it for granted. He valued nothing but wit and artistic talent. Sarcasm being his favourite form of wit, he used it indiscriminately, no matter how vulnerable the victim. Although Lara *felt* defenceless, she realised that if she showed it he would make her life a misery, so she responded vigorously to his wounding remarks with her own insults. Soon he was so addicted to alcohol that once, in the absence of anything else, he drank a bottle of eau-de-cologne that Lara had given to Anya as a birthday present. Then he started hitting Anya and openly making advances to other girls in order to hurt her and it was obvious the marriage could not last.

Edik had not been around at the time of Sasha's birth, having flitted off to Moscow to realise his dream of studying at the philological faculty of Moscow State University. He had taken the entrance exams two years running after leaving school but both times failed by one point. Then he had been called up. And then, finally, a married man of twenty-six, he had done it, and nothing else mattered, not even the birth of his child. He returned to Ufa the next spring, however, expelled after getting unwittingly involved in a students' mob fight. His documents being routinely examined in connection with his involvement in the fight, it was discovered that he had forged a character reference from his workplace (he was never any good at work). On his return, he could not stop talking about the unparalleled glamour of life at Moscow State University. He was still at it when Lara left school and was very much in two minds about what to do. Her maths and physics teachers suggested MIFI, the Moscow physics institute, to which she was not averse, having always wanted to excel in a predominantly male area and MIFI's ratio of girls being about one in twenty. Yet from the age of fourteen she had been spending a lot of time at Ufa's reading hall, determined to read every writer mentioned in the Art and Literature volume of the Large Soviet Encyclopaedia. Apart from the obvious and officially approved world classics she had struck upon Schopenhauer, Nietzsche, Kierkegaard and Freud, none of whose works was available but upon whom there was a good selection of monographs and learned essays. She carried Thomas Mann's *Dr Faustus* in her handbag for a year, trying to decipher tightly written pages where almost every other word sent her to consult encyclopaedic dictionaries. The study of the humanities appeared a compelling task. But really it was Edik who was responsible for the final choice. To surpass him in his own field would be the sweetest victory imaginable. It would show Anya too that there was nothing special about the hateful man she loved.

With what Lara has always regarded as the most incredible luck she landed nineteen points out of twenty at the four entrance exams and was accepted for the English department of Moscow State University's philological faculty. This success sent Edik, who was in Moscow with Anya for the announcement of the results, on a wild binge at the Aragvi, a Georgian restaurant of national renown.

Much as Lara loved Ufa and her family, she was glad of the chance to get away, and not only because of Edik. Too many of the young people of the town, including friends and acquaintances of herself and Anya, were turning into drunkards. Her friends had become unpredictable, so she could not relax with them as before. Drunkenness was spreading like a plague. It had become scary. She saw clearly she had to get out of Ufa or be destroyed in some way herself. So with no regrets and no doubts she became a *studentka* in the capital.

Chapter Eight
STUDENTKA

Moscow State University is one of the seven granite skyscrapers that dominate the capital's skyline, all built in Stalin's time in a style of architecture that reminds most visitors of a wedding cake and is called by Muscovites 'Repressionist'. The university's central tower is ringed with red lights to warn aircraft and is topped, like the Kremlin spires, with a red star. On one side is a giant clock, on another a barometer. It has thirty-two stories. All bodily, cultural and intellectual needs can be satisfied without leaving the building. Entrance to each block is through a narrow passage in a guardhouse, wherein is stationed day and night at least one beshawled *babushka*, at whom a pass has to be flashed. The building is surrounded by straggly gardens containing maple trees and apple trees. Apples can be collected each autumn from tree or ground by simply reaching up or down. Only students from the provinces are allowed to live in the dormitories, most of which are designed for four, two on each side of a thin wall with all four sharing a bathroom. Men and women are never assigned to the same cubicle but are often allotted adjoining places. Just before Lara arrived women had been segregated in a specially guarded wing of the main building – a system which lasted only four years. The most widespread of the theories as to why it had been introduced was that the first secretary of the university's party organisation had been perturbed when his daughter gained a university place, because he was Georgian, with a typical Latin-type concern for his daughter's chastity and honour. No one liked the segregation, and when he was sacked for some black market or political offence and sent to a job in Siberia, the original system was restored.

Lara's first neighbour was a man, one Zakharov, a *sver-khsrochnik* (someone who voluntarily re-engages afer completion of his statutory military service) who had therefore been accepted to the university with the lowest possible passing grades (fourteen points out of twenty). He was not as stupid as his younger fellow-students believed, but naturally the six-year break from scholarly pursuits while serving his country did not benefit his academic performance. He assumed the duty of waking Lara up at half-past six every morning with a yell of 'Reveille!'.

The previous occupant of Lara's half of room 432 had been a sloven who had left everything grimy and greasy, including the mattress. Sickened, Lara gave the place a thorough cleaning, dusting the mattress with bedbug powder and covering it with two clean sheets. She hoped her new room-mate would not be such a slob, for she could not stand living in filth. She then had a shower, made herself up and dressed to go out. Normally her straight auburn hair was worn long but at that time she'd cut it very short. Over it she put on a brown felt hat. She had on a smart brown costume and a black scarf draped loosely round her neck. Zakharov dropped in for a chat, and she was sitting on her bed talking to him, in her sophisticated outfit, smoking a cigarette and looking very suave, when a slender, dark-haired beautiful girl walked in – her new room-mate. They introduced themselves in the Russian manner, shaking hands and each saying her own name. The girl's name was Nadia. Zakharov left, and the two girls were alone together. Nadia unpacked her things. They were scared of each other, each seeming forbiddingly sophisticated, with Lara appearing positively exotic. Lara said something that seemed to the awestruck Nadia quite terrifyingly brilliant. Nadia meanwhile was of the cool, upright type that Lara had been scared of all her life. Nadia came from the Latvian capital of Riga on the Baltic, a region that, being the most Westernised of all the Soviet regions, had the reputation of being the most sophisticated. Its architecture was Western, it had cosy cafés and it set the pace in fashion. The truth was, both girls had a veneer of sophistication covering provincial uncertainties, and though wary, each felt interested enough to want to win the other over. Lara spoke immediately of her beloved Ufa, amazing Nadia with her experience. Nadia's childhood had been very sheltered. Lara spent nearly that whole night talking about Ufa, with Nadia telling a little about Riga, and by the next day there had developed the beginnings of a close friendship that endured throughout their stay in university, five years in which they talked endlessly and had only one argument. They were drawn closer together when Zakharov threw in the academic towel after only four months to become a PE instructor and they then had to share the dormitory with two girls neither liked, one being the sort of slob Lara had feared and the other a Tadjik 'sex bomba', with a face like Sophia Loren and an 'ironing board' body who could not leave men alone nor be left alone by them.

In their class was a boy named Tolya, with whom they formed a *troika* envied by the other students, especially Muscovites, for its warm companionship. Tolya seemed 'mysterious' to them at first, for he wore a black leather jacket and smoked a pipe, but they soon realised his air of mystery was the same as their veneer of sophistication. One other boy, named Seryozha, was allowed to join their select company. He was able to help them with their homework, as his class preceded theirs so he knew what questions would be asked. (Seryozha later married [and divorced] novelist Valentin Katayev's granddaughter, whose father was editor of the magazine for Soviet Jews, *Heimland*.)

The *troika*, inseparable, superior and secure, played cards instead of attending classes and held parties instead of doing homework, yet still managed to pass their exams – a dozen a term, in various relevant and irrelevant subjects – and learnt English better than many of the Muscovite students who had their mums to look after them. They recall it as 'a most beautiful experience', getting up at about eight, lingering over a big breakfast in the university canteen and then deciding not to attend classes but to return to their rooms and play *preference* all day instead.

Head of the English department was Professor Olga Sergeyevna Akhmanova, compiler with her late (reputedly fifth) husband, Professor Smirnitsky, of a world-famous Russian-English dictionary. She frowned upon mini-skirts, unconventional hair styles and smoking, the latter ostensibly because it damaged the vocal chords of the future interpreters and language teachers and also, in the English words of assistant pronunciation teacher Mrs Magidova-Metelitsa, because it was 'Oh, so dreadfully unladylike'. Students and staff were treated as guinea pigs for Olga Sergeyevna's eccentric experiments in the teaching of foreign languages. She insisted on English being spoken at all times within the department's walls. Very strong on pronunciation, she knew all the English class and regional dialects in spite of having been to England only once, when she visited Oxford in 1957 – her first contact with native speakers. When her younger colleagues returned from visiting England she always told them their English had deteriorated.

For three years Lara and Nadia remained convinced virgins, strong and chaste in their alliance. All that Lara had seen and experienced of men in Ufa had produced a contempt. At university she had to adjust her ideas to the likes of Tolya and Seryozha seeking her company in pleasant, innocent fashion, not necessarily with an ulterior sexual motive. She was agreeably surprised when she and Nadia walked about with these pleasant, friendly young men who were content to chat light-heartedly with no attempt at familiarities beyond the holding of an arm on icy patches. (Even this Lara disliked, though.) She began to feel more at ease, especially when she discovered that for all her provincial upbringing she was better-read than the men she met and that her quicker intelligence suitably impressed them. Used to outwitting the drunken men of her small provincial home town, she had not expected to be able to do the same at the country's main university. There was no dearth of admirers. It was obvious that many of them found her company more enjoyable than that of girls she privately considered lovelier, livelier and more accomplished than herself, so that, coming to regard herself as attractive, she regained the supreme self-confidence of her early childhood. Her feeling of superiority over men, formed at a highly impressionable age and reinforced by all that she had seen since, never completely left her. Tolya was a fine person, for whom Lara felt a deep affection, but the best times of all were when she was alone with Nadia, usually in their room, when they would spend hours talking easily in their different accents about plays and books, delighting in each other's sensitive, alert minds. They were so close there was gossip of lesbianism; and indeed, deep down Lara believed that no relationship with a man could possibly be as fulfilling as those she'd had with women. In discussion she liked to contradict men just for fun, to see their reaction. When they complained, she replied, 'If I agreed with everything you said it would be very boring.' This spirit of contradiction grew to such an extent that playing the devil's advocate became a habit extending to the lightest, most innocuous conversation and to the most piffling minor decisions.

Serious boyfriends arrived on the scene in the fourth year. Nadia told Lara there was one particular boy she liked. Lara said, 'Let's do something about it, then,' and, at a dance, to the music of Led Zeppelin, acted as matchmaker. And for a while Lara went around with a boy who had said interestingly, 'I don't care for Tolstoy or Gorky, I prefer fairy tales.' How singular, Lara thought, attracted. But it transpired he had meant exactly what he said and no more, because he was so thick.

The *troika* broke up when Tolya and Nadia met their future spouses, both foreigners. Tolya's fiancée was an East German called Gudrun, while Nadia fell in love with an American student named Ben. The final year at university was a difficult one for Lara, for she did not get on very well with Ben, partly because he was jealous of her close friendship with Nadia.

Ben and Nadia were married in Riga on April 3. Lara went with Tolya to the wedding, staying in Riga for three days. Lara saw for the first time, albeit through a spring mist and a drunken haze, Western architecture, a whole population dressed smartly, Latin script in shops and streets – and the sea. With a typically Russian sense of occasion, Nadia's brother and another man, getting her to close her eyes, marched her down narrow winding cobbled streets to the edge of the beach, where she opened her eyes to the panorama of the Baltic.

Asked if she wanted to see one of the *risqué* cabarets or floor-shows not seen elsewhere in the country, she said no, for, although curious, she suspected she would be too embarrassed to appreciate the spectacle. She did accept invitations to several of the numerous small cafés, however, and enjoyed the unprecedented experience of relaxing over a cup of coffee in a quiet, cosy ambience.

Nadia spent a lot of time and energy in her last few months at university in acquiring her exit visa, for she was planning to leave with Ben when his term was up. Prior to her departure for America, she held a big farewell party, at which Raisa Iosifovna alienated her mother, Natalya Ivanovna, by saying, 'My daughter will never leave me. I can't begin to imagine how you must feel but I have all sympathy for you.' By then Tolya had married Gudrun and was also preparing to leave the country, hoping to get a job in East Berlin.

Lara, though upset by the loss of Nadia and Tolya, concentrated on getting her degree.

Writing a thesis on 'The Linguistic Properties of the English Pun', she enjoyed herself drawing jolly material from *Winnie the Pooh*, *A Clockwork Orange*, *The Diary of a Nobody*, Nabokov, Shakespeare and John Lennon. She was awarded her philologist's degree in July, 1974. The document, a blue hardback passport-sized folder with the state emblem and the word *Diplom* embossed on the cover, qualified her to teach English at secondary school level. She was supposed to spend three years at a post wherever she was sent in the country, a custom designed to ensure a return on the investment made in higher education, the post to be decided by the State Appointments Committee. She did not want to live outside Moscow but it was out of the question that she would be assigned a post in the capital, and she knew that when the three years were up she would not be able to get back. Many graduates consoled themselves when accepting their post in the provinces that after three years they could return to Moscow, but they never did. They got married, or settled down in other ways, and became reconciled to provincial life, wistful thoughts of Moscow withering under the concrete necessity of securing a residence permit. It was a trap Lara was determined not to fall into. Of the forty students in the English department with her, only five were non-Muscovites, and jobs in Moscow could only be got with a Moscow residence stamp. Out of the five, two left the country (Tolya and Nadia), Seryozha took the classic way out by marrying a Muscovite (Katayev's grand-daughter) and one, a bespectacled, industrious girl named

Nina Chimodanova, went on to further studies in her native Novosibirsk, probably ending up in the neighbouring science town of Akademgorodok, where her father was a doctor of sciences. That left Lara. She waited to be informed of where she had been posted, and eventually the posting came: Murmansk, the fishing port in the Arctic circle. She had been appointed as a translator at the Fishery and Oceanography Polar Research Institute. She felt flattered because it was a post coveted by many, entailing a fifty percent northern allowance and contact with foreigners, but she could just see herself dealing with matters pertaining to cod and frozen oceans in Polar nights that had no end. She recalled a story about Rector Petrovsky, who had reputedly torn up a list of state appointments for one hundred graduates of the mechanics and maths faculty. The list suggested a variety of teaching posts in small village schools throughout the country, and legend had it that he said that handing out such appointments to these students was sillier than throwing millions of roubles into a fire to keep the stove burning: millions of roubles the state had spent on educating the country's best mathematicians, only to find no better use for them than to fill posts that any intelligent school-leaver was qualified for. This story was Lara's moral justification as she lied to the frowning committee that she would not be able to go where posted, for family reasons. 'Why should we waste this good post on you, then,' the head of the committee replied, piqued. 'Go and explain yourself in Irkutsk.' But she did not go to Irkutsk either. The years when the state exerted severe administrative pressure on postgraduates to put in three years working where appointed, were gone. She paid a visit to a lawyer who, parting somewhat reluctantly with the information, told her that there was no law, and never had been, forcing her to work where she was officially posted. Ten years earlier it had been common practice for education authorities to withhold the certificate of higher education, the actual piece of paper, until the postgraduate had finished the required three years. This was no longer done, since the thousands of universities, institutes and technical colleges throughout the country were now providing a steady supply of 'young specialists' sufficient to meet and even exceed demand. In some places the graduates were now even issued 'free diplomas', permitting them to look for a job wherever they wanted. This was what Lara ended up with after months of tedious formalities and string-pulling back home. The Ufa educational committee requested that she be sent back to Ufa – because of her ageing parents. So she returned to Ufa. But there were no jobs there. Ufa had its own university and pedagogical institute churning out English teachers. So the educational committee then gave her a piece of paper saying they did not really need her. Now a free agent, she returned to the capital. A regular job in Moscow being out of the question, due to the lack of a residence permit, for a few months she worked for the external relations department of the Academy of Sciences, a part-time job she had been delighted to land while in her third year at university. It involved looking after visiting scientists from socialist countries who spoke either English or French but little or no Russian. This had been fine when she was still a student earning a bit of money on the side. But with a *Diplom* in her pocket the role of general dog's-body irked. So she left it in the middle of her first independent winter to make her living solely from giving private lessons, many of which were found for her by her old university teachers.

In one year she lived in a dozen flats. Despite the chronic housing shortage there was always a number of flats temporarily vacant, some owners having gone off to do a stint of work elsewhere in the country while others had acquired two flats through marriage and were waiting for the opportunity to exchange them for a single bigger one. Sub-letting state flats was legal, provided the pretence was maintained that the lodger was paying merely for the use of the furniture. No one was supposed to make a profit from state property. So Lara, in the best of her flats, was happily paying eighty roubles a month in rent after signing an official contract for half that amount. Ironically, this flat was unfurnished: or, rather, the absentee landlord (away earning good money in Mongolia) had stored all his furniture in one heavily padlocked room. Lara had been thrown out of a previous flat after a downstairs neighbour, a frustrated latent homosexual recently divorced from his third wife, had complained several times to the *militsia* about the noise of her shower after ten o'clock at night, and about her male visitors, whose presence disturbed him. One day a young sergeant came to discuss the complaints and discovered the Ufa stamp in Lara's domestic passport. He was most apologetic about it, recognising the absurdity of the crank's complaints and clearly wishing he had never decided to investigate them. 'But I've seen your passport now. And you aren't registered in Moscow,' he said unhappily. The next day two millymen gallantly carried Lara's suitcases to a taxi. It was her twenty-fifth birthday. She was supposed to go back to Ufa, of course, but she continued to live in Moscow illegally without a residence permit, easily finding landlords and landladies ready to turn a blind eye to such irregularities.

Other work came her way. She translated a catalogue for the Academy of Sciences, which carried her name when published, and a novel based on the life of North Korean president Kim Il Sung for the North Korean embassy, which paid very well indeed, and took in some typing. She did work for VAAP (Soviet Authors' Rights Agency), translated into English for the magazines *Soviet Literature*, *Soviet Export* and *Moscow News* and, one memorable December, accompanied a group of forty Zambian dancers on a tour of Leningrad and the Baltic republics under the auspices of the Ministry of Culture. There were four interpreters altogether, plus a financial director who was normally a lighting technician at the Luzhniki sports complex. He came from an influential family, so although he did not speak any foreign languages he had been going on this sort of trip for years, and he was the nastiest person Lara had ever met, a slimy womaniser and alcoholic. Under a crazy system, he was simply handed a wad of money at the start of each tour and allowed to dispose of it as he saw fit. Naturally, a high percentage of it went on drink for himself. He was supposed to produce receipts but easily got round that. On the three-week tour, he drank expensive cognac the first week, cheap vodka the second and – money all gone – abstained in the third. The dancers, inadequately clothed for December and anyway unused to such a climate, kept falling ill with stomach upsets and colds. They turned to Lara for help because she was the only one who would listen to them and who cared. They were so miserable, feeling ill and homesick under unfamiliar cold grey northern skies, unable even to leave the hotel without permission from their own security man, that Lara spent all of her tiny allowance on presents and pills for them.

The Zambians were fantastic performers, spontaneous and genuinely creative in their music and dancing. The audiences loved them, even though the Baltic man in the street displayed some unpleasant racist attitudes. Spectators especially enjoyed an acrobatic dance by a sixteen-year-old boy with a supporting chorus. Lara recited the chorus in Russian: 'I'm a cauliflower. My twin brother has been picked. I squat here, lonely and maimed. Careful, don't step on me: I'm dreaming of my brother.' Among the drummers was a small middle-aged tribal chief who told Lara that having five wives was a formidable job and he was glad of the break. The financial director viciously objected to Lara's 'hobnobbing' with the Zambians. In Riga she called on Nadia's parents, and she was most impressed by Tallinn, capital of the republic of Estonia, which struck her as even more different than Riga. It had such a Western European atmosphere, it was so neat, its houses were so tiny, its res-taurants so cosy, she found it hard to believe she was still in the Soviet Union.

The trip was a welcome break from the daily grind of freelance work. Sometimes she wondered what sort of life she had let herself in for. Her pupils were scattered all over Moscow: some of them came to her flat for their lessons but many did not, so there was a lot of travelling. Few could afford to pay much, so Lara did not charge much. Some were Russians eager to learn English, while some were foreigners wanting to learn Russian. She was badly hurt once by an Australian couple who broke off the lessons and the relationship after she asked them to get some Marlboro cigarettes for friends next time they were in the special foreigners' shop. Lara, who had always had an aristocratic disdain of money, who had always lived as if it was beneath her consideration, was under-charging them, and the cigarettes anyway were not for her: but the silly outraged Australians said they had not thought their friendship was based on that sort of thing, as though she had been making calculated use of it; and they never contacted her again. Mainly however she got on well with her foreign friends, many of whom helped her with her translations, and she did become spoiled. Until then chicory coffee had been a luxury: now only pure coffee was good enough. Ben had arranged for her to buy a sturdy Smith-Corona typewriter from an American who was leaving and was glad to get rid of the extra luggage, so Lara got it cheap. This typewriter was in Lara's trade the means of production, and she accordingly valued it highly. And having free access to her American and English friends' private libraries was the utmost bliss, a justification and consummation of thirteen years of learning the English language. She read a book a day, reading on public transport, at the dinner table and in bed: in short, whenever she was not working. D.H. Lawrence was a revelation, followed by Kurt Vonnegut, Bernard Malamud and the entire bunch of modern American Jews; she read Richard Brautigan, then Doris Lessing and the subsequent feminists. This massive infusion of Western culture, consumed in an avid, dizzy rush, mixed with the deeply ingrained principles of a basically Victorian cast of mind. One moment she felt enlightened, the next, confused. Ideals of unbounded and adventurous personal freedom, ingeniously presented, clashed with ideas of self-righteous austerity. Lara lent Germaine Greer's *The Female Eunuch* to an Ufa friend who had made it from a wartime orphanage to a top job in Bashkirian administration, aided in his career by an attractive manly physique and a successful approach to women, whom he charmed with a condescending chivalry. He spent two nights reading the book and told Lara on the morning of the third day that it had upset the entire system of beliefs his life was based on. Lara's system of beliefs, too, was being challenged by all that she was reading.

Lara would take chunks of her work to parties, distributing pages of manuscript to native speakers for style editing. She used every possible opportunity to sneak a translation to a native speaker. Feeling alone in a battle for survival, she employed whatever cunning or subterfuge she thought necessary, including the turning on of feminine charm for men. She was so busy she never cooked proper meals, living on fried potatoes and diced garlic sausage, cooked in a frying pan that had lost its wooden handle so that it had to be gripped clumsily at the rim through a thick cloth. She could never find time to buy a new frying pan, and burnt her hands often. Her dangerous handle-less frying pan came to be referred to by everyone as the 'Mama mia padella', after the exclamation of an Italian pupil who burnt his hand on it. 'I'm going to cook some potatoes in the mama mia padella,' they would say, smiting their foreheads and waving their arms in a parody of Italian gesturing.

Some of the work was interesting. She was commissioned by a Mosfilm director to translate 'the most exciting parts' of the novel *Jaws*, which turned out to be all the sex scenes and every time the shark gobbled someone up. The director never paid her but left her the book. Lara was helped in this *Jaws* work by an American couple, John and Kris Bushnell, who were doing two years as translators for a Moscow publishing house. They were excited about her incipient career, helping her and showing great interest in it, and she blessed them for that. They shared the pleasure of her successes and the pain of her disappoint-ments. On the publication of her first translated story in *Moscow News*, they held a celebration party. She actually lived with them in their flat for a while. They drank a bit and, with them, she also learnt to drink. She would probably have begun drinking sooner or later anyway, for the strain of her way of life was starting to tell. She was in effect learning a trade with no teachers, no curriculum and no schedule, on her own. John showed infinite patience. And he and Kris even gave financial support when it became necessary, as, for all her chasing about and hard work, it occasionally did. The journals and organisa-tions she did work for were all notoriously tardy payers. Giving Lara financial support was in itself a huge achievement, for her pride was such she was quite capable of rejecting money while starving. John managed it with a clever ploy: he would give her some of his own translating work, saying he had not enough time to do it, and then carefully go over her translation, which really meant he did it. He then paid her seventy-five percent. And in this joint work, he taught her to translate.

Lara was not helped at this time by a need to go often to Ufa, where Anya's marriage was finally breaking up. Anya was persuaded to take Sasha and go to live with Lyalya in Obninsk. This meant in fact that Anya and Sasha were a lot of the time in Moscow, for poor Lyalya was not up to the extra responsibility of providing for her sister and nephew. With all three sisters departed there was nothing to keep Raisa Iosifovna in Ufa and she too moved in with Lyalya. The regained togetherness, after years of nothing but loving letters and brief visits, caused more strain than any of them had foreseen. Each had got used to her own way of life, to being her own boss. Readaptation was slow and painful, not helped by having to be achieved under the disapproving gaze of Lyalya's pedantic, strait-laced husband. Lara often had to act as mediator.

In the middle of this period of punishing hard work, deep financial insecurity and heavy family responsibility, the Bushnells, their two year contract ended, returned home to America. Lara was distraught. She had to sit up the whole of the night prior to their departure finishing a translation, which she asked John to check in the back of a van on the way to the airport. When kissing them goodbye she tottered in her high heels and nearly fell. Exhausted through lack of sleep and knowing she would never see John and Kris again, she felt so limp she could hardly stand. In the van on the journey back into Moscow she cried as though her heart would break. Tired and lonely, she felt shattered.

She discovered the Bushnells had left four hundred roubles for her with a mutual friend. They had not given it to her direct because they knew she would not have accepted it. She used this money to pay for a month-long holiday in Yalta, on the Black Sea, where she did nothing but sleep long hours, sunbathe and swim. She said afterwards this holiday probably saved her sanity.

Back in Moscow, she gathered up the threads of her work and settled down again to hard graft, aided by replacements for the Bushnells. Nina Muller, a petite Welsh girl in Moscow on a British Council grant to write a thesis on contemporary short-story writer Yuri Kazakov, helped in spite of being exasperated by Lara's perfectionism. Barry and Joy Jennings, there on the same basis as the Bushnells, helped as much as they could but they had a baby, so that was not much, and Lara helped them more by baby-sitting. Diana Miller of *Moscow News*, met at a boring party, had helped Lara immeasurably early on, introducing her to *Moscow News* and several other journals selling abroad and turning her early awkward renditions into fairly readable English, and the two women now worked together on bigger projects. Diana received commissions to translate books, work which Lara did some of for half the payment.

As the long, dark winter progressed, Lara felt things getting on top of her again. She missed terribly Nadia and John and Kris. Although she lived a social life at as punishing a pace as her professional one, she felt desperately lonely. Rarely alone in her flat except when working late at night, she nevertheless felt its cheerlessness, for though she had always liked to have lots of people around her, she had also always had a need for one or two especially close friends. Even allowing for the bad luck of Nadia marrying a foreigner, she wondered what she, so undeniably attractive, had done wrong that she could have reached the age of twenty-six and be so alone. She knew she was demanding of her friends, but surely she gave a lot in return? In particular, having experienced the pleasures of warm companionship, she yearned for the intimacy of a successful marriage. And she wanted a child. The maternal instinct was strong in her. Wanting as many experiences as life had to offer, she could not ignore the primal experience of having a baby. She wanted her share of happiness. Confronted with the plight of both her sisters however, which reinforced her deeply ingrained distrust of men, she was wary. She did not want to go the way of either of her sisters. Lyalya had taken permanent refuge in ill-health. She had become a semi-invalid, a sultry gypsy drooped listlessly across a divan, a martyr to recurring aches and pains and depression, resigned to never again feeling fine. Lara's visits, or a similar pleasing or interesting event, revived her for a little while, but she always afterwards sank back into her habitual languor. Summer heat she found debilitating, winter cold unhealthy. She had become a typical miserably married woman.

Surely, thought Lara, between the two extremes of wildness and dullness represented by her sisters' marriages there was a happy medium? Or was marriage always tremendously difficult, an endurance course strewn with obstacles to contentment? A perfectionist by nature, she was in danger of either waiting too long for the perfect man, who of course would never arrive, or of compromising, to her lifelong regret. When things were going well, this dilemma could lightly be lived with. In bad times, it drove her mad with dejection.

Meanwhile, she worked. Deadlines dominated her nights and her days. The work had to be done, and done on time. Procrastination was paid for dearly in panicky races against the clock. By the end of the winter she would have had a lot of money – if all those she had worked for had paid up. As it was, she was broke.

By then, when the sun had been warm enough on a few days to melt the snow a little on south-facing pavements, sills and roofs, she was toying with the idea of taking another holiday, and wondering how she could rake up enough money to pay for it. She resented having more work than she could handle at the same time as not having enough money to pay for a holiday. In the last days of February her routine of working through most of the night and sleeping till midday was broken by a caretaker clumping about on the roof above her bedroom each morning, hurling down masses of soft snow with an aluminium shovel. Able usually to sleep through any noise, this clumping and scraping, combined with her current restless state of mind, woke her up and prevented her going back to sleep. Dark, blueish rings appeared under her eyes. Just before half-past ten on the night of March 4, she was debating whether to do some work or have an early night for a change when the room shook. Scared, she rushed down the fourteen flights of stairs out to the street, along with neighbours. Someone phoned the seismology institute to confirm it was an earthquake, and was told it was but only a small harmless tremor and was advised to go back indoors, where it would be perfectly safe. Most of the neighbours stayed outside, however, too excited to go back and watch television, but Lara returned to her flat, where she continued her ruminations about work, sleep and money. Of all her debtors, the only one she could put pressure on for payment was Diana, who owed her hundreds of roubles for work done months before. So she phoned Diana. Diana could say only that she was expecting a large amount any day now and would pay Lara as soon as it came. Lara had not seriously entertained hopes of any other answer. 'By the way,' she said, 'I just felt an earthquake.' She told Diana all about it. Affected like everyone else by the excitement of the experience, she could not now think of going to sleep, so after her call to Diana she did some work, breaking off as usual in the early hours of the morning.

The next day, she was woken up too early, not this time by the caretaker on the roof but by the phone ringing. Bleary-eyed and cursing, she jumped out of bed and answered it. It was the *Morning Star* Moscow correspondent wanting her impressions of the earthquake.

Chapter Nine
THREE SCORE YEARS AND THEN

Lara's Victorian prudery and my shyness meant we never discussed birth control, except for one day when she asked me point blank, out on her balcony, with guests inside, what I would do if she became pregnant. 'Is she?' I asked myself, going to pieces.

Birth control for unmarried people in Russia is difficult, for it is state policy that devices be freely available only to women who have had at least one child. I could have bought sheaths but all the shop assistants in chemists were young women whom I could not face for such a purchase; I had read that Soviet sheaths were thick, clumsy and unreliable; and I did not know the word. 'There would be three alternatives, I suppose,' I replied. 'Abortion, illegitimate birth or marriage.' Abortion was the most widely used form of birth control. It had been legalised again in 1955 after Stalin had banned it twenty years before. Young women often had four or five abortions in as many years. It is nevertheless still a traumatic experience, and Lara was appalled at my apparent insensitivity.

She said to herself, 'All right, let's call it a day.' Only the fact that she had guests stopped her throwing me out there and then. That night, in bed with my back to her, I said casually, 'What do you think about us getting married?'

She said, 'I think it's a good idea.'

She was having to leave her flat, and plans were well advanced for her to move to another in the far north-east of the city, to be shared with a friend called Galya. This flat was as far from mine as it was possible to be and still be in the same town. I thought she might as well move in with me for convenience and to save money but she did not want to let Galya down. I had not even met Raisa Iosifovna yet and Lara wanted to keep her independence until our marriage, so she moved to this other flat. There we had our first row. Typically it was over nothing. We had been out for the day, and, nearing home, Lara got it into her head that I was 'mean'. It was important, she said, for she hated meanness in people more than anything else. I knew that I was not mean and that time would prove it, but nothing I could say or do would help at that moment. Lara was so upset that for about thirty minutes it seemed our romance was finished. We sat in a children's sand pit in the desolate space in front of her new block, Lara crying while I did not know what to do or say. Then the mood passed. She apologised, we dusted the sand off her clothes and continued our day together. It was as though a lone cloud in an otherwise clear sky had drifted over the sun to cut off its warmth. Soon after this Lara did become pregnant.

By now it was summer. The dry air of the surrounding plain drifted into the city. The *topol*, or white poplar, shed its fluffy seeds, which slowly sank to gather in bleached drifts along the edges of pavements and in sheltered corners. On breezy days the air would be thick with this fluff, so that it clogged your nostrils and got into your mouth. I had been looking forward to my month's holiday in London but once there I missed Lara and felt I should be with her, so returned to Moscow after only a fortnight. The expense and inconvenience of her new flat proving too much, she finally moved in with me.

Sam visited Moscow on a free holiday. Lara and I entertained him at our flat one evening, as an obligation. Sensing romance in the air, he made a point of saying that if the hard-line group that had recently broken away from the British Party, called the New Communist Party, was allowed to have a correspondent in Moscow, as seemed possible, I would be withdrawn, so Lara and I would be separated. I did not tell him we planned to marry for I did not regard him as a friend and felt it was none of his business. He heard it later from someone else. For some reason this infuriated him. 'I resent not being told by you,' he said over the phone. As always, I was cowed. Instead of telling him to get knotted I mumbled something resembling an apology. Then he said, 'Has there been sign of any official disapproval?'

Of course there had not been, nor could there have been. But I had lived in Russia only a few months and knew nothing about the country beforehand. He was an expert on the place, with thirty years' experience. One had to assume he knew what he was talking about. I felt that Lara, unregistered, unmarried and pregnant, was horribly vulnerable. Lara herself did not feel vulnerable, knowing that in her condition no one would hurt her. The only thing that would have hurt was me bottling out. We discussed this and I assured her I was only a physical coward, not a 'moral' one. But certainly, not knowing what to expect in an alien country and unnerved by Sam's question, I was confused and worried to the point of paranoia. One morning the phone rang at 6 o'clock and I leapt out of bed to answer it, half asleep, and could not understand what was said. It was a man's voice, speaking Russian, and it sounded sinister. The man called me '*Gospodin* Bushell' – Mr Bushell – the form of address used before the revolution and now only applied to 'bourgeois' foreigners. I was usually called *Tovarish* – Comrade. '*Gospodin*' might be a sign of disapproval, signifying I was no longer considered a friend. 'Is this the way it's done?' I thought. 'Is this how they start to express their disapproval?' The next day, at a more civilised hour, my old teacher of Russian in London, Mr Purves, phoned to say he was in Moscow on a short visit and apologised for phoning so early the previous day.

Several of Lara's old friends re-appeared at this time, to her delight. Whether childhood friends from Ufa or university friends, whether working-class or intellectuals, they shared one characteristic – they liked to talk till the early hours of the morning. They would sit in the kitchen, drink tea or wine or vodka, smoke, nibble dried sunflower seeds – and talk. International affairs, Russian affairs, affairs of the heart, all would be discussed animatedly, with never a pause. Sometimes they were happy *tochit lyasy*, to chatter, while at other times the talk would be *po-dusham* 'soul to soul'; or the talk would flow effortlessly from one type of conversation to the other and back again. Petty gossip could precede observations on great issues, for they did not rigidly demarcate small-talk and big-talk and the transition was effected easily. I could clearly picture past events and old acquaintances from their unaffected and exuberant descriptions. Such sparkling talk displayed a talent that transcended mere social accomplishment. Most were ordinary people working in mundane jobs, to whom little luxuries (and sometimes necessities) that in England would be taken for granted came rarely, usually requiring some inordinate effort on their part: and yet their talk sparkled with a far superior basic intelligence than would have been found in their English counterparts. They reminded me of the two young boys Thackeray overheard in Ireland as, dressed almost in rags, they 'lolled over a harbour wall and talked brilliantly about one of the ancient Egyptian Ptolemys'. Voices did not grow shrill in these sessions at our flat, no matter how heated the discussion. Sometimes they deepened. The friends came from different parts of the country, and they usually brought something that was currently available where they came from and not in Moscow – good linen, fresh salmon, sub-tropical fruit. Lara had a large number of such friends, from whom she exacted much and to whom she gave much. Friendship for her was not a casual relationship: it entailed duties and obligations nearly as demanding as those of familial relationships. Because this feeling came naturally to her, the demands did not seem heavy.

Lyuba, a sinuous acrobatics coach from Moldavia, would get gorgeously drunk and impersonate a dancing *tsiganka*, gypsy woman, which, with Lara and Anya clapping and singing an old song, 'Dark eyes, passionate eyes, burning and beautiful eyes . . .' transformed our kitchen into a *tabor*, gypsy camp. Tanya, a Siberian, I remember describing a Chukchi holiday: 'Many Chukchi still breed reindeer, travelling with the herds in summer,' she said. 'Each year each family, which under Soviet power means a team, sell to the state two thousand deer at ninety kopecks a kilo. As a deer weighs two hundred to three hundred kilos they should earn annually about two hundred thousand roubles. But as they do not know the value of money the clerk simply throws notes at them until they think they have enough, which is usually less than half that amount. It is government policy not to allow them to be served in shops until they have washed. Because of the climate traditionally they do not wash or change their clothes very much. The showers are such that you stand under either scalding steam or freezing water. Rarely do the two merge to make hot water. So a woman waits outside the

shower to check as they come out whether they have had a
proper shower or not. This she does by sliding her fingers along
a hair on their heads. If it makes the correct wet noise she lets
them go. If not, they have to go back. Rich and clean, they now
go shopping. They are interested in only one thing – the "holy
water" – vodka. In the wine shop money is again thrown down
by the handful – this time by them. Again they are the losers.
The shop assistant tells them when to stop. Having got the
vodka they go in search of a type of mushroom which when
immersed in the drink gives off a laughing gas. They drink the
gassy vodka, roll about laughing for an hour and then collapse
for two. They wake up, vomit and begin again. Their pleasure
would kill a softer European. Then they go back to their work
herding the deer.'

I enjoyed these evenings. Many of these people had had a
hard, buffeting, struggling life; and it had imparted shrewdness
and earthy humour. Those that had remained Lara's friends
were the most generous when need arose, the ones who, though
endlessly busy and overcrowded, always found time and space
for a chat when someone's troubles needed airing. They were the
ones who had no idea of thrift. (It was true, Lara could not stand
mean people.) Their genuineness and earthiness shone out as
cardinal virtues, leaving dim and unimportant their less admir-
able traits. They were the ones who had passed Lara's uncom-
promising test for sincerity. Undepleted by superficialities, they
had an affinity with the earth and its basics. Sometimes the
extravagant emotional atmosphere they created had a chaotic,
anarchistic edge but it was always vibrant. It tired me, I must
admit. I usually had to give up and go to bed soon after
midnight. If I was still awake when Lara joined me later, I
noticed she was invigorated by these sessions rather than
exhausted.

One of our guests was an attractive, petite, dark-eyed Tatar
from Ufa, a waitress named Zameera. As she had not seen Lara
for several years, was meeting me for the first time and had an
important personal decision to make, she talked at length about
herself, speaking Russian with a Tatar accent. Born just after the
war, she was her parents' fourth child but the only one to
survive infancy. One boy had died of dysentery, one girl of some

other disease and another it seemed had died simply of starvation. Zameera herself was very sickly. At the age of five she still could not walk unaided because of rickets (she remained bow-legged). Her father disappeared when she was seven. She shared one room with her mother and a sick cousin. Married life was even worse, for she was still in one room now with three other people – her husband and their son and daughter. Her husband took to drink, so she left him. Her big decision was whether to go back to him or not. He had been for treatment and was currently not drinking.

Another guest was Vera, one of the few who did not have a mundane job. A philologist, she had just been set a peculiar task by the Ministry of Food – to find the origin of the word vodka. She was not sure why the ministry wanted this information – 'It's a trade problem, I think,' she said – but it seemed clear to me that the ministry had decided it would be profitable to have a monopoly on the use of the word vodka just as France had on the words champagne and cognac. Vodka however is a Polish word also; and Vera had come across it in Polish in 1600 while the earliest she could find it in Russian was 1649. 'We have a good chance though,' she said once. 'All the Polish sources have been fully investigated but we have many Russian manuscripts absolutely untouched.' Later however she lost her optimism; and she never did find the word in Russian before 1600 – which is why you can still buy in Britain all those British vodkas with Russian-sounding names. The Soviet Union had actually complained to these companies about calling their stuff vodka and had already taken its case to an international court but the Poles were unhappy about it, as Polish vodka is a valuable export, and without the early word the Russians stood no chance of winning this particular game of monopoly.

Vera had a two-year-old daughter whom she saw twice a year. The girl was living with Vera's mother in a small town in the southern Ukraine, one thousand miles from Moscow. Vera had made this arrangement because she wanted maximum freedom for herself and a good climate for her daughter. 'It's better for a child to be in the south,' she said. 'There's more fruit and vegetables, more sun, and she's near the sea and a river.' She paid a nanny fifty roubles a month to help her mother with the child. Neither she nor anyone else considered it a strange arrangement, for grandmothers in Russia have always played a big part in bringing up children.

Preparations for the marriage went on apace. I put up the banns at the British embassy and swore an oath with the consul, Miss Borland. The consular offices were installed in the grounds of the palatial embassy building on the embankment opposite the Kremlin. Each of the two entrances at either end of the courtyard wall was guarded by two policemen, one of whom would stand firmly in your path if you did not flash your British passport. You would not pass until you showed you were not a Russian seized with a desire to move in diplomatic circles. I believe I could have chosen an atheistic oath but Miss Borland had the holy one all ready and I did not care enough either way to warrant making a fuss. We were alone in her small office but because I stumbled over a sentence halfway through she insisted we begin again from the beginning, even to the extent of both of us sitting down again and standing up again and her handing me the Bible again. 'You serious?' I said. She was. I suppose if you are taking a holy oath there is another Presence, Who does indeed have to be taken seriously.

Soviet law provides three ways of registering a marriage: the wife may take the husband's surname, the husband may take the wife's or they may each keep their own name. Lara had no intention of changing her name, so we decided on the third way, a decision that caused problems with British documents.

When we registered we were given a booklet like a ration book, to be used at special Wedding Shops where you could buy gold rings and all the other traditional necessities of marriage. Each type of product had a section in the booklet, and when you bought something that section was cut out so you could not use it again. Things were not cheaper in these special shops but were simply always available: that was what made them special and why rationing was necessary. We bought our wedding rings at one of them, and a pair of shoes each without the aggravation that usually accompanies this transaction. The shop, which was a big department store, was crowded, because that time of the year (after the harvest had been gathered in) is traditionally the time for weddings in Russia. We had been worried about this, doubting that we could be fitted in quickly, but were lucky in that we were available any day of the week.

We notified Lara's departed friends of the impending marriage. I phoned John and Kris Bushnell. Kris congratulated me sincerely, saying I was lucky. 'You'll never be bored,' she said. It was a phrase I was to recall many times.

We went for long walks in the country. Deep in a wood once we engaged in some desultory mushroom picking, sifting the fallen leaves with dry, dead branches or long twigs. (Serious mushroom picking entailed getting up at five in the morning, which Lara had been known to do even though for her it meant only two or three hours sleep.) I picked several beauties, all of them bright red and firm and poisonous. Lara always returned from these walks with at least one twig or branch she had been attracted to by its peculiar shape. She kept any that in her eyes resembled some animal or the human figure. Several stood in our flat as decorations, Lara being so attached to them she carted them with her in her various removals. Large yellow maple leaves covered the forest floor, over ankle deep in some places, so that you waded through them as though paddling in water.

We were lucky enough to be in the forest on the final summer's day, when shafts of sunlight filtered through the trees and dappled the ground and the mouldering, acrid smell of loose foliage being burnt was wafted to us from nearby garden plots. We saw the bonfires on our way to catch the bus home, the flames flaring brighter and the smell growing sharper as the day gently declined, melting away in the damp warmth, peacefully and sadly, smallholders chatting to each other in between tending their fires, their voices reaching us clearly. After that day the weather deteriorated sharply. Soon every branch was bare, a couple of strong winds having been sufficient to dislodge the few leaves still clinging. Now the air smelt fresh from puddles that each night were covered by bright, glassy ice, from clods of earth dappled white, and from the fallen leaves which, though they still rustled loudly as we pushed through them, were now damp from night-frost. The smell of the bonfires was increasingly one of smouldering ashes rather than leaping flames.

Both of us viewed the actual wedding ceremony much as students view an examination and job-hunters an interview. We were not looking forward to it. It being unavoidable, however, we made preparations. Galya made a wedding gown out of two large traditional white-and-flowery Russian shawls. We booked a small room in a restaurant on Leninsky, the Moldavanka.

Preparations were going on at the same time for another celebration, a somewhat larger affair – the Day of the Sixtieth Anniversary of the Revolution. Nearly every day in the Soviet calendar is a Day of Something-or-Other. October 7 was two Days in one – Constitution Day and Teachers' Day. May Day and Anniversary Day are the two great public holidays however, with the latter taking pride of place that year as the sixtieth anniversary. Press, radio and television had been preparing the people for the occasion for months beforehand. *Pravda* editorials had urged workers to complete production schedules before time in honour of the anniversary, and there was a rash of solemn and impressive pledging. Three weeks before the event all the national and local newspapers had published on their front pages the slogans. There were seventy-three to choose from, number one being 'Long live the Sixtieth Anniversary of the Great October Socialist Revolution!' and number seventy-three proclaiming 'Under the banner of Marxism-Leninism, under the leadership of the Communist Party – forward to the Victory of Communism!' All domestic and international issues were sloganised. Subtle changes and additions and omissions in these slogans from year to year give Kremlinologists clues as to the thinking of the Soviet leaders on domestic and foreign policies. Every Soviet citizen was covered by at least one slogan. Trade unions, the armed services, women, industrial workers, the intelligentsia, 'veterans of the revolution, the war and labour', health workers, athletes and coaches, schoolchildren – all had their own slogan. All institutes, factories and districts had a ready-made banner stored away to be dug out and unfurled twice a year. The actual holidays were Monday and Tuesday, making it a very long weekend, a welcome break, but all the preceding week there was a festive atmosphere. On the previous Monday a woman groaning under the weight of two full shopping bags from the market turned to me in the street and said, 'And this is only the beginning!' In that week, schools and kindergartens held 'morning parties' that went on till the evening while offices and factories had 'evening parties' that lasted till the morning. There were numerous seminars, conferences and meetings devoted to the Great October, climaxing on the Wednesday and Thursday in a celebration meeting in the Palace of Congresses at the Kremlin, where delegates from about one hundred countries listened to leading figures of the international working-class movement. Top Soviet citizens from all fields of life and work were also at the Kremlin meeting, and in the intervals you had to shout to be heard above the clinking of medals as all the heroes of socialist labour, war heroes and other honoured Soviet citizens walked by. Among the guests were Alex Kitson, representing the British Labour Party, and Gordon McLennan. I had to arrange for a photograph of Gordon speaking at the meeting. Under a long-standing reciprocal arrangement, TASS correspondents in London obtained photographs from the *Morning Star* picture department, while the *Morning Star* Moscow correspondent got pictures from Fotokhronika Tass, where I dealt with one Galina Lantseva. I had told her days in advance I would be needing this picture, Gordon spoke in the morning and Moscow was three hours ahead of London. Believing it would be a routine job done calmly in plenty of time, I phoned Ms Lantseva at one in the afternoon to ask when it would be convenient to collect the picture.

She said, 'Comrade McLennan has not spoken yet.'

I said, 'Oh yes he has.'

'Just a second. . . Correct. It is just that our photographer did not take any pictures.'

'I'm sure he did.'

'Just a second.'

Three-quarters of an hour later: 'Terry? Hello, there! We have checked. The picture can be collected tomorrow afternoon' – which, for a daily newspaper, was useless. I remonstrated. She then said it could probably be ready within a couple of hours and would call me when it was. I eventually sent a picture by telegraph at five o'clock. Another photograph that had been arranged of Gordon with politburo member Dinmukhammed

Kunayev was indeed not ready until the following day, and even this was after Ms Lantseva had claimed she knew nothing about such a picture.

On the Friday evening, street lights and illuminations gleaming through an early dusk and drizzling snow and people doing their last-minute shopping gave Moscow the atmosphere of an English Christmas Eve. Laughter was a bit louder than usual, steps a bit lighter, shopping bags a bit heavier. It had been ensured that shops were well stocked for the occasion.

Finally the great Day arrived. I got up at seven to make my way into the centre of the city before the crowds became too dense. Every building had red flags fluttering on metal flagpoles permanently embedded in its brickwork or stucco. By the Universitet metro station two men were hurriedly installing one last portrait of Brezhnev on a wall. I overheard two tourists – American ladies who had learnt a smattering of Russian for their trip – translate a slogan as 'Yes Hello Leninist Communist Party of the Soviet Union'. 'Yes Hello' is a close translation of the Russian equivalent of 'Viva' or 'Long live'. The streets were only just being brightened by dawn. Slush covered the pavements, caused by heavy weekend snow and a sudden thaw. Aware that I would be standing for two or three hours on freezing concrete, I had put on my Arctic reindeer boots, great furry clodhoppers that made my feet sweat even in the coldest weather. I shared an underground carriage with a gaggle of schoolgirls colourfully attired in tracksuits for the gymnastics display part of the procession through Red Square. Each carried a large paper carnation. Only they and I were using the metro because only we had passes enabling us to alight at Marx Prospect station adjoining Red Square. At the top of the elevator stood the first of several police cordons. Between the station and the next cordon at the square I had to jostle my way through crowds so thick that soon they would be impassable. Manege Square and all the streets leading into Red Square were filled with tanks, missiles and khaki lorries awaiting the military parade, while further back, out of sight, the participants in the main citizens' procession would be forming up in their groups from workplace or district. A few days before I had gone to Ball-bearings Factory Number One in the south-east of the city, where the factory's party committee was discussing anniversary matters such as who of the staff would represent the factory in the parade. It was decided that their contingent would have nine hundred workers. They, along with five thousand other people of the district contingent, were to meet at the factory at nine forty-five and march through Red Square at eleven twelve, led by fifty-year-old metalworker Mikhail Kondakov, who had worked at the factory since he was twenty. This contingent would now be in its place on one of the roads approaching the square. By the Bolshoi Theatre building big groups of Young Pioneers, red kerchiefs around their necks and balloons clutched in their hands, were being coaxed and nudged into position by men resembling scoutmasters. The excited children broke ranks as soon as the scoutmasters' backs were turned, while in one place a full-scale fight developed, two boys violently disputing who was at fault over the escape of a blue balloon now floating away up Kalinin Prospect.

I took my place alongside my fellow wordsmiths in the area next to the Lenin mausoleum reserved for journalists. The Soviet leaders ascended the tomb. The spectacle began on the stroke of ten – on the third stroke of the chimes of the Kremlin clock, to be precise. At twelve minutes past eleven I looked out for Mikhail Kondakov and his workmates from the ball-bearings factory but the square was too packed. Small children were carried on fathers' shoulders and bigger children walked hand in hand with parents, although taking children on the parade was not advised because of the early start and long wait. The columns filed through the square for nearly two hours with complete informality, laughing and joking and singing. Paper flowers were everywhere, done up as garlands and bouquets, woven into designs (including one beautiful portrait of Lenin) or worn in buttonholes or simply carried in hand. Hot wine was on sale to spectators, but even with that stimulant towards the end I was frozen all over apart from the two appendages cosily zipped up in reindeer fur. When I left, the columns were still filing in. Outside the square, by the Lenin Museum, you could still see thousands of people converging from over a mile away. Some broke out into impromptu dances while waiting for their column to move, or teased the young soldiers standing duty –

then the column would suddenly surge forward and there was a need to run to catch up.

I had miscalculated the time. After the parade there was a buffet banquet in the Kremlin attended by all the bigwigs, to which only Communists had been invited, me included. But now there was no time to get home and change into more suitable footwear, so I had to attend the banquet in my fur boots. I felt such a fool. Brezhnev was there, shaking hands with everyone, and Premier Kosygin, looking bored, as he always did on formal public occasions. Everyone who was anyone was there. The large hall was a splendiferous sight, gold and white mouldings on marble walls ablaze under huge crystal chandeliers. The politburo sat at a table at one end of the room, a band played soft music on a platform at the other end, while we stood in the middle at long buffet tables, digging in. The tables, which ranged down both sides of the hall and down the centre, were laden with caviar, crab, sturgeon, salmon, cooked meats and fruit and vegetables, vodka of all flavours and colours, Georgian wines and five-star Armenian cognac. Waiters served dinky little jugs of hot mushrooms and coffee from silver trays. I shook hands with ambassadors, conversed with cosmonauts, joked with ballerinas, all of whom politely tried to keep their eyes off my great furry clodhoppers.

I could not stay long anyway, for I still had my day's work to do – write a report on the parade and send a photo. I went home and wrote my story and telexed it to London and then collected a photo from Ms Lantseva and took it to the telegraph office. All traffic being banned in the centre, Gorky Street was an unbroken mass of heads. The whole of Moscow had a carnival atmosphere, with everybody out promenading. Even prams had tiny flags affixed. Music was piped throughout the main streets, while from nearly every courtyard came the sound of an accordion and singing. Knots of spectators gathered round dancers. At eight o'clock the Kremlin clock and a dull booming in various parts of the city signalled the start of a fireworks display. For fifteen minutes, red, green and yellow stars cascaded in the sky, the sparks falling like a golden rain, cheers going up as each firework scattered its colours against the black sky.

After viewing the fireworks display from our window, Lara and I went for a walk. Snow was falling now, making the streets blustery white. This, the illuminations and sound of singing in the distance, again brought to mind Christmas. Some people leaned out of a brightly lit window and shouted to us and waved. All barriers were down and the whole of the city was one big family celebration.

And then Lara and I got married. The ceremony was held at Wedding Palace Number One in Griboyedov Street. Our witnesses were Peter Tempest and Campbell Creighton. We drove to Griboyedov Street in Peter's flash West German car, the day clear and sunny. Parked outside the pastel green building of the Wedding Palace (which was an aristocrat's mansion before the revolution) was a long, sleek, black Chaika limousine hired for the occasion, and two humble borrowed Zhigulis bedecked in ribbons and balloons. Tied to the front grille of one was a teddy bear, symbolising the couple's wish for children. A group of guests dressed in their best clothes stood on the pavement, some carrying bouquets to be presented to the bride, each bouquet consisting of an odd number of flowers, as an even number is for funerals. Hair lacquer and after-shave made for a festive odour. We climbed up a one-flight, red-carpeted staircase, at the top of which was the cloakroom, a closed gift shop and a woman selling bouquets. A newly-married couple passed us on their way out. The women in our group accompanied Lara to the bride's waiting room while I went with Peter and Campbell to present our documents. We booked the resident photographer but declined a recording of the wedding march. Music cost extra. Separate knots of people, each a bridal party, went about their business, each oblivious of the others, the brides dressed in white gowns and clutching bunches of roses or carnations. A loudspeaker instructed me to collect my bride. Anya and Raisa Iosifovna, stifling giggles, informed me they would not let Lara go until a dowry was paid. This threw me. I did not know this oriental custom persisted and anyway they had left it a bit late. No one had mentioned it before. I turned to the gift shop but it was still closed. Then Campbell, an old hand, came to my rescue with some pre-wrapped solution. Everyone laughed, and we passed through high double doors to the ceremony in that condition, chortling, a merry crowd. The ceremony was brief but dignified, performed by the director, Mrs Klara Yemeshkova, a middle-aged woman with short dark hair. Over her plain polo-necked black dress was draped a red sash bearing the emblem of the Russian Republic. We stood on a red carpet in the middle of the high-ceilinged room while our guests arranged themselves along a wood-panelled wall on our left, next to a bust of Lenin. Lara was holding a bouquet of seven long-stemmed roses wrapped in cellophane. At the far end of the brightly lit room, in front of tall windows draped with elaborate white curtains, stood Mrs Yemeshkova's large, ornate wooden desk, on which was a tray containing our plain gold rings, a crystal vase with white carnations, and our passports. Mrs Yemeshkova picked up the two rings, approached us and had us exchange the rings, without vows. It is the custom in Russia for the groom to have a wedding ring as well as the bride. Wedding rings are worn on the right hand. I had reminded myself of this many times beforehand but forgot at the instant it mattered and held out my left hand. The photographer clicked at that instant, to show for posterity Lara, her ring on her right hand, sliding my ring onto the finger of my wrong hand. Mrs Yemeshkova then said she hoped we would be a good family as the basic unit of Soviet society, shook our hands and gave us our passports, Lara's domestic one and my British one, both already stamped with the registration of the marriage. The tall, burly official photographer snapped us signing on the dotted line, us kissing and a group scene: and that was it.

It was a bit conveyor-beltish (you got the impression Mrs Yemeshkova could hardly refrain from bawling 'Next!' before we were out of the room) but no more than weddings in urban register offices anywhere else.

The walls of the Moldavanka were covered in murals of peasants in traditional Moldavian costume. About thirty guests feasted on *zakuski*, vodka, wine and champagne and a meat dish, at ten roubles a head. As an economy measure, we had ordered as little drink as possible, bringing our own to supplement the restaurant's. The guests danced to recorded music coming from the main hall of the restaurant. Lara and I were pestered throughout by cries of '*Gorko, gorko*' (bitter, bitter) meaning, 'Life is bitter, give us something sweet', which was a call for us to stand and kiss. About half the guests were foreigners. Because of that our party was subdued compared to the usual boisterous Russian wedding party. Every guest made a toast in our honour at some point in the evening, some of the toasts elaborate, some joky. Vladimir, my teacher of Russian, had composed a poem for the occasion, which he recited. Someone else quoted some appropriate verse from Pushkin. The corner was stacked with gifts. Raisa Iosifovna was seated next to Donald, who conversed with her throughout in his faultless Russian. Afterwards she asked, 'Who was that charming man sitting next to me?'

'His name is Donald Maclean,' we said.

'What a charming man.'

'He was a spy.'

'Oh.' Raisa Iosifovna's kindly face suddenly developed a fastidious pout. 'I thought all through the evening there was something fishy about him.'

Chapter Ten
A MAN IN THE MOTHERLAND

We honeymooned in Yerevan, where there was still warm sunshine, before settling down for the winter to await the arrival of our baby. Lara had stopped smoking. We walked long distances together every night. Our life was quiet and uneventful. I had a certain amount of researching and writing to do but not much, as the job, which I had never properly got a grip on, was slipping ever further from my grasp. While I did what little work I had, Lara sat reading or translating.

We bought a cumbersome, heavy, ugly and broken second-hand cot for nearly as much as a new one would have cost, if we had been able to buy a new one. We made it ready for its occupant, with blankets and blue eiderdowns. Everything was blue. Lara so definitely wanted a boy we never considered getting anything pink for a girl. We even chose only a boy's name. We decided on Daniel, as it was so similar in both languages (Daniil in Russian).

Raisa Iosifovna moved in with us. This move seemed so natural to Lara she did not even discuss it with me. *Babushkas* always move in to help with babies, no matter how crowded it makes the flat and despite the additional differences of opinion. On our walks Lara clung tightly to my arm the whole time for fear of slipping on the icy pavements. She said she could not remember a winter when she had not slipped and fallen heavily at least once. Such an accident in her condition could, of course, be a disaster. With her equilibrium all upset she was exceptionally clumsy, so slipped every few hundred yards, each time

jerking at my arm, to my intense irritation. Because of her round
stomach I called her 'Mr Pickwick'.

I must be one of the few Westerners ever to have attended a
Soviet antenatal clinic: and, judging by the reaction of the
obstetrician, the first-ever man. I had asked the head of the
maternity home housing the clinic if many men accompanied
their wives to these talks. 'Oh yes, many,' she replied. This
turned out to be Russian flannel.

The squat, yellow-brick building stood down a side-street, off
the main road, though, in the complicated Soviet fashion, its
address was number seventeen of the main road. The first time
we went there we had a hard job to find it. In its grounds stood
silver birches taller than the building itself and young men
calf-deep in snow looking up at its windows. Behind the
windows were the top halves of young women in dressing-
gowns. Some windows were white-washed over completely,
while the ground-floor ones were made of frosted glass, behind
which moved blurred white figures.On the wall, over a pile of
empty orange boxes, a small fascia sign said Maternity Home
No. 25.

The inmates were not allowed visitors, so they stood behind
the double-glazing gesticulating to their outmates. Some inmates
were still pregnant, others had already given birth. Lara was
waddling like a penguin, scared of slipping over. A cold wind
blew falling snow all over the place. Settled snow lay all around.
We walked through a courtyard and entered a green outer door
at the top of a few concrete steps. The middle of the steps had
been swept clear of snow and ice. Mounds of hard snow
remained at the sides. After the green outer door we were
confronted with a glass partition and two more doors, both
glass, one to the left, one to the right, an arrangement designed
to keep out freezing draughts. In that arrangement sometimes
the left-hand inner door was locked, sometimes the right-hand
one. I approached the left-hand one and pulled and pushed.
That day it was the right-hand one that was not locked. Now we
were in the reception hall. The reception was cool. On one side a
blank-faced receptionist behind a counter and a pane of glass
was denying to an angry pregnant woman that she had given her

a wrong appointment time, which had led to a wasted journey across the ice. On the other side an old kerchiefed cloakroom attendant was refusing to take any coats. 'I'm full up,' she was saying. 'Where do you all come from? Too many people.' Women in various stages of pregnancy were in various stages of coming and going. As no overcoats were being accepted, we went in still wearing ours, under a sign saying, 'The Soviet Health Service is the Best in the World'.

'Where do you think you're going!'

We turned around. It was the receptionist who had screamed. Lara told her. She replied, 'Not with your coats on, you're not. Overcoats are not allowed.'

'The cloakroom attendant won't take them.'

'Overcoats not allowed. Leave them on the chairs in the hall here.'

If we had done that in the beginning, she would have screamed that that was not allowed. As it was, I was wearing my expensive British sheepskin overcoat and was reluctant to leave it in the hall. I told her this. 'Can I leave it with you?' I asked.

'No,' she said.

While we were discussing what was to be done, two women came out and collected their coats. Now there were two free hooks, so we could leave our coats with the cloakroom attendant. We took them off and handed them over the counter to her and she, still grumbling at the number of people in the world, slammed our numbered discs onto the counter for us to pick up. We went again under the National Health Service advertisement.

That maternity home had a terrible reputation for infections. My friend Igor told me that though it was his local one, his wife had not gone there to have her baby. He said it was reckoned over half the deliveries there were complicated by infections. Lara also did not intend going there for the birth. But it was our local one, too, and was convenient to attend for the antenatal talks.

On a wall of the concrete corridor hung an anti-abortion poster: a picture of a foetus and the text, 'If you, young woman, terminate this beautiful budding life you are committing a crime. And by starting this life you will prolong your own.'

These posters distressed many women. There were many complaints about them. (Abortions were carried out in the same building.) We climbed up two flights of concrete stairs and entered a room at the end of the corridor. A dozen swollen women sat round two sides of it, those on one side on chairs, the others at right angles to them on a long low gymnasium bench. Opposite the bench were windows, beneath which were radiators and beyond which the snow was hurtling horizontally. The fourth wall was taken up by a blackboard. Behind the bench were wall bars. In the middle of the parquet floor was a sunray machine. By the windows stood a white-coated obstetrician with a set of diagrams. She was a middle-aged woman wearing glasses, with fair hair piled up in a bun. She had not started her talk. Upon our entrance, the women giggled and the obstetrician said, 'You are together?'

'Yes,' we said.

'We'll be talking about intimate things,' she said unhappily. Clearly, the head of the maternity home had lied when she said many husbands attended these talks. Lara and I went to the only free place, the far end of the bench. Most of the women were overweight, pudgy and sallow and altogether unhealthy-looking. Only Lara and a couple of the others were not. Most were wearing a fluffy woollen hat, thick woollen tights and boots. None had maternity clothes. Instead they wore ordinary clothes bursting at the seams.

The obstetrician began. Very solemnly, she said, 'You should remember that giving birth is a physiological process.' At first, confused by a male presence, she was not very articulate and spoke too loud. But soon, her themes and the situation being so familiar, she talked normally. She constantly made two comparisons: between humans and nature and between the Soviet Union and the West, mainly France. 'In France,' she said, 'sixty-eight per cent of mothers have a natural delivery, with no complications nor help needed, while in the Soviet Union in sixty-two per cent of deliveries there is something wrong with either the mother or the baby and help is needed.' She went on with some frank warnings. 'Every twenty seconds a defective baby is born in the world and unfortunately it is not such a rare occurrence in our socialist motherland,' she said.

'The trouble with our women is obesity. In the Soviet Union fifty per cent of the population is overweight. Woman, because of their physiological make-up, should eat less than men. Our ballet dancers and gymnasts eat a twentieth of what an ordinary woman stuffs into herself every day although their professions demand much more energy. Fat takes up a lot of oxygen so an overweight pregnant woman has to breathe hard to satisfy her layers of fat, leaving little for the baby, who needs oxygen for his proper growth. It can be especially bad during labour because the baby works as hard as the woman. If you are overweight during labour your baby is liable to asphyxiate. It is also bad for the baby if it is too big itself. Smaller babies, up to 3.7 kilos, grow and develop better than giants. Napoleon weighed six hundred grammes at birth and he was put in a beer mug and placed on the stove to "bake" and warm milk was dripped into his nose. Turgenev and Lomonosov both weighed less than a kilo at birth. When they grew up their brains alone must have weighed several kilos. To make your labour natural and produce a healthy baby you should move as much as possible during your pregnancy making not less than fifteen thousand steps a day – that is, two hours walking a day. In order to lose thirty grammes you should make six thousand steps extra. Lack of movement is the curse of our time. Women should be more active during pregnancy, not less. They should not be mollycoddled. When a herd of deer is running the pregnant does run in the vanguard. Why? Because in pregnancy the entire organism is doubled in strength and energy. So, whereas usually a pregnant woman is treated like an invalid she should in fact take a broom in her hand and clean and wash the flat and do all the household chores with even more energy than before. Then she will have an easy and successful labour. That is not to say she should be treated roughly. On the contrary, she needs to be surrounded by a kind atmosphere. The foetus is affected by anything upsetting the mother. If something hurtful is said to the mother and she is about to cry the foetus is already crying: if you tell her something funny or nice the foetus shows pleasure. It has all been filmed, in Sweden.

'Unfortunately Soviet doctors are not allowed to experiment on humans even though there can be no harm to either mother or baby in such experiments. But we have made experiments on rabbits. We discovered that if you apply some irritant to the pregnant doe's ear the foetus reacts to it before the doe. Also, we found that if you keep a pregnant doe forcibly immobile the weight of her foetus can become ten times bigger – four hundred grammes instead of forty – so that the poor doe cannot deliver it.

'We do not believe that birth necessarily has to be painful. When we say that a cat or dog cries when giving birth and therefore labour is naturally painful we are wrong because we have spoiled cats and dogs by domesticating them. The same is true of horses and cows. Among wild animals screaming is always an appeal for help. If a wild animal screams in labour it means it cannot give birth and should in fact be killed. When a monkey has a pathological delivery it screams and tries to jerk out the foetus by pulling its legs and arms, not caring whether it hurts the baby or not but trying to save its own life. Her partner helps. If a woman cannot deliver her baby naturally, strictly speaking it should be killed. This is the law of the wild. But in the Soviet Union we fight for the life of every baby because we have no population growth. Every fifth Soviet citizen is a pensioner. Soon there will be no one to do the work.'

She spoke of other things, 'intimate' things that embarrassed nobody: not her, for she was now warmed up in her talk; not the women, for they had too much to worry about to bother about me; and not me, for I was not listening. I was bored. I did notice however that she showed few of the diagrams, probably because of me.

I resumed paying attention when she asked if there were any questions – and, when a woman with light shiny hair, blue eyes and a bad complexion asked about breathing exercises, ignored the question. Instead she said something not only irrelevant but untrue as though it were a vital fact she had forgotten to mention before. 'In the West,' she said, 'a doctor goes with you to the hospital. You have to pay for it but it creates a better psychological atmosphere for the woman.'

A girl in a pink fluffy hat and tall black boots said, with a glance at me, 'Can't our husbands be taught to help more? And why are they not even allowed to visit us in the hospital?'

The obstetrician deigned to reply to this question. 'Our men are not yet up to it, to be taught to help their wives,' she said. 'Their psychological level is not yet high enough. If you start talking to our men about sex they get embarrassed and become frivolous. But I believe they will be taught in future. We are preparing television programmes. After the pleasure of intimacy and conception you have to work hard to deliver your baby and when our men are educated properly they will understand that they also have to pay for those moments of pleasure. The husband will have to be taught to help take care of the baby and be considerate to his wife, not to touch her during the pregnancy and after the birth until she has stopped breast feeding.

'As for visitors not being allowed, it is because maternity homes should be absolutely clean. There is a danger of infection if fathers visit. Six days is not so long to wait.'

'But,' the girl said, 'in other countries the husbands are even allowed to be present at the birth, and these countries do not have epidemics of infection.'

'Our men are too irresponsible,' the obstetrician said. 'If we let them in, many would come in drunk or dirty. There are different traditions, different medical rules. We think our ideas are well-founded. We believe our system is the best. There is simply the danger of infection.'

A pale girl with brave brown eyes asked about books and information pamphlets. 'You can't buy any anywhere,' she said.

The obstetrician agreed. 'Everyone is agitated lately about these books that are impossible to get. There are virtually no books or information pamphlets. In theory there are a few in bookshops but, as you say, it is in fact impossible to buy any. Most practising doctors are not at all happy about the literature that is available on the subject. There is a recommended new book translated from Polish but none of you will be able to get hold of a copy.'

Two women asked questions simultaneously, Blue Eyes again about breathing exercises, another about that abortion poster downstairs.

'Is it really necessary to have an abortion poster in a maternity home?' she asked. The obstetrician chose to answer the poster question.

'It is official policy not to recommend abortion, even though it is legal,' she said, adding some more misinformation: 'Abortions are prohibited everywhere in the world except the Soviet Union. In Mexico they only abolished capital punishment for the crime of abortion seventy-five years ago and they still send people to labour camp for it. We are humane enough in the Soviet Union not only to make it legal but to provide free medical service for those wanting an abortion. But the state needs babies, so we do not encourage it.'

A girl in a blue frock said, 'You said expectant mothers should be surrounded by kindness. What about the hags downstairs? Haven't they been told this?'

'I also said that one in five in the Soviet Union is a pensioner and there is a labour shortage. We can't afford to let an able-bodied person do those cloakroom jobs. So we have to get pensioners to do it at a pitiful wage. We cannot choose our cloakroom attendants, we have to take what is available.'

'What about the receptionists?'

'They are trained and qualified people and do their job. Any more questions? I should also tell you to look beautiful during your pregnancy. No one wants to have a Quasimodo around. So buy yourself a few beautiful dresses. Don't stint your money when it comes to nice things.'

'But maternity dresses are not sold in our shops.'

'Make one yourself then. Women in pregnancy can actually look beautiful. It is our prejudice that pregnant women are ugly. In ancient Rome they made statues of pregnant women in black marble and the statues were beautiful.'

Blue Eyes, valiant to the end, asked again, 'What about breathing exercises?'

The obstetrician, unable now to avoid the question, said, 'God taught you to breathe, didn't He? Breathe as He taught you.'

'But Soviet doctors pioneered all that sort of thing.'

'We don't believe in it anymore.'

She was wrong. Psycho-prophylaxis was and still is the official Soviet method of preparing expectant mothers for childbirth. It has been ever since a law passed in 1951 made it obligatory for all Soviet clinics and maternity homes to use it.

The talk was over. We queued up at the cloakroom counter for our hats and coats. There was a different cloakroom attendant, another kerchiefed old woman. As I walked away with my hat and coat I heard her say to the girl behind, 'A man here!'

'It's as well,' the girl said. 'It was getting boring with only women around.'

Those that had taken off their fluffy hats combed their hair in front of a mirror before putting them back on. The receptionist was turning away an expectant mother. At least five months pregnant, the woman had only recently moved into the area and had not yet got round to registering at the local police station. Consequently her domestic passport still had her old address stamped in it, the other side of Moscow. Because of this, the receptionist was refusing to let her attend that maternity home.

'But,' the woman said, almost in tears, 'why should I come to this maternity home if I didn't live in this area? You think it's such a magnificent place I would travel from the other side of Moscow?'

'If you're not registered locally, I'm not letting you come here.'

'But I'm pregnant! Or do you think I've got a pillow stuffed up my jumper and want to come here just for fun?'

The receptionist was adamant. The expectant mother left the building crying. Lara and I followed her out into the hurtling snow.

'Her foetus must be in a right state,' I said.

'Poor woman,' said Lara. 'This is a bad maternity home. They're not all like this.'

Some boys were playing a gun game – cowboys and Indians or cops and robbers or partisans and fascists, whatever it is that Russian boys play. They were not wearing overcoats but had on fur hats, the earflaps of which hung casually down. They were playing their gun game as though the cold wind and the snow and ice did not exist. Their trousers and anoraks were covered with snow from where they had slipped over or lain down on account of being killed. A building had sheltered us from the snow blowing in the wind. Now we turned a corner and got it smack in the face. We turned our faces sideways and down and bent our bodies against the snow.

'Those women are unhealthy because of the food and the climate,' I said. 'Pregnant women can't go for long walks on this ice.'

'I did,' said Lara.

'You had me to lean on. And they're scared because of the lack of information, and that woman, instead of giving it to them, frightens them still more with nonsense about animals and the West.'

We came to our tram stop. We waited a while, our tram came, grinding in its tracks, its windows opaque with frost, and we boarded it. It was crowded but a young woman gave Lara her seat.

Chapter Eleven
PICKWICK PAPERS

At the end of February we were lying in bed in the early hours of the morning when Lara gently woke me and said, 'Terrichka, I think it's started.' I kissed her sleepily, and drew her into the hollow of my arm, and we lay there cuddling and talking softly and dozing. According to what her doctor had told her, she was three weeks overdue but in fact probably was not. Expectant mothers in the Soviet Union are entitled to fifty-six days paid maternity leave but doctors habitually put the date back a couple of weeks to deprive the woman of the full amount of leave.

At dawn the contractions were still far apart. I got up and made tea. The morning passed and still she did not feel it was time to leave: the afternoon came and went and it was not until dusk that she said it was time to get a taxi. We put on our winter clothes, sat for one minute in silence for luck, Raisa Iosifovna kissed her, I picked up a suitcase and we left.

It was snowing again, this time a heavy wet snow coming straight down. The air was raw and cold. I was steeled for a bad few minutes, standing on a frozen pavement with a wife in labour and no taxis stopping. Anyone who resents the way taxi-drivers tout for custom in some countries should go to Russia. But we were lucky. One stopped and we got in. The streets were busy. Lights were shining everywhere, gleaming through the snowy dusk. We drove right past Maternity Home Number 25 to Maternity Home Number 23, another four-storied building. I was worried that they would not take Lara in, and that they would send her back to Number 25, but she said that there would be no problem. Fresh snow lay all around the courtyard, smooth, pristine, with a lovely texture. Lara clung tightly to me while taking the few steps to the Admissions entrance. This time it was not ice that made walking difficult, but deep powdery snow. All the windows were lit up. White-coated staff stood at some of them, having a cigarette in the corridor. Some inmates stood at the windows also, looking down. Their outmates stood down in the courtyard, looking up.

'I'm not going to do that,' I said. 'It's pointless and undigni-fied.'

This was hardly the most appropriate thing to say in the circumstances and I immediately wished I had not said it.

'I don't want you to,' said Lara. 'Quick, give me fifty kopecks. I'll have to give something to the doorwoman. No, better if you give it to her.'

The Admissions entrance was in a left-hand wing. The door was locked. We rang the bell and waited. An old woman in a white coat opened it and let us in without speaking. Two thick wooden doors crashed shut behind us as we entered a small bleak undecorated room. In it were two chairs and a table and nothing else. Yellow paint on the walls was grimy, chipped and peeling. The floor was bare concrete. A blue radiator gave off dry heat. A naked light bulb illuminated the bleakness. The room, as Maxim Gorky said about an English church hall, was 'unadorned to the point of absurdity'.

I shoved the fifty kopecks into the old woman's hand. Lara gave me a dirty look. She had wanted it done with more finesse. The old woman pocketed the money without saying anything. Because she had some trouble with her nose she was breathing through her mouth, so you could see lots of false teeth even though not a word passed her lips. Maybe she did not speak because she was ashamed of her mouth full of false teeth. Or maybe she was simply just another grumpy old pensioner being paid a pitiful wage. She opened an inner door which we assumed we were to go through. Lara did so but the woman stopped me. At last she spoke. 'You can't come in here,' she said.

Beyond her, already in, Lara said, 'Wait here. They'll bring out my clothes for you to take home.' The old woman shut the door between us. Because I had thought I was going in with Lara

I had not kissed her or said anything loving or reassuring. She was not allowed to take in anything with her. In the bleak room I waited. And waited and waited and waited. There was nothing to look at, not even a list of Party regulations or a slogan, not even a picture of Brezhnev or Lenin. This must have been the only public room in the Soviet Union without at least one of those things on a wall. It bothered me a lot that the last thing I had said to Lara at that extremely important time in our lives was that stupid remark about not standing outside to see her after the birth. Outside the window there was nothing but darkness and falling snow and anyway the window was covered in frost and dirt. And, not knowing I would be sentenced to solitary confinement like that I had brought nothing to read. I sat on the radiator. This too became hot and boring so I moved to one of the chairs. I was sitting on the table, growing quite desperate, my brain exploding with boredom, when the old woman emerged and silently handed me Lara's clothes. I put them in the suitcase and took a tram home. Snow was still falling in huge wet flakes. The tram steps were covered in khaki slush. The young lady driving the tram announced the stops through a microphone. I sat on a rear seat. The ribbed floor was strewn with tickets. The tram rattled on, screeching at the bends, the wheels grinding on the rails. The windows vibrated in the frames. They were covered with frost patterns, so you could not see out. The patterns were intricate and beautiful. With my glove I made a peephole.

At home, Raisa Iosifovna waited an hour, then phoned the maternity home. Lara had not yet given birth. Raisa Iosifovna was told the Enquiries service closed at eight. She phoned again just before eight but the number was continuously engaged. She phoned again immediately on getting up in the morning but there was no answer till nine. Then the answer was, still not. Throughout the day she phoned. Always the answer was, Lara had not yet delivered. Raisa Iosifovna and I were very worried and started imagining terrible things. At best, Lara had been in labour for over twenty-four hours and at worst something was wrong. In the evening I was sitting at my desk and at last Raisa Iosifovna, smiling joyfully, entered the room and announced, 'It's a boy! Both are fine. Glory be to God!'

The next morning I bought a bunch of flowers and took a tram to the maternity home. This time I entered the right-hand wing, where the room was bigger and full of people. Two middle-aged female orderlies in white coats and hats sat behind a glass partition, one under a sign saying 'Enquiries 9.00–20.00', the other under 'Messages 12.00–15.00 and 16.00–19.00'. I handed the Messages lady the flowers and a letter. She told me to wait there for the answer. On a board were cards, the size and shape of visiting cards, on which, under the appropriate day of the week, the details of each birth were written. Girls had red cards, boys blue. Under Saturday, there was our blue card. I took it. The baby weighed 3.5 kilogrammes and was 5.1 centimetres long. His number was 582. I put the card in my pocket and sat down in a chair and waited for Lara's answering note. Pot plants drooped in containers on the walls. On one wall were photos of home-sweet-maternity home scenes, some in colour but most in black and white. Chairs were ranged all round the room, nearly all occupied. Every time someone entered or left, the door creaked on its thick wire hinges and banged shut. The Enquiries lady gave a piece of graph paper to a young husband for him to write a note on. Another young husband borrowed a pen from an expectant grandmother. The Messages lady called out, 'Kuznetsova?'

'Yes, yes,' said Mrs Kuznetsova, jumping up from her seat. The orderly handed her a note. Mrs Kuznetsova read it and said to her female companion, 'I wonder at which window it's possible to see her.'

'Ask what floor she's on.'

'Next time.'

They left with a creak and a bang. Then there was silence except for the Enquiries lady on the phone. 'She's in ward twenty-one. No news yet. Phone tomorrow.'

A dark, flashy young man entered and walked briskly to the Messages window. 'I have to speak to the doctor,' he said firmly.

'Write down the message and give it to me,' said the Messages lady, equally firmly.

The Enquiries phone rang incessantly, the Enquiries lady answering all the calls: 'A girl, three kilogrammes' . . . .'She's in ward fourteen' . . . .and even once, 'She feels fine,' as though she could possibly know the feelings of one woman out of the hundreds in the place.

A new batch of notes arrived from the inmates. There was a rush to the Messages window. 'We can answer, yes?' asked one young husband, I suppose meaning he had already written one note that day and was he allowed another. It seemed he was.

A big sign in the middle of the partition listed some of the things allowed in and some of the things forbidden.

Allowed: biscuits, 1 packet; milk, 1 packet; cheese, 200 grammes; fruit, 1 kilogramme; butter, 100 grammes.

Forbidden: fruit juice; home-made produce; fish; sausage; meat products; strawberries.

'Is Baikal allowed?' someone asked. Baikal is a soft drink allegedly made from the root of the ginseng plant. The answer was yes, a bottle of Baikal was allowed.

Lara's answering note came and was handed to me by the Messages lady. Lara thanked me for the flowers, said she was fine and the baby beautiful, and added a list of things for me to bring tomorrow; indicating which of them were prohibited, and would need to be smuggled in. It seemed that almost everything was prohibited, including books. The most important things, she said, were a book to read and small change with which to tip the staff and make phone calls.

The next day was Monday and Mondays were Cleaning Days, when the building was closed completely to all visitors, so I took the things the day after, in a plastic bag, the forbidden things hidden away at the bottom and *Martin Chuzzlewit* in an emptied macaroni packet. The orderly did not look carefully through the contents of the bag, so Lara received everything.

The day after that I received a scribbled note from her. She wrote, 'I'm grievously upset because me and another girl are the only ones in the ward without milk yet. And Danya has a huge appetite. And I don't know what to do. Will you try and ask the doctor what can be done. You know they don't talk to new mums. Try and be insistent, will you? Otherwise by the time we get home there'll be only half of me, the other half being dissolved in tears of grief. Please don't accept no for an answer! My doctor simply says, "You'll just have to bottle feed, won't you?" What a fool! As though it was that easy!'

It was a hundred times worse for both of us because we could not see each other and talk. But her milk came the next day. Then she was allowed to go out to the public phone in the corridor, and phoned me every day till she came out, a week after the birth. I had cleaned and disinfected the flat, helped by Raisa Iosifovna, Anya and Sasha. We all went and collected her and the baby, me carrying her clothes in a suitcase.

I handed the clothes over to the orderly. Lara came out wearing them and carrying the baby. Danya was swaddled and wrapped up in a blanket tied in the middle with a blue ribbon. He was screaming his tiny wrinkled head off. We kissed Lara. Her face was thin and drawn, her eyes dark and sunken. She had told me to bring three roubles to give to the nurse. It is a superstition that if you do not give the nurse some money the baby will be unlucky. The nurse was very young, standing shyly in the inner doorway, and when I gave her the three-rouble note she blushed.

We covered Danya's face before taking him out in the cold to the waiting taxi. If it had been one or two degrees colder Lara would not have been allowed to take the baby out that day but would have had to wait for milder weather. Later, when Danya was asleep, we sat and drank tea in the kitchen while Lara told us about the birth. She was wheeled into the delivery room where another woman was already giving birth. This other woman's delivery was difficult. At one point the midwife's white coat was splashed with blood. 'Damn you!' she said to the woman in labour. 'Can't you be more careful!'

Lara's midwife remonstrated with her and she apologised. 'It's my second coat today,' she explained.

Lara herself, once she was at this stage, had no trouble at all. She even gave a little laugh of joy, as mothers are supposed to do, when she saw her baby for the first time. She thought him beautiful and marvellous the instant she saw him. She was very pleased she had gone to this maternity hospital and not Number 25 because another objection to Number 25 had been that in the event of a long or difficult labour they would be more likely than elsewhere to administer an anaesthetic against her wishes. In the Soviet Union anaesthetics in childbirth are supposed to be used only in emergencies, as it is believed they can harm the baby.

Lara shared this belief and anyway wanted the full experience of having a baby, no matter how difficult.

I had called Lara 'Pickwick' because of her bulging belly: the bulge, though now a baby, kept the name, and we called Danya 'Pickwick'. Later it was shortened to Pick. When we registered him we received our Pickwick papers – a cardboard birth certificate of the same shape and size as wedding certificates and domestic passports and a card of congratulations from the Executive Committee of the Moscow Council of Workers' Deputies. 'Dear parents!' the card said. 'We congratulate you on the birth of a son, wish health and well-being in life, hope that you will bring him up as a worthy builder of communist society and a patriot of our motherland.'

Everyone who asked about the health of mother and baby, all Foreign Ministry and central committee secretariat officials, all Communist Party members and Young Communists, said the same thing when informed both were fine: '*Slava Bogu*' – 'Glory be to God'.

Chapter Twelve
DANYA BOY

The arrival of Pick complicated our lives to an extent I would not have believed possible. A baby is always a full-time job for someone: we contrived to make it a full-time job for three. The horizons of our world narrowed to Pick's digestive system and his nether regions. The burning topic of each day was whether or not he had done a pooh.

For the first few days he was wrapped in such a tight cocoon he could not move. I felt sorry for him but they defended the practice, saying it stopped him scratching himself, with special fear for his eyes and belly button, and that he slept better. Far from abandoning the advocacy of this ancient Russian custom, Soviet doctors have evolved a new theory in support of it: that swaddling simulates life in the womb, so that the baby actually feels more secure and this possibly explains why he sleeps better. Western commentators have made much of the psychological implications of swaddling, claiming that the baby's inability to move its limbs freely restricts its sense of individual independence when it grows up, and that the rigid discipline of swaddling alternating with the thirty minutes' freedom allowed at each feed is the cause of the orgiastic outbursts for which adult Russians are so famous.

Pick was showered with love and attention from all of Lara's family. Sometimes there would be five gooey females leaning over him in his cot. No amount of fussing was considered excessive. Pick became the focal point of the entire family, his prerogatives the concern of all. 'A baby is nothing but joy,' said Anya. I was more concerned about him growing up in this pampering feminine cocoon than I was about swaddling, which after all only lasts a few days.

Our lives were complicated further by the difficulty in getting things. I have mentioned in passing that we disinfected the flat prior to Lara's homecoming with Pick. The cleaning had been preceded by a week of desperate search for disinfectant. Not even the main chemists, Number 1 in the centre of Moscow, had any. Disinfectant was *defitsit*, as they say. I wrote an article about the shortages of household necessities which provoked indignant letters from *Morning Star* readers. I mentioned in the article that, coming across tap sprinklers, I bought a dozen for friends and relatives, as is the custom with *defitsit* goods. One reader wondered whether it was compatible with 'Socialist morality', where shortages were 'alleged' to exist, to buy in bulk, a thought that would never occur to any Soviet citizen. And why the 'alleged'? Did he believe the *Morning Star* correspondent was fabricating shortages? These readers were indeed living in another world.

Some of these letters were published, while the editor sent others on to me with no comment, which seemed to imply that he agreed with the criticisms. So much for Sam's desire for a picture of how ordinary Russians lived.

We bought with no problem a pram and a plastic bath. Everything else was acquired with difficulty or from foreigners or not at all. Carry cots, pram nets, plastic bibs, high chairs, cot-mobiles, playpens – all these things were either *defitsit* or simply unheard-of. Even nappies were a problem. Lara was advised to make nappies out of old sheets. In fact disposable nappies were occasionally available, and by keeping a look-out, dashing to a shop where they were being sold and queuing and buying in bulk, we stayed ahead of the nappy problem: although, I am ashamed to admit, at the expense of our Socialist morality.

As a washing machine was indispensable, we bought a small 'semi-automatic' which, though brand new, was badly scratched. '*Nichivo*. That doesn't matter,' the shop assistant said airily. 'It works.' Lara informed me much later that dearer, fully automatic machines were available but she did not mention this at the time because we were short of money. I would willingly have paid anything to avoid the sort of washdays we had with this contraption, a tinny tub that did no more than gently agitate the water. It needed attention and manual operation every few minutes. The only labour it saved was in the actual agitation. It could take only tiny bundles. The soaking clothes then had to be put through a wringer turned by hand. Rinsing also had to be done by hand, under the cold tap in the bath. Our washdays used to end in the early hours of the morning, with the bathroom floor awash, but Lara seemed to enjoy the work and she definitely loved the feeling of satisfaction afterwards.

There were clinics and distribution points where you could get special milk products and baby foods such as thin cereal: but we could not find out where our local one was. Raisa Iosifovna did not trust these special products, anyway. So we made our own, even though milk was often off at the time of purchase.

I have never brought up a baby elsewhere so I have nothing to compare it with, but I strongly suspect our concern for hygiene was excessive. Nothing was allowed to touch anything else for fear of contamination. Once, after we had bathed Pick in the bedroom in his plastic bath, I started emptying the bathwater by scooping some out with a bucket to make the bath lighter to carry to the bathroom. 'What are you doing!' exclaimed Raisa Iosifovna. The water had to be emptied straight out, for a bucket was not allowed anywhere near Pick's plastic bath. She looked so horrified you would have thought I had put Pick in the bucket. Her hands were frozen in mid-air. Her mouth was open. That particular bucket, it so happened, was the one used to wash the floor with. Naturally, I had picked up the dirtiest poxy bucket in the whole flat.

We had the usual problem of nights of broken sleep, of course, made worse by Pick sleeping in our room. With Raisa Iosifovna kipping on the settee in the other room, we had no choice but to have his cot next to our bed. He would wake up to be fed twice a night and sometimes be woken up again by my snoring. We stayed awake in the daytime by quaffing coffee. Although coffee was *defitsit* we had a large stock due to a marvellous piece of luck. We had been to the *Moscow News* offices in Pushkin Square one late afternoon and walking down crowded Gorky Street on the way home came upon a surrealistic scene opposite Moscow's main food shop, Gastronom Number 1 – the Harrods of Moscow – which is an ornate, chandeliered shop still known to everyone by its pre-revolution name of Yeliseyev's. There was a permanent sign up in this gastronom saying No Coffee Today. Across the road a long queue led down into a dark alley, the head of the queue curling in to a hole in the wall. 'What are they giving?' we asked.

'Coffee,' we were told.

(Russians always speak of 'giving' and 'taking' rather than of 'selling' and 'buying'.)

We joined the queue. It was a cold evening. Lara went off to find a phone to tell Raisa Iosifovna we would be late home, and the reason for it. We counted our money. Luckily, we had enough on us to make the long cold wait worthwhile. Eventually we disappeared into the hole in the wall – and emerged a minute later with coffee. There was no shop sign. It was just a cellar, bare except for tins of coffee being sold surreptitiously like prohibition liquor.

I later attended a press conference held by Prices Minister Nikolai Glushkov, where he announced that several items were to be substantially increased in price, including coffee, which was to be increased fourfold. Simultaneously, coffee appeared in great quantities in all food shops. Most shoppers took one look at the price and decided to stick to tea. By another linguistic quirk, they were telling each other coffee was now 'free' – meaning it could be freely bought, without queuing.

That summer I had to cover the trials of the dissidents Alexandr Ginzburg and Anatoly Shcharansky. It was a pointless, provocative assignment. No other Communist newspaper in the world placed its Moscow correspondent in such an invidious position. And then, while the trials were still going on, Reuters reported that a rock concert at which Joan Baez, Santana and The Beach Boys were to appear in Palace Square, Leningrad, had been cancelled at the last minute, and hundreds of pop fans, many of whom had travelled vast distances from all over the country, had rioted and been dispersed with smoke grenades and water hoses. Sam phoned. He wanted the story from me. This seemed to me silly, for two reasons: one, he already had the story from Reuters, and two, this was not the

sort of story the *Morning Star* correspondent should be covering. I voiced these considerations. 'I want *you* to do it,' he
insisted. I phoned Reuters' Moscow bureau for the source of the
story: it was the American consul in Leningrad. I phoned him
and received the facts already lying on Sam's desk in London.
Joan Baez was in Moscow, having arrived for the aborted
concert, and I got her hotel phone number from the American
embassy and called her for a quote. She did not know of the riot.
I informed her of it. 'Oh, my Gahd,' she said, which quote I
added, suitably anglicised, to my story that was in every other
regard a repeat of Reuters'. Three days later I received a phone
call from a Soviet official. He was furious. He said that the story
of the riot was a complete fabrication, that we all knew what
American diplomats were in Russia for, that in any case Soviet
police never used water hoses. And he demanded that the
Morning Star publish a retraction. This the paper did, under my
name, like the original story. The whole affair made me and the
paper look stupid and it had all happened because I had done
what Sam had told me to do.

I find it hard to be clear-minded about my relationship with
Sam at that time. I know what it felt like from my point of view:
it felt as though he disliked me and was deliberately making life
hard for me; and I was baffled. On the other hand, I am unable
to judge to what extent my soft nature and tendency to fold up
in the face of unsupportive behaviour was maddening. Or was I
being actually paranoid in feeling so acutely that I was being got
at? Whatever the case, coming on top of everything else – all my
new experiences of Moscow and marriage and fatherhood – it
was too much for me. I felt I could not cope. All my old
inferiority feelings returned and I showed every sign of relapsing
into the self-harshness of my youth. I was increasingly nervous
and irritable. I again looked inwards instead of looking around
me, which hindered my work badly. The articles I wrote were
not poor: there were simply too few of them. I was in a huge
country teeming with life, yet feeling very little of it would be of
interest to anyone. My self-respect had gone again. It seemed I
had been allotted five years of energy and self-confidence and
had used them all up on the sports desk.

I discussed my plight with Lara. She was not harsh. She, too, thought I was being given a hard time. But she did not want a submissive husband, one who flinched from confrontation: she wanted a man who could stand firm for himself and for her and her child. However timid one felt, one should not show it, but should hold one's own, stand up and fight. Accepting, however, that I could not possibly sustain an all-out open campaign against Sam, she suggested I go to London and have a word with Gordon McLennan, and, if nothing came of this, turn the job in and find another job in Moscow. I had several times expressed admiration for the incisiveness of Gordon's mind. So I arranged this. I informed Sam I was coming to London but did not tell him I was making an appointment to see Gordon. I was fool enough not to realise that going to see the general secretary without consultation would annoy both Sam and the editor. The interview was a failure anyway, due to my inability to explain the real cause of my discontent. How could any adult in a responsible job complain about feeling bullied? So I resigned. On my return to Moscow I looked for another job, as translator or style editor, could not find one, and withdrew the resignation. Luckily the editor accepted the withdrawal, with the stipulation that I did not make a habit of resigning.

The summer that year in Moscow was like an English winter. Thick dark clouds permanently obscured the sun. Pick caught a cold and an infection causing pimples, and the doctor who came to see him was amazingly nasty. In her thirties, she was not ugly but her deep-grained nastiness was already souring her face. She arrived in an ambulance with a nurse – all part of the service on the Soviet National Health – but the good service was spoiled by her attitude. Pick had not done a pooh for three days. 'What were you doing for three days,' she snapped. 'Standing there looking at him? He should go four times a day.' She prescribed enemas. Full of nonsense as well as nastiness, she also prescribed twenty times the stated dose of vitamin D drops, recommended that we prick his pimples with a pin, and said, 'Plastic pants make boys impotent.' There had never been any plastic pants in the Soviet Union – she was just repeating handed-down folk wisdom. Then she said he had rickets. Badly, she said. We, naturally, were shattered. I remembered Lara's friend Zameera, unable to walk till she was six, and bow-legged ever after. Was our beautiful baby to be like that? It was unthinkable, impossible.

Lara said later she was gratified at my reaction to the crisis. Dr Nasty had snapped that Pick should get as much fresh air and sunshine as possible (though he was not to go out while he still had his cold). She strongly advised that he go to the country. The answer was a *dacha*, a country cottage. My reaction was to make acquiring the use of a *dacha* top priority, no matter what the expense or inconvenience. The battle against Pick's rickets should be regarded as a war in which all other considerations became irrelevant. Within two days we had a *dacha*.

When we told other Moscow-based Westerners Pick had rickets, they laughed. It seemed that ninety-eight percent of babies born in Moscow in the winter have a very mild form of rickets, which goes in their first summer. The lack of sunshine in that exceptionally cold summer had possibly slightly held up Pick's development. Dr Nasty had just been having fun when she added, 'It's very bad, very serious.' We had a *dacha* by then anyway, and saw no reason to give it up. Fresh air never hurt anyone. And we were fed up with all the interfering neighbours whenever we took him or left him out. If he was asleep after being taken out in his pram we used to leave him in the pram in our yard, below our windows, which we left open so we could hear him crying when he woke up. We never had time to dash downstairs before, at the first plaintive yell, from all sides of the block, including top balconies, would be heard calls of '*Rebyonok, rebyonok, rebyonok* – the baby, the baby, the baby.' No one else left a baby unattended even for one minute. When we asked the head of the nursery adjoining our block if we could leave him in the nursery garden, in full view and sound of our flat, she said no, adding, 'I had wondered what sort of parents could leave a baby alone like that.' She said crows might peck out his eyes. So a *dacha* seemed a good idea even though he did not have rickets.

Our *dacha*, rented from friends, was about ten miles north-east of Moscow on the banks of the river Klyazma. Built in the 1930s as a co-operative, it was a big, two-storey wooden building that had been divided into four quarters, each self-contained, with its own separate entrance porch and large garden, giving the impression it was four separate buildings. Facilities were primitive, the only mod con being electricity. Heating was provided by a traditional brick stove in the downstairs room, while water had to be fetched from a well in a nearby lane. The toilet was a stinking wooden shed by the garden gate. The *dacha* had been allowed to fall into decay, and its owners, our friends, a young couple who lived and worked in Moscow, were just getting it back into shape, decorating the rooms with the customary wood panelling and bringing in carvings. Our section had a wooden porch, one big room downstairs and two small rooms upstairs. Cooking was done on a small calor gas ring in the corridor. Thousands of empty bottles stood upright against the corridor's back wall.

The place needed to be thoroughly cleaned. All of Lara's family rallied round to help, even somnolent Lyalya. The weather continued to be so bad that we could not go there for several days and when we did finally make a dash for it we could not do much: rain smashed down incessantly, falling in long perpendicular lines like pencils, pouring off the roof in rods as thick as walking sticks, descending with tropical ferocity, covering everything in sight as though with a net. Huge yellow puddles flooded the paths. Lyalya said it could continue like that for the rest of the summer, but that was wishful thinking on her part. It cleared up, we cleaned the place, and we took Pick there each weekend. Ideally Lara would have liked to remain there with him but she was engaged in acquiring a visa to accompany me on holiday in England that autumn, a process requiring her full attention.

We would take the suburban *elektrichka* train from Yaroslavsky station to the small town of Bolshevo. The train was invariably even more packed than the metro in the rush hour, the passengers carrying baskets and picnic hampers instead of briefcases, and it was a relief to get off and wander across the station square to a small local market before catching a bus out to the *dacha*. There was usually an ice cream vendor in the square as well as the inevitable old women selling sunflower seeds from a sack. The square was earth that became rutted and dusty in hot weather and a quagmire in wet. Mangy stray dogs rummaged or slept. Goats would be tethered on long ropes at a side of the busy square that opened out onto a wild-looking field. It was a timeless peasant scene that reminded me of India.

The bus journey to the *dacha* was very pleasant, the bus rumbling down a hill to the Klyazma, bumping in and out of big potholes, crossing the river and then passing through a semi-suburban area until it came to the end of the road, where it turned round and went back. A short walk up a dirt track, past other *dachas* standing in a rustling pine forest, in big gardens protected by high slatted fences, and we were there. The garden was overgrown, waist high with grass and weeds. It contained several apple trees that were to give so much fruit in the autumn that although we picked and collected hundreds each weekend, hundreds more had to be left to rot. There was a big strawberry bed, too. If the weather was fine we ate outside, at an old garden table. There was a swing on which Pick could be entertained while meals were cooked or wood cut for the stove. Sometimes on Saturday evenings we cooked *shashlik* over an open air fire. The forest was quiet, the air clean.

The Klyazma lay only about five minutes' walk from the *dacha*. Its sandy banks invited sunbathing and swimming, although some stretches of the river were reserved for fishing. There was the constant sound of frogs croaking, and herons were a common sight. It was a beautiful, tranquil, pine-scented place, only ten miles from the swarming capital, yet untidy not with people's untidiness but with sprawling undergrowth and shrubs and the long roots of the trees. We would stroll along the river bank, me always enchanted by the unspoilt wilderness. There were no small, trim fields, no paths or flowerbeds, only the gently undulating Central Russian plain, uncultivated and rambling, stretching away from the slow-moving river for unimaginable distances. A cornfield on our side of the river was vast, seemingly a natural field of corn, a yellow waving sea. A narrow, deeply rutted dirt road ran through the cornfield to a tumbledown, one-street village, where tethered cows were grazing.

We would occasionally make a long detour on the way back for provisions. Most had to be bought in Moscow before setting out, for the only shop within a mile of our *dacha* was a little wooden hut called the *palatka*, which sold only soya beans, tinned cabbage, old bits of pork fat and cheap wine and whose opening hours were erratic and unreliable. Still we went there sometimes, usually for some pork fat for cooking.

Pick would kick and gurgle in dappled shade in our garden and when we took him for a walk in his pram would sit up wide-eyed and open-mouthed, looking around, fascinated by all the new things in the world. The instant his pram was set in motion he would start humming. He would continue to hum throughout the journey. We called the hum his 'travelling song'. He had a way of sighing with contentment. His face was lightly pinked by the sun. He was a sturdy, beautifully healthy baby, and anyone could see now that talk of rickets was laughable. I wished I could stay there at the *dacha*, taking Pick for walks and tending the vegetable patch, instead of having every Sunday night to return to Moscow and stuffy press conferences, turgid TASS news and the nerve-wracking telexes from London. But then autumn came anyway and all *dachniki* had to return to town.

Pick started to crawl. A playpen became desirable. The only place you could buy playpens was the huge Children's World department store in the centre of Moscow, and then only once a month. Lara phoned one day to ask if they had any in and was told yes. We went the next day. Too late. We saw some behind the counter with 'Sold' stickers on them. There would not be another delivery for another month. Lara then phoned to ask if there were any high chairs in. Yes, there were. She went the same day. Again too late. The wasted journeys and the insolent shop assistants were upsetting. We bought a playpen from an American couple, exchange students whose year was up and who were returning home and did not want the encumbrance of such a bulky object.

We followed Pick's progress to the biped stage with concern as well as enjoyment, for he had been born with a slight malformation of the feet, which we had been told would straighten itself in time but could prevent him walking properly at first. The paediatrician at the clinic had advised that his feet be swaddled very tightly but refused to show us how to do it. 'You'll learn,' she said. He had been about two months old when she suggested we take him to an orthopaedic specialist. I asked Yuriah Heep to make an appointment.

Yuriah Heep was still around, making mistakes and forgetting things and phoning to say he was ill and could I manage without him. Often he was genuinely ill. Hardly any part of him functioned normally. His stomach was in a state because he had not eaten properly while a student and because of the quantities of vodka he quaffed. He had back trouble because of the way he stooped. Toothache and headache were frequent complaints. As for his brain . . . . Though he could never remember anything, he refused to keep a notebook. He took a course of acupuncture, telling me of its efficaciousness without informing me which of his ailments it was treating.

He lied prodigiously. He would lie to get out of chores and to cover up mistakes and omissions, and the lies begot more lies till the atmosphere was heavy and dark with them. He always gave the impression of squirming in a web of self-woven complications. The ordinary duties and obligations of life and work were too much for him, and his deceit, which was supposed to help him cope, only entangled him even more.

For months I had been regularly assured he would be replaced within a few weeks. A pattern had emerged: he would take outrageous liberties, not doing a stroke for days; his superior would reprimand him, after which he would come and say, 'Terry, are you satisfied with my work?' I would give him some soft answer to avoid unpleasantness, for a while he would be marginally better, then he would start taking liberties again. I began to suspect my soft answers were contributing to the delay in getting rid of him, for he could convey to his superior the impression I was now satisfied. So one day I replied, 'How is it possible to be satisfied with your work? You never do any.'

'So I have to find a new job?' he said.

'Yes,' I said.

He looked glum. A new job meant he might have to work. He sealed his fate with this orthopaedic business. Lara and I took Pick to the children's clinic on a crowded bus in a blizzard, only to be informed that no orthopaedic specialist (*orthoped*) was on

duty that day. Yuriah Heep, it seemed, had made an appointment with a tooth specialist (*orthodont*) instead. A second's
thought would surely have been sufficient even for someone as
stupid as Yuriah Heep to realise that a two-month-old baby
could not possibly need a tooth specialist. We carried Pick back
home through the blizzard. I phoned Yuriah Heep immediately
and, informing him of his mistake, told him I never wanted to
see him again. He was not to phone me in the morning. I then
informed his superior of my action. Yuriah Heep phoned me the
morning after next as though nothing had happened. He even
used his usual mechanical phrase: 'Will you be needing me
today?'

'I told you not to phone me again,' I said.

'I thought you meant just yesterday.'

'No, no,' I said. 'Ever. I don't want you to phone me ever
again.'

That was the end of his job with me. I heard however that
many months passed before he left the department for another
job. He was lined up for a post in the Foreign Ministry but it fell
through. They even tried to promote him as a way of getting rid
of him, but that failed too. After a long delay I was appointed a
new secretary, a girl called Olya, and she described his routine in
the department: 'He comes in in the morning,' she said, 'leaves
his jacket on the back of his chair, puts two piles of paper on his
desk – and vanishes for the day.'

The head of the department had heart trouble. He spent a lot
of time in hospital. Olya told me once he became dangerously
agitated in his hospital bed when informed that Yuriah Heep
was still in the department. 'I said months ago, he's got to go!'
he yelled, as nurses rushed to calm him.

Eventually, Yuriah Heep got a job in the embassy at Addis
Ababa. Amharic was his main foreign language. He despised the
language and its native speakers, for racialism was another
characteristic of this charming person. He once had the gall to
say about Uzbeks, 'Those people are always liars.'

Chapter Thirteen
VIS-A-VIS A VISA

A visa normally took three months to be issued. We had wanted to go to England in August but had lodged the application too late for that, due to having Pick to care for and the preliminaries taking so long. In fact Lara began the process in the middle of May, before we had the *dacha*, when she had her photo taken. Six photographs were necessary. In the absence of automatic instant booths she went to a photographer's studio and waited some days for the pictures to be ready.

Then her domestic passport needed to be renewed. She handed it in to the local ZHEK (the official abbreviation of the Russian words for housing office), who dealt with such things, and was told to collect the new one in a week's time from the local *militsia* (police) station. She was told that the passport section at the *militsia* station opened at midday. In fact it was scheduled to open at three and it actually opened at four. Luckily, Lara did not go at midday or at three, but a little after four. There was a lengthy queue, and after a long wait she was told it was the wrong police station – it served our neighbouring block but not ours. We then went to the correct cop shop, just off Leninsky Prospect. Over the entrance inside a banner read 'The Party is the Mind, Honour and Conscience of our Epoch – Lenin'. There was a portrait of the eponymous leader. On a 'Wanted' notice board outside were pinned three mug shots, two men and one woman, with descriptions of their crimes. One man was wanted for refusing to pay alimony, the other was a dangerous criminal wanted for all sorts of felonies, while the woman was a confidence trickster. I was memorising their faces as requested when Lara emerged with a brand new shiny red domestic passport, which had cost two roubles and another day.

It was now June 1, a Thursday, which was fortunate because the local OVIR, the 'visa and registration department', opened on only two half-days a week – Mondays from three to seven, and Thursdays from ten to two. We got there at one o'clock. The visa office was on the sixth floor of a Ministry of the Interior building, across a dingy courtyard. The lift was not working so we carried Pick all the way up. There was no sign, but we deduced the nature of the waiting-room because about forty people were in the room waiting. On a table under a pane of glass were two separate lists of documents that would be needed, one list for socialist countries, the other for capitalist countries. Ten documents were needed for both. Several of the applicants had cardboard files to hold all their documents. Ninety per cent of them were applying to visit socialist countries. There were not enough seats. Some of the applicants were sitting on the window sills while others were standing. A man gave up his seat to Lara and Pick. Not one person in the room was reading though all must have known they were in for a long wait.

To keep the queue in order a baldheaded man had voluntarily drawn up a list of those waiting. He was sitting at the glass-topped table, the list in front of him. It covered both sides of a piece of paper, with the names numbered 1 to 45. We were 35, and number 23 was being seen at that moment. A bespectacled woman tried to push in, saying she was there at opening time to establish her place in the queue and then went elsewhere, a common practice, but she was not on the list and Baldy did not remember seeing her before. Another man said he had been there since six in the morning, standing in the courtyard, and he had not seen her before either. He added that this was his second day. A frizzy-haired woman holding a Camus Napoleon Cognac bag said she had been there since eight and she, too, had not seen this woman before. The queue-jumper retired, her ruse unsuccessful. Number 31, a blonde girl, returned from having done some shopping. Baldy said to her, 'You've come running back early.'

Number 46 arrived, a dark-haired girl wearing a yellow blouse and foreign denim skirt. She did not understand the system of queuing. When it was explained to her, she said, 'Maybe it will go quick?'

'Quick?' Baldy gave a satisfied chuckle. 'No, it does not go quick. It goes very slow.'

She considered leaving before she began but then sat on a window sill. Numbers 47, 48, 49 and 50 arrived. Baldy registered them. The first three were young women, all dressed flashily from head to foot in foreign clothes. A young man offered number 48 a place next to him on the window sill. She was loath to sit down, feeling that it would be acceptance of the situation. She did sit down, however, as that *was* the situation. Number 50, a short, thick-limbed man with bandy legs, simply wanted to go in quickly to ask a question. He asked if he could but number 24, due in next, a slight woman with dark, melancholic eyes, said, 'No, I'm sorry, after waiting three hours I'm not letting anyone in front of me.' Bandy retired to lean on a wall.

Number 23, a broad-shouldered man with short black hair, came storming out of the inner sanctum. In the doorway he turned and said, 'This is not the last word on it!' He stumped off and the slight, melancholic woman went in.

Number 25 had gone away some time ago and had not returned. The waiting was too much for some, while others simply had other things to do.

'Number 26?' said Baldy. No number 26. 'Number 27?' No number 27 either. So number 28 was the next in line to go in.

Number 30, a fat woman, returned breathlessly from some unfinished business, exchanged her position with number 33, and hurried away again.

A lady clerk came clattering in from the corridor on high-heeled shoes, carrying a big bundle of files. Bandy bounced from his wall and asked his question. Ignoring him, she knocked on the inner sanctum door and while waiting for the call to enter silently stared at the ceiling, studied the walls and carefully considered her high-heeled shoes. Then she went in, leaving Bandy standing by the door like an invisible man. Biding his time, he collared her again on her way out. She said, 'I'm not allowed to talk to you,' and clattered her way back down the corridor of power.

A baby aged about eighteen months was crying. Pick had been lying in Lara's arms asleep most of the time till then, but was now sitting up awake and was getting restless. He was bored and hungry. We heard the chimes of an office radio. Someone said, 'They should have a television set in here.'

Numbers 26 and 27, two attractive young women dressed in three-quarter length foreign frocks, returned, late, and wanted to go in anyway. 'We've had some little things to do,' one said.

'Everyone's got little things to do,' said Baldy. 'I called your numbers earlier.'

'Can't we be fitted in?'

'Sorry, I can't negotiate.'

'We don't want to set up a trade deal, we just want to be fitted in.'

As they were, like us, at the first stage of the process of getting a visa, needing only to hand in the letter of invitation from abroad and collect the application forms, and as they were pretty young things, Baldy relented and let them take the place of missing applicants. They re-emerged, forms in hand, almost immediately, giving Baldy a smile for his trouble. Next in line was Baldy himself. He handed over his list to a very tall man. Then our turn came. Lofty called out, 'Number 35?'

'Here,' said Lara.

'Name?'

'Putsello.'

'Correct.'

And he crossed us off his list.

Behind the desk in the little office sat a woman in her early thirties, wearing a flowery blue summer frock, her hair tinted a glossy auburn. The room's window looked out onto a brick wall. On the sill were three flower pots, all containing African violets.

'Sit down,' she said.

We sat down and Lara handed her my letter of invitation, carefully worded according to British embassy recommendations, with the round embassy stamp at the bottom, and Lara's shiny new red domestic passport.

The woman said, 'You are together?'

Lara said, 'He is my husband, who is inviting me to England.'

'A foreigner?'

'Yes.'

'Foreigners are not allowed in here. Only Soviet citizens.' The woman said to me, 'Please wait outside in the street.'

Taking Pick, I left the room. I waited in the corridor however, not in the street. Lara joined me a few minutes later. The department would soon be closing. We had only just made it. Most of those still waiting would have to come back another day and start again. 'She told me foreigners are not allowed in here because they would see the queue,' said Lara.

Pick was now screaming to be fed. Lara handed me the application forms to hold. They were two identical forms, folded in four so they opened up like maps. We looked for some quiet place where she could breast-feed Pick. We walked along the concrete corridors. There was nothing except numerous identically painted doors, all numbered on small wooden squares at head height, and all shut. Finally Lara started to feed Pick at the end of a corridor. A young typist emerged from one of the doors and invited us into her quiet room. She sat at her desk while Lara fed Pick, then when he fell back content and smiled at her, went all gooey.

'How old is he?' she asked.

'Four months,' said Lara.

The typist cooed.

Lara asked her if she would type out her forms as she had no Cyrillic typewriter. The sale of typewriters was controlled and yet it was stipulated that all answers on the forms must be typewritten. And the identical forms were so folded that carbon paper could not be used, even in the unlikely event of carbon paper being available. A list of all relatives was necessary, 'alive and dead'. There were twenty-one questions, plus a big blank space on the back page numbered 22 for 'any other relevant information'. The typist said she was forbidden to type out applicants' forms.

One of the documents necessary was a certificate from the army. Like other students of a Western foreign language, Lara did military training and theoretically was still in reserve. She had a piece of paper that should have been converted into a certificate, only she had never bothered to get it done. Such a certificate was now necessary. She had to go to the central military headquarters. She could not go on the Friday and then came the weekend.

Monday, June 5: Lara went to the central military headquarters. The soldiers yelled at her. 'What if a war had started!' they bawled. 'We wouldn't have known where to find you!' They stamped her piece of paper with a 1976 date and told her angrily to go to her local military place. This was open only on Wednesdays.

Wednesday, June 7: She went to the local military place. The woman there was very nice and did not shout at her. She put another stamp on her piece of paper. It was now certified and this seemed to be sufficient. Lara came home, fed Pick and then went to our ZHEK to collect forms to fill in to confirm that she did in fact live where she claimed to be living. These too had to be type-written. Lara asked the woman there, a pleasant Jewish woman who spoke Russian with a slight accent, if she would type them out for her. When the woman agreed to, Lara asked her if she would do the main big ones as well. The woman said she would. Lara left all the forms with her, with the answers handwritten on pieces of paper, and came home and fed Pick. Then she returned to collect the filled-in forms. She gave the woman three roubles and a box of Maltesers.

Thursday, June 8: A hectic day for Lara. She got up at six to feed Pick, then went over to OVIR to be there by eight to get a place in the queue in the courtyard before it opened at ten. She got seventeenth place and asked the man in front to hold it for her while she went elsewhere, as is the custom. Then she went to the nearest *Notarialnie Kontori* office where for a fee they make certified copies of documents. Lara needed such copies of some of her documents, including our marriage certificate and Pick's birth certificate. This office opened at eleven and there also she found a big queue at the door before it opened. But she got it done relatively quickly, then went to a bank to deposit 20 roubles for the 'first payment' on the visa. The total cost would be 200 roubles. (The average monthly wage was 160 roubles.) If a visa application was refused the 20 roubles deposit was not returned. The remaining 180 roubles was payable on receipt of visa. The total cost used to be 20 roubles, then it went up at the time of the mass Jewish emigration to 400 roubles, now it was 200. This was for capitalist countries. For socialist countries the total fee was only 30 roubles. After paying in the money Lara came home, fed Pick and then returned to the OVIR queue. It was now midday and she was just in time as the man in front who was holding her place was just going in. Then Lara went in. The woman told her that three extra things needed to be typed in, emphasising that the same typewriter as before must be used. In the blank question number 22 she must state when and how she met me, when we got married (though this was on the marriage certificate, which they had), and that she had not worked since 1974. In fact she had worked, but only as a freelance. Being freelance, she had no document saying she had worked. So therefore she had to state that she had not worked. The Russians have a ditty that begins, 'Without a piece of paper you're a creepy-crawly'.

An experienced queuer had told her it was impossible to satisfy them first time. They always made you come and queue again at least once more. This number 22 was their catch-all section, their Catch 22. They probably wanted to know how we met so that if possible this unauthorised avenue for meeting foreigners could be closed. They wanted to know who the contact was. I thought it pointless, for anyone could simply lie and say they met at a bus stop.

Lara asked the woman, 'Do I have to do all that queuing all over again?' The woman shrugged and said, 'Of course.' Lara told her she had a young baby to feed and the woman said that was not her fault.

Lara came back home to feed Pick, then returned to the ZHEK Jewish lady for the extra typing. The Jewish lady did it while Lara waited and did not want to take another two roubles but Lara insisted. It also cost another four days.

Monday, June 12: Pick woke up screaming at four in the morning, it took us half an hour to quieten him, then Lara had to get up again at six to feed him. He never went back to sleep after his six o'clock feed so we could not either. Lara was feeling sick from exhaustion. She needed to be back at the door of OVIR by half-past twelve in order to have a reasonable place in the queue when the office opened at three. She also at some time in the day had to deliver a translation. She got to the OVIR door at twelve-thirty: there were twenty-two people in front of her. She waited a respectable time before asking the person in front to hold her place while she returned home to feed Pick. Back home at one-thirty, she fed Pick and herself, went back to the queue, waited a while for appearances' sake, and left to deliver the translation. She got a taxi back but still missed her place in the queue, but only just and people let her in. I took Pick down to her there as it was already an hour past his feeding time. She fed him in a corridor and this time no friendly sentimental typist offered the privacy of her room.

Beginning of July: We received a card from the central OVIR demanding a *kharakteristika* (a reference) from Lara's current workplace. A *kharakteristika* was not on the list of documents needed and anyway they had already forced her to say she had not worked anywhere since 1974.

Lara wanted to know what information should be in the *kharakteristika* so phoned the central OVIR. The woman who answered the phone refused to give the phone number of Inspector Bogorodskaya, who sent the card, saying Lara had to go personally to the office. Lara said she had a young baby to feed every four hours but the woman insisted.

Unable to find time to go to OVIR, Lara decided to get a *kharakteristika* without asking exactly what was wanted. She got one eventually from her main source of income, *Moscow News*. The *kharakteristika* had in it all the information possible and confirmed that Lara had done freelance work for them for at least the last two years.

Tuesday, July 25: We went to the central OVIR with the *kharakteristika*. Lara wanted me present because there was a chance they would be less unpleasant with a foreigner around. There was no ban on foreigners at the central OVIR. We left Pick at home with Raisa Iosifovna. We did not post the *kharakteristika* because we feared we might never hear from them again. The central OVIR waiting room was bigger than the local one and there were fewer people. We had not been waiting long before we were called in. A stout woman behind a desk took the *kharakteristika* and read it without asking us to take a seat. She looked up. 'What's this?' she said. 'We don't need this kind of *kharakteristika*. Wait outside.'

We waited outside. Then another woman, who turned out to be Inspector Bogorodskaya, came from upstairs and called us into the room. She sat at one end of a small table, Lara at the other, while I stood. Another visa applicant was being grilled at the proper desk in the room.

'This *kharakteristika* is no good,' said Inspector Bogorodskaya. 'There's too much information on it. We don't need all this stuff about how much you've earned.'

Lara said, 'So ignore that bit.'

'This *kharakteristika* will make me a laughing stock. You'll have to get another one.'

'I have a young baby to feed. You'll only be laughed at: my baby will go hungry again.'

'Bring it when you bring the new *kharakteristika*. You can collect the visa on the same visit. There's no need to hurry. Your documents are still being considered and the visa is not yet ready.'

In the heat of the moment, Lara did not ask the obvious question: if the visa would be ready for collection when she took the new *kharakteristika*, why did they need it?

Instead she asked, 'What if *Moscow News* won't give me another *kharakteristika*?'

'They will,' Inspector Bogorodskaya answered. 'You're not the first person to go abroad from there.'

On the way to OVIR Lara had been in a bubbly mood. On the way out she was deflated. 'I'm fed up with being spoken to as if I was a whore,' she said. 'I don't care what they think of me but I don't like being in their power.'

Friday, July 28: Head of the Soviet Tourist Board Sergei Nikitin wrote in the weekly newspaper *Soviet Culture*, 'There are still quite a few factors that influence negatively the development of Soviet citizens visiting capitalist countries: specifically, a rather long and complicated procedure connected with the granting of visas to Soviet citizens still exists in several Western states.'

Friday, August 4: We phoned *Moscow News* to ask for

another *kharakteristika*. Again there were no problems at *Moscow News* except it meant the nuisance of another journey halfway across Moscow to Pushkin Square to collect it.

Monday, August 7: We collected the new *kharakteristika* from *Moscow News*.

Every day: I went morning, afternoon and evening to our letterbox in the entrance hallway downstairs to see if the card from OVIR informing us the visa was ready had come. We were worried it could come and be stolen, as children kept taking things from our letterbox.

Thursday, August 17: As we had been getting more and more worried that the card could be sent and stolen, we phoned Inspector Bogorodskaya to ask if the card had been sent. She said she did not know and gave us the phone number of the Enquiries Department, open from ten o'clock till one. Lara spent the whole morning trying to get through to the Enquiries Department. The number was permanently engaged. Probably the phone had been left off the hook, a common Soviet practice. The Enquiries Department that day brooked no enquiry.

Friday, August 18: Lara finally got through to the Enquiries Department. She was told the visa was not ready.

Thursday, August 31: She phoned again. She was told to phone again in ten days. This meant ten working days, which meant September 12, which was three months to the day from when she lodged the application. Obviously they wanted their months' worth.

Thursday, September 7: As we desperately did not want to take Pick to England in the winter, Lara phoned again in the hope the visa could be speeded up a little. A young woman said it was not ready and to wait until we were summoned. Lara was about to ask why she was being spoken to like a criminal being summoned to appear in court when the young woman hung up on her, another common Soviet practice.

Wednesday, September 13: I went down to our letterbox and there was a card telling us the visa was ready for collection. Now we had the problem of raising the money. We needed 332 roubles for Lara's plane fare (mine would be paid for me), 33 roubles for Pick's fare, 196 to change into pounds (twenty-eight days at seven roubles a day, the maximum amount per day allowed) and 180 for the visa: 741 roubles. We did not have it. We would have to borrow it.

Meanwhile, we collected the visa. There was almost a last-minute hitch. Lara had earlier gone to a bank and paid in 180 roubles and got the receipt to take to OVIR. While leaving the flat to go to OVIR she noticed that the card said to take 181 roubles. She returned to the bank and paid in another rouble.

At OVIR she was given an external passport in place of her domestic one, which she had to hand in. The external one was not as impressive-looking as the domestic one. The visa for Britain was stamped inside. It emphasised, and she was told orally as well, that she could go only to Britain, not anywhere else. She had to sign a form saying she knew what was expected of a Soviet citizen abroad and that she would uphold the honour and dignity of the motherland, and she was ordered to report to the Soviet embassy in London immediately on arrival.

Chapter Fourteen
WESTWARD HO HUM

We flew to London at the beginning of October. Lara reported to the Soviet embassy as ordered and was told she would be watched throughout her visit by British security. This was one of ten items on a declaration *Warning to Soviet Citizens Abroad*, which she had to read and sign. Among the other items was: 'When shopping you should be very careful not to forget to pay for what you have taken as there are special personnel watching over shoppers: if you walk out with something in your bag you have forgotten to pay for you will get into grave trouble and could be prosecuted.'

There was also a warning to be particularly careful with the traffic as it drove on the left and the traffic regulations were slightly different. And again there was, 'It is your duty to uphold the honour and dignity of the motherland'.

This trip to England was the biggest disappointment of my life. I had looked forward to it so much, not doubting for one minute that Lara would be favourably impressed with the high standard of living and the public politeness. It is not a small thing for an ordinary Russian to visit Britain, and here was Lara making the journey when less than two years ago such a trip had seemed as likely as a trip to Mars. I was fully aware of the romance and uniqueness of a Cockney marrying a girl from the steppes of Bashkiria and looked forward to the impression we would make, Lara as an individual and us as a couple. But no one seemed interested. After the vibrance of the Russians, the English seemed so blasé about everything they might as well have been dead. Nothing stirred them. My brother Ken drove us from the airport. I had been in an interesting part of the world and had not seen him for a year and yet he asked no questions and we barely spoke. That should have warned Lara. Even I thought it a bit weird.

She was surprised at the flatness of London. She had expected skyscrapers and tower blocks but on the road in from Heathrow there are only flat factories, squat offices and terraced houses and we were in London before she was aware of it. She met my parents. Everyone was uneasy, the normal unease of a first meeting between daughter-in-law and husband's parents being heightened by her foreignness. My mother appreciated the romance of the situation though, and enjoyed the meeting. My father kept farting. At first he left the room to do so (not without a muttered ribald comment to Ken) but then he remained flatulently with us. Most of what he said was so distorted by twisted vowels, dropped consonants and glottal stops Lara could not understand it, but she caught enough (and anyway there was the farting) to gain some idea of what sort of person he was. After the introductions, cups of tea and presentation of gifts, Lara fed Pick. As she was changing him my old man exclaimed, 'Gor, 'e's got some chopper on 'im, 'ern 'e.'

When Pick was in bed Lara and I went out. As it was too late to go very far I took her to the nearest pub, somehow believing that the mere astounding fact of sitting in a London pub would enthral her. The pub was called The Standard. It had been a clean, brightly-lit place before and was to be so again. In the meantime, while we were there, it was one of the dingiest, dirtiest pubs around. I hesitated in the doorway, said, 'Maybe we'd better . . . ' but then, not knowing where else to go, led her in. A young slob fiddled with a Space Invaders machine. An old drunk slobbered at the sopping bar. 'What did we come in here for?' Lara asked.

'It's a pub,' I said. 'Typically English.'

'It's horrible,' she said.

She was upset by my dithering. Immediately I saw how the place had deteriorated I should have led her straight out. I had said how much more sure of myself I was on home ground. She saw in that instant how hard life with me was going to be.

We stayed in the following evening to watch television. My father had gone out for a drink. My mother, who liked plays, especially drama, wanted to watch the dramatisation of Frank Harris's autobiography, *My Life and Loves*. Unlettered, she did not know it was pornographic. I knew but believed they would tone it down for television. They didn't. Soon Lara, my mother and I had for our delectation all the grapple and grope, grunt and groan of real live telly sex.

In the following days, my profoundly insensitive father alienated Lara more and more. She had told him what a great baby Pick was. 'He only cries when he needs something,' she said. And then when Pick cried once while she was changing him, my old man exclaimed, 'Ah-ha, I thought you said he never cried for nothing,' as though he had discovered that Pick was not a great baby after all and that Lara had lied. And he kept on about how much money our stay was costing him, what with us using electricity and the gas cooker and hot water for the bath. It was said in a half-joking manner but you could see it bothered him, and this was the worst possible thing he could have said, for it showed he was *mean* – for Lara the cardinal sin, the worst possible fault anyone could have.

Ken's indifference, my uncouth father, the absence in our house of any communication except the shallowest, puzzled and surprised her. There was a strange feeling of disharmony, which, after her own warm family life, greatly upset her. Discomposed by the weird company she found herself in, wholly beyond her previous experience or anything she could have imagined, she went up to our room, threw herself on the bed and cried her heart out. I did not understand the cause of her misery. She needed emotional support, comfort, interest and attention and all she saw in my eyes was confusion and even annoyance. I held her for a moment, then patted her briskly on the back, the way professional wrestlers do when they want to disengage from a pointless clinch.

I had believed she would be fascinated by everything and full of unreserved admiration at the fantastic riches all around. It did not work out like that. For a start, like her compatriot Dostoyevsky a century before her, she was appalled at the litter in the London streets. And as for the abundance of things - it overwhelmed her. The first time we entered a clothing store the sight of the long rows of jeans openly on sale so disturbed her she nearly cried. And when we first went to a bookshop she stood in the doorway stunned by the vista of open shelves of books. (Books in Russian bookshops are behind counters: you have to ask an assistant to hand you one if you want to have a look at it. Browsing is unheard of.) She remained in the corner by the door, among the science fiction, in which she was not the least bit interested, feeling vaguely, weirdly, humiliated. She felt she had no right to be there, confronting an array of books so superior to anything she had ever seen before: it was not for her to appreciate, it belonged to another people. She could not enjoy something she had neither worked for nor possessed as a birthright. She had no clue as to which books to look for, nor did she know how to go about looking. All were so beautiful the natural thing to do was to buy hundreds. To choose just a few seemed ridiculous, like picking just a few mushrooms in a forest full of them.

Pick was a burden. My parents had borrowed a carry-cot that he was supposed to sleep in at night, but it was too small for him. Every time he moved he woke up. And anyway he too was disturbed at the change in surroundings. As we did not have a car we had to go everywhere by public transport. Often we would be standing in a crowded bus, trying to get out the fare, hanging on so as not to be swayed over, clutching a pushchair and holding Pick – and not one passenger would offer us a seat. This would never happen in Russia, and Lara, expecting better from the famous 'English gentlemen', was shocked. Shopping was an important part of our plans but Pick would not let us shop in peace. We wanted clothes for Lara and presents for her friends and family. Once we had a big row because she was a long time in a clothes shop while I had to wait outside holding screaming, squirming, kicking Pick. I knew how incumbent on me it was to display patience and understanding, but I was not up to it.

Fares stunned me as well as Lara. In the time I had been away bus fares had leapt astronomically. Going shopping the first time I said to the driver/conductor, 'Two to Lewisham please,' with a 50p piece in hand, expecting change.

'Eighty pence,' he said.

I honestly thought he was joking. He was a young man, and looked the sort. I duly laughed at his little joke, then said, 'No, seriously, how much?'

A bus journey in Moscow, any distance, costs the equivalent of 3p.

A friend took us out to the Kent countryside in her car and we visited Barry and Joy Jennings in Portsmouth by train. Lara was surprised that small, industrialised England had so much countryside, though she did say she had the feeling all the time that a town was just behind each rise in the ground and always just beyond the horizon. After the vastness of Russia, with its huge skies and wild scenery, England seemed tiny and quaint, with toy trains gliding through a miniature landscaped countryside. She was struck by, and I appreciated for the first time, the extraordinary manicured neatness of the English countryside – beautiful, yet seeming only a garden of the towns. Russians have a big thing about nature, the word for which has the same root as the word usually translated as motherland and all the words to do with birth. In Russian, 'nature' strongly connotes origins, beginnings. In England, on the other hand, as William Golding says, what we call nature 'is something so lived in, so brushed and combed that it is hardly to be distinguished from a garden or a park. Five thousand years of grazing has carpeted our downs with short and perfect turf . . . Even the clumps of trees that stand up elegantly here and there on the downs are the work of eighteenth-century landscape artists.'

I was even disappointed in my role as cicerone. I had looked forward to showing Lara around but she asked unexpected questions revealing my ignorance about my own country, and when travelling she always seemed to me to be missing interesting or beautiful things, looking left when I considered she would have been better employed looking right, or vice-versa; and, because Pick was not letting us get much sleep at night, she often had her eyes closed.

Another problem was *ctenocephalides felis felis* – the cat flea. I had often complained in Moscow about the cockroaches. Now Lara had the chance to return the complaint, about a pest she thought much worse, because it bit. My parents had a cat called

Tiger. The humid weather that summer and autumn so suited cat fleas that their numbers constituted a national record. Pick and I, with our cutaneous susceptibility, had an itchy time of it. We dusted our bed and Pick's cot with anti-flea powder, my parents all the while disclaiming all knowledge of the pests.

So the month passed, a disaster. Lara liked some things, of course: fish and chips, jumble sales – and, above all, roses. Greenwich Park and the gardens in London and Portsmouth were ablaze with the most marvellous blooms. And the scent! If we could have lived in Greenwich Park and the roses could have remained in bloom, Lara would have been blissfully content.

'We'll have a garden with roses,' I said.

'I would like that,' she said. 'D'you think we will?'

'Why not?'

And she did acknowledge the superior workmanship, noticing small things such as crates on lorries being tied on securely, unlike the haphazard way it is done in Russia. Also, she left her change on a pub counter once and the barman came over to our table and handed it to her, which impressed her.

As for me, I felt strange throughout the entire trip, as though in a daze, horribly disorientated. Seeing my own country through the eyes of someone from a relatively backward country, I realised for the first time just how fantastically rich and developed southern England was. Juggernauts and flash cars zoomed along magnificently paved roads. Shops were packed with goods. Towns, as well as the countryside, were so much more tamed than I had been used to in the last year. I had the feeling there were more layers of concrete. Even the dereliction of slum areas was of a different quality to the roughness of the older sections of Russian towns. There was a very strong, distinct impression of one society having nowhere to go, expending energy on silly advertisements, pap and gimmicks in all fields — and another society still building.

Of the former society, Lara used the word *meshchansky*, which the Oxford Russian-English dictionary defines as 'Philistine; bourgeois, vulgar, narrow-minded.' English values seemed to her overcomplex, shoddy and absurd. Culture for most people seemed to be only the meretricious, inane pop culture, which, rooted in an entertainments industry, was really no culture at all. (None of these observations are new or profound, any more than my perceptions of Russia are new or profound. I am simply retailing our experience.) So, both Lara and I were glad when the holiday was over and we could return to Russia, where life was governed by simpler necessities, was more straightforward and basic. It had been pleasant for me to share old jokes with friends who understood the shorthand, but the trip had revealed in stark relief the problems caused by being aliens in each other's country. Now that Lara had seen England and been unimpressed, we began to have childish exchanges at the level of, 'My country's better than yours, nah.' Most people seem to feel more comfortable in a foreign country if they can be disparaging about it. In a mixed marriage, this is a luxury that cannot really be afforded. We both recognised this eventually but only after the habit of disparagement had firmly taken hold.

We arrived back at our Moscow flat to a traditional bread-and-salt welcome from Lara's family. She'd only been gone a month but it *had* been abroad and her family possessed the usual Russian sense of occasion. The flat was decorated with fresh-smelling birch branches, while on the table were set burning candles and bunches of wild autumn flowers specially picked. Embraces and kisses were heartfelt and unrestrained, with no inhibition to tangle and confuse. There was a strong feeling of harmony, of deep communication, of empathy. Emotions were strongly felt and clearly expressed. Presents were given and accepted with a deeply satisfying joyful simplicity. It was good to be back.

Chapter Fifteen
A FREEZE OF GLORY

Another Moscow winter came, that winter which is unlike any winter anywhere else, to begin its laceration of nerves, its wearing of patience, its sapping of energy. Peasants used to liken it to a priest: both contributed nothing and exacted a lot. It wearies, consumes and wastes. Huge efforts have to be routinely made simply to keep the roads and pavements and courtyards clear. Dealing with winter is a full-time job for millions of people. They all have to be paid and in a temperate country they could all be doing something else. The deformities inflicted by frost are everywhere, scars and pockmarks on peasants' faces as well as on roads and buildings. The streets are full of cold, hurrying, hostile people with no energy to spare for the niceties of etiquette or even for normal good manners. There is a reluctance to allow doors to be opened, even in the most public places such as shops.

But the land can be beautiful. On sunny days and moonlit nights, the snow and the rigid trees glitter and sparkle. And it provides the perfect setting for the New Year celebrations. All the trappings of Christmas – the white-bearded, red-cloaked old man delivering presents (called *Dyed Moroz* – Grandfather Frost), the greetings cards, the fir trees – have been transferred to the New Year holiday. The custom of standing a fir tree, a *yolka*, in the corner began in this land of fir forests, and, as neither holly nor ivy grow in Russia, the evergreen fir remains the great symbol of renewal and awakening. The symbolism has more meaning here also, for, unlike in England, where bulbs can poke through the earth in a mild spell as early as January and buds can appear on trees and bushes soon after, and where the grass continues to grow, the long Russian winter is uncompromisingly, rigidly barren. Plastic trees, though available, are not popular, understandably when 'fir tree bazaars' are erected on pavements with real firs piled up for sale as if a forest had been uprooted and deposited there by a flood and trees growing only a bus ride away can be chopped down (illegally) and surreptitiously carted home. The tree, plastic or real, purchased or poached, is set up in a corner and decorated exactly as in the Christmas version except it is usually topped not by an angel or a fairy but by a red star. It is draped with coloured lights and tinsel decorations, including a tiny silver cosmonaut, and laden with gifts. For a fee of five roubles a Grandfather Frost from the Children's World shop will deliver presents to your home on New Year's Eve, accompanied by a Snow Maiden. He reputedly travels through the night sky in a horse-drawn *troika*, and it is the custom to treat him to a glass of vodka when he delivers the presents.

We saw that New Year in huddled up in the living room, dressed in overcoats, scarves and hats. Lara even wore my Arctic fur boots. The old year was going out in a freeze of glory. As the newspapers reported at the time, 'This frost has already gone into legend. Heroic tales are already being told about it.' The last days of 1978 were the coldest in the hundred years that records had been kept, with the mercury freezing solid in thermometers as the temperature plunged to an Arctic minus 45 degrees centigrade. In our flat in the mornings there was ice on the inner side of the inside pane of the double-glazed windows. Television programmes throughout the weekend were interspersed with repeated warnings from the Ministry of Health to be careful with the drink in such cold, and to parents not to let their children out for too long – preferably not at all. Cases of frostbite in the capital were reported and the Moscow newspapers carried advice on treatment of frostbite and how to recognise it. If anyone was out in the open for prolonged periods they had to look for white, bloodless patches on their skin and treat them quickly or, as one paper said in a euphemistic phrase, 'Spontaneous amputation may supervene'.

The few people out of doors on Old Year's Night heard 'the

stars rustle', a North Siberian phenomenon rarely heard in that latitude. A faint rustling could be heard coming from the invisible particles of ice in the air. After midnight we went out for a short walk. The snow on the ground was frozen solid, as hard as concrete. The treachery of vodka was proved, for I felt no colder than on normal cold days in Moscow. As in Norilsk, I again forgot to pour out a glass of water to see if it would freeze before hitting the ground. It was said also that if you spat in such cold your saliva would turn into a gob of ice in mid-air but I forgot to test that as well. Vodka itself froze at that temperature. This fierce weather followed several relatively mild winters and an unusually mild November so that people had been saying Moscow no longer had the really 'hard' winters it used to have. The Meteorological Office said that the big freeze was caused by very cold air masses coming from the Arctic. No matter what measures were taken, the cold got in everywhere. Even winter sports events were cancelled or curtailed. The food shops were open throughout as usual and the poor sales assistants were dressed up like polar bears, so encumbered by clothes they could hardly handle the money or pass over the goods. As in Norilsk, milk froze solid in the cartons. But that uniquely Russian sight, people eating ice cream in the street in the middle of winter, could still be seen, the ice cream kiosks doing as brisk a trade as ever. In spite of the warnings about children, open air parties continued to be held for them as planned, and children from all over the country were taken to see the huge, eighty-foot decorated *yolka* in the Kremlin and the very tall revolving silver tinsel tree in Children's World, on which coloured searchlights were focussed so that it changed colour as it revolved. Older children skated round the lit-up fir trees on the boulevards, while younger ones were pulled along the streets on small sledges, so wrapped up against the cold they could hardly move when they had to get off to walk.

The town was enveloped in a frosty veil. The flow of traffic was hidden in billows of steam from the exhausts. No birds could be heard. All cats and dogs were sheltering indoors. The trees were white and frozen rigid. There was a weird stillness about the streets, even when they were full of people. On our way to an evening at the foreigners' ghetto in Kutuzovsky

Prospect, ten minutes walk from Kievskaya metro station, Lara and I had to take shelter in the Fotokhronika Tass building because our faces hurt so much. We confused the millyman on duty inside by talking to each other in English and by the time he realised we had no business to be there we had thawed out enough to continue our journey across the snowy streets. Bodies of sparrows lay on the pavements, birds that had died in flight and turned stiff in seconds. When we reached the foreigners' block only five minutes later Lara would not take the lift up to the flat immediately to meet strangers because her 'mind was frozen'. We stood by a radiator in the hallway for a few minutes to recover.

I wrote a news story about the freeze-up that was considered interesting enough to run as a page lead. Then the editors wanted a piece on the way winter was dealt with in general, using the big freeze as a peg. Over the next few days we heard more and more tales about the freeze. One group on their way to a new year's party had been stuck in a lift between floors till two in the morning. They 'celebrated' in the lift, the vodka probably keeping them alive. Heating broke down completely in one block so that there were sub-zero temperatures actually inside the flats. This block was evacuated. In other blocks it was still so cold that the inhabitants preferred to sit round bonfires outside. Many sought refuge with friends or relatives. One friend of ours made a phone call from a public box and bits of skin from his ear stuck to the receiver. Another friend was luckier: when he tried to phone the dial was frozen so it could not be used. Our radiator, which should have been too hot to touch, was lukewarm. The mains pipe outside our flat burst. A children's doctor said the number of respiratory infections had increased by fifty per cent. In our flat the hot water kept going off. Typewritten notices were pinned on the street doors of our block: 'Comrade tenants!' they read. 'More strong frosts are expected. Please ensure that all windows are tightly sealed and all balcony doors are insulated.

'At the coming of the frosts it is necessary to ensure free access of warmth from the radiators into the rooms (to remove furniture, curtains and decorative screens from in front of them).

'Special danger comes from street doors left open. Do shut

them properly behind you. Party committee, tenants' committee.'

A rumour circulated that the temperature was going to fall to
an unprecedented minus fifty.

It was from these things heard or experienced personally that
one drew up a picture of what that winter, the most severe in
living memory, must have been like throughout a large part of
the country. Nothing was reported in the media. Piecing it all
together, I wrote my story. Naturally, it told of a certain amount
of disruption, 'though nothing spectacular' as the country was
'too well equipped for snow and ice for that'. But it had to be
said, so I said it, that the degree and length of that cold spell was
straining resources to the limit.

This story was rejected as being 'far too negative and nark-
ing'. The editors wanted a picture of life going on normally.
Since when, I wondered, has life going on normally been
considered a good subject for a news story by any British paper?
In fact there had been severe dislocation, the real extent of which
was only gleaned gradually over the following weeks. Trains
from the Ukraine continued to run a day late for ages. Casualties
from frostbite proved to be so numerous that the Ministry of
Health issued a decree authorising hospitals to instal extra beds.
Gangrene developed in many cases. On February 16 a report on
local elections added, 'This winter's unusually severe frosts . . .
to a certain extent disorganised life in some cities and at some
plants.' And on April 19, at the end of a routine commentary on
a forthcoming parliamentary session, was, 'The two years
remaining before the end of this plan period will be more
difficult than expected: the weather of the past year upset the
rhythm of production in oil, rolled steel, cement, mineral
fertilisers and other items.' A television commentator reported
'certain complications' arising in the functioning of factories.

The editors and I could not even discuss the weather without
disagreeing.

Everything seemed to combine against me working. The
situation at home was appalling. It is difficult for four people to
live together in a two-roomed flat. When one of them is
supposed to work in one of the rooms and another of them has
just reached the perilous biped stage of his growth, work

becomes impossible. Pick was fascinated by all aspects of my work, in particular the typewriter and the telex machine. He found the tape of the latter irresistible. Sometimes two hours' work would be punched on the tape and Pick would come toddling in to see what I was up to. If he grabbed hold of the tape I would have to laboriously type out the whole of it again. Once, when he came dangerously close at a critical time and I expressed a certain amount of panic, Lara said to him in what seemed to me sarcastic tones, 'Come away Pick, we mustn't disturb Papa while he's working.' She, bothered at how little I was doing, often asked, reprovingly, 'Why don't you work?' The answer was obvious. The flat was too small. Even if it had been just the three of us with me going out to work in the daytime and returning home only in the evenings, it would still have been too small. I could not lock the door of my office because it was also Raisa Iosifovna's bedroom, where she kept all her things, and the main living room. Lara wanted me to work but could not provide the conditions for me to do so. She and Raisa Iosifovna each considered they did not interrupt me very often – but taken together their interruptions were many. One would come in and ask something without realising that the other had been in with a question only a few minutes before. And then there was always Pick. Often before I could even begin to think about work I had to gather my pens and pencils that had been strewn all over the floor, or disentangle the typewriter ribbon that had been pulled about, or remove a pile of clothes from my desk. Raisa Iosifovna could never accept that always while seated at my desk I was working. Only when I was actually pounding typewriter keys did it resemble work as she knew it. While going through the newspapers I seemed to her to be relaxing, just reading the papers. And she considered I could have been better employed – taking Pick out for some fresh air, for example. 'Have you finished yet?' she would ask. 'When will you be finished? When are you going to take Dannichka for a walk?' If this direct assault did not bring results she would stand outside the door and keep up a kind of soliloquy, ostensibly addressed to Pick: 'Dannichka, we must not make a noise. Papa is working. We must not disturb Papa when he is working. He will take you for a walk when he is finished. He should not be long now. We must not go in to him yet. He would not like that. But you will not have to wait much longer, I am sure.'

Then, my defences weakened, she would attempt another direct assault, standing in the doorway and asking if I was nearly finished yet: 'Dannichka has to go for his walk, you know.' Pick would usually find a way past her legs at this point and scurry into the room to attack my pens and typewriter. I would get rid of them both, he possibly crying, my concentration gone and my mind full of guilt.

One of the reasons Pick was such a sturdy child was that I gave in to this pressure. I stopped working. With no secretary to help me with the bureaucracy and with Sam Russell spiking perfectly good stories, I felt anyway as though I were swimming in a sea of mud. So I stopped trying to work, taking Pick for a three-hour walk every day instead.

Wherever we went Pick was the subject of unsolicited comments from all kinds of passers-by about all sorts of dangers. Strangers' dangers included traffic, running before he could walk, animals and, the most common, improper dress. In cold weather passers-by objected to his not being bundled up as stiff as a plank of wood, while in hot weather everyone considered a hat indispensable in order to keep off the sun. The admonitions varied in tone from barely audible muttering in passing to a full-scale harangue from a *babushka*, usually preceded by the dreaded '*Molodoi chelovek!*' – 'Young man!' Over-reacting to the incessant annoying warnings, I would let Pick toddle far ahead of me so there really was a danger of him crossing a road in front of a vehicle, and take him out in clothes that were by any standards unsuitable for the weather. And at the zoo once, sick of zoo-goers' warnings of dangerous animals, while lifting him up to feed a camel with a bunch of leaves I let the beast's enormous teeth chomp dangerously close to his tiny fingers.

Pick, of course, loved animals. One Saturday we took him to the big open-air Kalitnikovsky pet market, still called the 'bird market' from when it began long ago as a place to buy and sell canaries. Commercial pigeon breeders joined the canary fanciers on the big vacant lot, then other animals were fetched to be bought and sold and informally discussed. Now birds take up only one corner of the two-acre site.

Across the road from the high fence surrounding the market, four sunflower seed sellers had set up their sacks, two men and two women. The men wore fur hats with ear flaps flapping, the women woollen scarves over their heads. All wore felt boots. Each had a small queue of customers. One customer was holding a new birdcage. Another new birdcage was set on the ground behind the sellers, next to a briefcase. Two arguments were being conducted. A male customer had complained to one of the male sellers about the quality of the seed. The seller was loudly telling him that the seeds were all identical. Meanwhile another male customer was telling a woman seller that her hands were dirty. She told him it was from handling the sacks. He told her she should wash her hands and she told him she would in a minute. The weather was freezing but there were so many people milling about that the snow had turned to slush, trampled into a dirty porridge. Pick's pushchair kept getting stuck in it. The market was too crowded for a pushchair anyway so we folded it up and took turns carrying it and Pick. The first section of the market was the aquarium fish section. Just inside the crowded gateway stood amateurs with only one brightly-coloured fish to sell, contained in a jar held against the body to keep it warm. Most of the jars had foreign labels because Soviet jars did not have screw tops. Beyond these were rows of little tanks on stands, all crowded with exotic fish. Each dealer seemed to specialise in one breed. The tanks steamed in the cold, heated by small boilers fired by portable gas cylinders. One dealer was fishing out with a small net vivid bettas, putting them one by one in a jar for a customer, a young man with a neatly trimmed beard.

'Don't push them in like that,' the young man said. 'You'll injure them.'

'Don't tell me how to handle fish,' said the dealer. 'I'm not injuring them.'

The young man insisted he was, so the dealer said, 'Don't take them, then,' and poured them back into his tank.

Three middle-aged men, their faces red from the cold, were consulting a book, the spirit of mutual counsel having survived from the early days. Many use the market as a club, a place to meet fellow enthusiasts and chat about their hobby. One of the men, it seemed, had had trouble with his pearl gouramis. They had spawned twice without producing any fry. Perhaps his fluorescent lamps were the problem, his friend suggested. Maybe he should get ordinary electric lights? The other man claimed it was all due to hard water. Next to them one enthusiast was excitedly telling another he had had a spawn of discuses. Beaming with pride and pleasure, he explained that the water had been acidified and that he had correctly chosen a hundred-litre tank, which he had given indirect lighting from one side only. He would not be bringing the discuses to the market as they were too valuable, but they were available for view at his home.

Fighting fish were kept in separate jars in the tanks. 'How much?' we asked one dealer.

'These males 1.50, other males one rouble, females 50 kopecks.'

'Dear.'

'Fighting fish are the pride of an aquarium.'

Other dealers were selling all the paraphernalia of tropical fish keeping – the rubber tubing for air pumps, the pebbles, decorative stones, plants, feed and tanks. There were aquariums for sale, new and second-hand, all home-made.

'The ones you buy in the shops all leak,' one dealer told us.

'How much is that one?'

'Ten roubles. It holds eighty litres.'

A woman in felt boots was selling tiny wriggling red worms, the writhing scarlet mass heaped on a stand in front of her. She thrust her hand into the squirming pile. 'Very small, suitable even for fry,' she said. 'Fresh, clean, small. Come on, come on.'

One customer was enticed by her description of her wares. The woman tore off half a page of *Pravda*, twirled it into a cornet, scooped a heap of the tiny scarlet worms into it and handed it over as though she were selling ice cream. Next to her stood a man selling maggots. One passer-by was attracted by them. He had a look, then took the bait. The last part of the fish section was reserved for goldfish, selling at a mere 15 kopecks each.

The two-acre site was overcrowded, jammed so tight with people that we could not put down either Pick or the pushchair.

The dealers stamped their feet on the icy ground while we pushed our way on to the rabbits.

A small brown bunny poked its head out of a battered shopping bag and twitched its nose in the freezing wind. Two other rabbits huddled together in a cardboard box. Alongside the row of fluffy bunnies being sold as pets was a row of big grey bucks being sold as meat. 'Three kilograms of meat,' one dealer said of one of his bucks. And water rats were on sale for their fur. 'Good for collars, hats, fur coats,' said the dealer.

'How disgusting,' said a girl hurrying past.

Cats and dogs were, for some reason, supposed to be barred from the market, but men and women stood under the trees near the exit gates with puppies and kittens tucked under their coats. One smartly-dressed woman had a wriggling something under her overcoat. 'I've got a boxer,' she said. 'Do you want it?'

Another woman, saying, 'Here are my children,' unbuttoned her coat – and out peeked two little furry heads. Details of dogs for sale were pinned up on a notice board, some accompanied by photos. There were no prices, just phone numbers. Among the photos was one of a beautiful Russian borzoi. A rough drawing of a lost fox terrier accompanied a plea to anyone finding it to return it.

In the street outside, cats and dogs were openly on sale. Two young men selling kittens left their charges with a dog seller. He was unhappy about it but they promised to bring him a glass when they returned. A retriever sat shivering on a piece of cardboard in the snow. We had not seen a single mongrel. In the difficult Moscow conditions anyone wanting a dog would want a pedigree dog. The weather, limitations of living space and strictness about where dogs were allowed in the city ensured that one did not buy any old dog or young puppy on a whim. Freezing ourselves, and worried about Pick being out in such cold for so long, we took a taxi home.

Our weekend excursions were memorable pleasures lighting up drab days, days that began drearily and continued along the same lines. Usually I would be woken up at five-thirty by noises in the basement. It was our *dvornik*, our caretaker, a simple young man who every morning at that time in the winter came to collect his tools to break up the ice in some part of the courtyard. Often he would decide to start his day's work right underneath our window. No one else seemed bothered by the noise. Lara would occasionally stir, I would murmur 'The iceman cometh' but she would already be fast asleep again so my wit fell on deaf ears. If the iceman went to some other part of the yard to begin his scraping, sweeping and shovelling of snow and ice, I would be kept awake by one of several other noises: by the two heavy wooden doors directly under us crashing shut; by the stoutly padded young cleaning woman dragging and banging her steel bucket on the concrete staircase; by the decrepit lift clanking or its iron doors crashing; or if none of these noises did the trick then the people upstairs began moving about on their uncarpeted floor and banging the lid of their litter chute.

Reluctantly, I would get up and go to the toilet, waiting a while in the toilet doorway after switching on the light in order to give the cockroaches time to run for cover. After I had used the toilet, I could not flush it as Soviet toilets are made to gush rather than flush. They gush permanently, incessantly, so that everyone lives with this soothing 'white noise', which time-study experts reckon is conducive to maximum production. It did not seem to help me in my work. My production was minimal. And anyway I would have preferred the water to remain in the cistern for when needed for a specific practical purpose. Each visit to the toilet ended with a manipulation of the ballcock in the chest-high cistern. This done, I went to the bathroom. Our bathroom light switch required the delicate touch of a surgeon's hand if the switch was to remain in position and the light to stay on. At five-thirty in the morning I lacked this sureness of touch and so would herald my arrival to the bathroom cockroaches with a signal of blinking light. My ablutions finished, I would go to the kitchen to put on the coffee. Igniting the gas usually took a minute or two, for we had only Soviet matches. On average, one in three Soviet matches ignites. Occasionally I would strike it lucky. But usually three or four of the matches broke, being pin-thin. Russians as a matter of course strike three or four together. Outside it was pitch dark except for the yard's yellow lamps and a few lighted windows. On the wall outside the kitchen window the thermometer would be registering some frighteningly low temperature. I would sit and drink my coffee to the sound of the outer portals downstairs crashing shut in harmony. The two heavy wooden doors were held to the wall by hinges that did not slow them down to soften their closing. The iceman had fixed a huge spring to the inner door but it had never worked properly from the day he did it. The caretaker had not taken enough care. Later the same day it broke away from the door and had dangled uselessly on the wall ever since.

After I had finished my coffee I would put on my sheepskin coat and fur hat and descend the two flights of chipped, cracked stairs to the rows of blue-painted tin postboxes on the wall of the ground floor corridor. The aged postwoman, her body bent by many years of carrying heavy loads, came very early, and if I did not collect my post, boys, having discovered that I received interesting letters with foreign stamps, would take it on their way to school. As soon as a new lock was put on my box, or the existing one mended, they broke it again. Now the lid hung permanently lockless and lopsided, the contents available to all.

The corridor would be freezing. I often saw the postwoman. She would be muttering to herself as she shoved envelopes and newspapers into the boxes. (In the Soviet Union newspapers and magazines are delivered by post.) She knew me and sometimes, knowing my problem with thieving schoolboys, fetched a letter to me on the third floor. 'Anything for me?' I would ask, and she would mutter something inaudible so I would have to look for myself. By now, the building sounded as if it was being demolished. Crashes and bangs came from all directions. Joining in the cacophony would be Pick. He would invariably wake up in the few seconds I was downstairs. When I returned he would be standing in his cot, dummy in hand, crying, while Lara, not knowing I had gone downstairs, would be calling for me to attend to him. Raisa Iosifovna would be *hors de combat* in the bathroom. I would lift Pick out of his cot, an action that nearly always precipitated a wee. We were trying to dispense with nappies. Often he called for the pottie but sometimes he forgot or could not be bothered. I would mop up the puddle and change his rompers. Lara would say it was too early for him to get up and couldn't I have got him back to sleep and I would reply crossly that he was already wide awake and that there was too much noise.

I would be feeling intensely irritable. We were overcrowded, with no defined tasks, so that each little chore was preceded by a discussion on responsibility. I knew that the morning would go on like this, a pile-up of minor domestic duties and petty vexations. Some days I felt as though I were on stage in a farce. Complications followed hard on each other's heels with theatrical timing. I remember one morning the tap water that was rinsing Pick's washed clothes suddenly turned as brown as mud, staining them, but mostly I cannot now remember what the complications were, precisely because each one in itself was so petty. Pick weeing or poohing himself was a common occurrence. We might be cleaning this up, say, when Raisa Iosifovna, who was out shopping, would phone with the news that they were 'giving away' Bulgarian tinned tomatoes (in jars), a stock of which would be useful as an ingredient in *borsch* for months, and she had a place reserved in the queue and one of us was to take some money and help her buy as many jars as we could carry. Pick's pram came in handy for these bulk purchases until the day it collapsed and broke under the weight of six big cartons each containing twelve jars. Whoever went on these shopping expeditions felt obliged to take Pick. This meant he had to be dressed. Dressing Pick in winter was the biggest complication of all. First, tights had to be put on. Then the first pair of trousers. Then the second pair of trousers. Then the first pair of socks. Then the second pair of socks. At this stage he usually grew sick of the whole procedure and began wriggling, stiffening and arching backwards. Lara and I would use our respective methods of overcoming this difficulty. Lara adhered to the cajoling, reasoning method. I adhered to brute force. We would argue over our respective ideas while Pick screamed.

'I'll do it on my own,' Lara would tell me angrily.

I would gladly leave them to it. First he had to be calmed down. With me out of the way this was relatively easy. Over the two pairs of socks went a pair of *valenki*, knee-high felt boots. These did not go on easily. They had to be pushed and pulled, the dresser all the while making appropriate noises so the dressee thought it was a game and did not get upset. With the *valenki* pushed and pulled on, the bottom half of him was ready. Now the top half had to be covered: two pullovers, two pairs of gloves and two hats, followed by an overcoat firmly buttoned up and a scarf tied round the neck. His ears had to be properly covered, as he could easily get an ear infection if they were exposed. Now cream was applied to his face. He was ready.

Whereupon he would want to do a wee. His coat was hurriedly unbuttoned, the scarf unwound from his neck, the layers of clothing covering his legs pulled down, his two hats removed and his pottie fetched. He would proudly do his wee, then while I emptied the pot Lara would pull up his tights and trousers, put back on his two hats, re-button the coat and tie the scarf again. As he was now much too warmly dressed to remain indoors I had to take him downstairs while Lara got ready. When they were gone I might want to take the opportunity to do some phoning, and find either that all the officials I wanted to talk to had left their receivers off the hook or my phone had gone dead.

I would listen to the BBC World Service midday news if the reception was good enough, fearful I had missed something important through switching off the clacking TASS teletype machine for the night. If the BBC had picked up on TASS something that had appeared in that day's *Pravda* I had a choice of translating the *Pravda* piece or going over to the Reuters bureau in Sadovo-Samotechnaya, the other side of Moscow, to see what weight they had attached to the story. Reuters might also have some other bits of news. Really I should have been putting together features but visits and interviews necessary for this could only be set up by a secretary working at it full time, and I had no secretary. So I would go over to Reuters instead, spending over an hour getting there and over an hour returning, the trip taking up the whole afternoon, often with nothing gained other than the knowledge when I telexed Sam in the evening that all really was quiet on the Eastern front.

I did acquire over the months an insight into how a consensus of opinion is built up among journalists. Only one or two are ever really expert in any field, capable of an independent informed assessment of events as and when they occur. The other reporters get their interpretation of news from these. The head of the Reuters Moscow bureau, Bob Evans, was an authority on the Soviet Union and international affairs. Other correspondents exercised their right to obtain information from

Reuters, as their newspapers paid the agency a lot of money for the service of news and information, and gleaned at the same time Bob's interpretation of the news. I saw this done many times. I observed the sowing of ideas, their growth and their fruition. Someone like Bob Evans lightly introduces a personal interpretation, which is repeated unquestioningly by other correspondents, whose journals then develop and expand the idea in features and editorials, after which, allowing for a few weeks more of common usage, it becomes an accepted Truth. In some circles, and among some types of people, after a bit more time has elapsed it becomes a fact so obvious as to be beyond discussion.

Returning from Reuters I would telex Sam, a task that threw its shadow over each entire day, much as I disliked myself for being so affected by him when he was 1,600 miles away and I did not even have to hear his voice. Logically, there was nothing he could do to hurt me, but it was strange how he could convey irritation over a telex machine. Choleric by nature, he would occasionally let himself go. The Moscow correspondent by tradition bore the brunt of his wrath. He was said to be disappointed in the Soviet Union, as though that country owed him something personally. (Lara was disdainful: 'We of this country have got enough problems without worrying over the delicate feelings of liberal foreign Communists,' she said.) The telexing done, with varying degrees of unpleasantness depending on Sam's mood, we settled down for the evening. To me there always seemed to be pandemonium. I could not switch the TASS machine off till later, so that would be banging away: Pick would be trundling around in his tractor: Lara would be going frantic two minutes away from some translating deadline: Raisa Iosifovna would be fussing over some chore that needed doing that instant: and Anya would often be with us on a visit – vivacious Anya, exuberant, full of bubbling life, making plans, loving and loveable but adding greatly to the turmoil. I felt we were overcrowded: Lara said I did not know how lucky we were.

We rarely went out in the evening, even though we had Raisa Iosifovna to babysit. It always seemed to me more trouble than it was worth, and I missed a lot through this apathy. Unpardonably and foolishly I was ruining a unique experience. I had 'gone native' to an extent rarely known in Russia and was wasting the experience through my old habits of introspection and self-doubt, encased in my closed universe. I would never again have such an opportunity to record everyday life in what was not only the biggest country in the world but was for millions of people the most interesting. I knew it. The thought was there, alongside the thought that there was no point in shaving, polishing my shoes or finding a clean shirt. The acrimony with which all public life was conducted and the hostility of the weather provided justification for not venturing out. I remember once Lara did persuade me to go with her to see a film at our local cinema. Pick played up when going to bed, making us a few minutes late. We hurriedly bought our tickets, and were about to enter when an imposing doorwoman descended on us. 'Where do you think you're going!' she yelled. 'You're too late!'

'We've had to put our baby – '

'Out!'

Snow was falling, an unpleasant fine wet snow that melted immediately, not much more than white rain. Humiliated, we went back out into it. On the corner was a cocktail bar. Called the *Luna*, it displayed exotic Western bottles of whisky, gin and brandy but they were all empty and the bar in fact sold nothing but a sickly sweet cocktail. We had one each of the vile concoction, then returned home in the wet snow.

Before our marriage I had dreamed of Lara sitting in one corner calmly doing her translating, me in another writing my articles, with both of us occasionally consulting each other: it would be bliss. It never worked out like that. I had wanted the peaceful routine of normal family life with its simple joys and privacy for work, and I had not got it. Pick and Raisa Iosifovna came along too soon. My vision had turned into a hectic family drama, crowded with supernumeraries. We would usually watch television till about eleven, after the nightly announcement: 'Comrades, it is late, tomorrow is a working day, please think of your neighbour's peace, turn down the sound on your radio and television sets.' Then Lara would begin work: and I would go to bed. Her work had to be done, or she did not get paid. I received my wages whether I wrote one article a week or twenty. She had the greatest incentive to work of all: I had none. Each night I lay in bed, chafing and fuming, waiting for her to finish, having achieved nothing during the day and yet knackered.

Vodka. The tender diminutive of *voda*, water. The 'water of life', the Russian wine, 'wild cow's milk', the green snake, the damned, the bitter, the green devil. Vodochka. Dr Gregory had asked me if, in view of my father's example, I thought there was any danger of me ever succumbing to the allure of drink and I had airily replied, 'No, I don't like the taste.'

'That's all right, then,' Dr Gregory said reassuringly, certainly knowing that those who really need to drink are not put off by the taste. Before going to Moscow I hardly drank at all. I had not once in my life been properly drunk. In fact I was worried about all the boozy receptions I would have to attend. Now the main attraction of the receptions was the booze and the taste was no longer a problem, for I threw vodka down my throat as adroitly as any Russian. I often felt I needed a drink. I took to surreptitious swigs when left alone in the kitchen, diluting the vodka that remained in the bottle to keep it at the same level. And it was vital to have a snifter for a meal, an *impératif* before dinner.

In the spring we moved to a bigger flat. It was in the same neighbourhood, just off Universitetsky Prospect. It improved nothing as far as my work was concerned because in the discussion on how best to utilise the extra space the question of the respective ages of Raisa Iosifovna and Pick was raised, with the attendant suggestion that they be the main beneficiaries. This suggestion was subsequently elevated to the status of a resolution, which was passed unanimously, with one abstention (mine). I possibly made mild noises of dissent before giving in and shutting up. I cannot now remember. My aversion to argument, which at cocktail parties led me to agree with anyone on anything so that I could appear to be a hard-line Stalinist and a die-hard royalist and anything in between, all at the same do, also led me to fall in peaceably with other people's arrangements, even when it would have been clear to anyone else that the arrangement was against my interests. I could persuade myself that almost any arrangement was unimportant, and see good points in it, resolving to save my strength for the really vital issues. So it came to pass that I ended up sleeping on the floor. The new sleeping arrangements were that Raisa Iosifovna would kip on the divan in the living room, Pick would have the extra room and Lara and I would doss down on the floor of my office. The bedding took up half the length and the whole width, from door to desk and from wall to bookcase. Lara, unable to break her old habit of late retiring and late rising, was usually still recumbent at midday, when in normal circumstances I might have thought about the possibility of starting some work.

I ceased to function. My feelings of frustration, despair and failure led to what I believe was some sort of breakdown, for what is a breakdown but a ceasing to function? Like a convict awaiting the day of his release, I waited passively for the day I could go home, caring about nothing else. I stopped contacting Sam every day. It was a very quiet time politically anyway, a sort of protracted Moscow correspondents' silly season. So I languished, like Oblomov or Andy Capp, dull and forlorn, rotting.

My biggest mistake of all was not to enjoy my son. Pick was a strikingly healthy, sturdy child, with blue eyes and a mop of loose golden curls, intelligent and lively. He loved our walks. Often they coincided with the schoolchildren going home, and he would go off and play with them if they let him, or simply stand watching them if they did not. Adults loved him, and gushed as only Russians can over little children. Guests would always generously fetch him a gift – a soft toy (to which he was never attracted) or, more to his taste, a plastic animal on wheels or a tinny toy car. Passers-by gave him so many sweets when he went out that on his return he would produce sweets for minutes on end from all over his body like a magician producing rabbits from a hat. You would think there could not possibly be room for any more and start to walk away, and Pick, with an entertainer's timing, would – hey presto! – bring out another sweet and hold it up triumphantly, laughing. On crowded public transport even the elderly and infirm offered to yield their seats to him, while I had only to sit him on a counter and shop assistants would actually serve me. He was a great joy to everyone except his father. I did not realize how quickly children grow up, and even if I had realized I do not think I had it in me at that point to dredge up interest.

My apathetic listlessness ended only when I went on a trip to the Caucasus in the spring, a trip that was so adventurous only a zombie would have been unstirred. It was Anya's suggestion that we go. Anya had at last got herself a steady, genuinely caring young man. Zhenya, whom she called her husband for the sake of convenience, was one of a group that every spring went off to some remote mountain river to shoot the rapids. This year they intended to shoot the rapids of the Avarskoye Koisu river in the Caucasian Mountains. Though Anya, Lara and I were unqualified to take part in this tightly controlled sport, we could hitch lifts on cattle trucks while the others were on the river, meeting up with them at their camp at the end of each day. Zhenya would probably travel with us part of the way instead of going on the river, as he suffered from jealousy and rarely let Anya out of his sight for longer than a couple of hours. The group aimed to cross the main range from Georgia to the Caspian Sea, hiking and taking buses and lorries at the beginning and end and rafting in the middle. They had been preparing and training for it all winter. What did we think? asked Anya. Should we go? We were keen but I doubted if I would be granted a visa. I applied however, giving the exact itinerary, and, to my surprise, was given permission to go without even needing any piece of paper. So at the end of April, rucksacks on back, we set off for our Caucasian torrent.

Chapter Sixteen
CAUCASIAN TORRENT

      As we stood on the platform waiting for the train to start, Gennady Aleksandrovich Tsip entertained us. Gennady Aleksandrovich Tsip played the Fool not because he was stupid but because he had been very unhappy as a boy and thought his quick wit could hide his misery. It could not, of course, but he thought it could and when he began his military service he felt an even greater need of something as camouflage. By the time he got married to a woman he loved and had a son he was proud of, the mould of Jester had hardened. I have never appreciated his type of loud tomfoolery but I liked him and recognised that it served a purpose in a group such as ours. There were eighteen of us altogether, including four girls and six Sashas.

We piled into the train and trundled slowly southwards, through the Moscow suburbs where winter had barely ended and the trees were not yet even budding, laughing at Gena Tsip's exuberant silliness. For Russians, going to the Caucasus is like going abroad, the equivalent of the British going to Italy or Spain. As is the tradition, the first meal was shared by all, squeezed thigh to thigh, tin plate of noodles in one hand, tin cup of vodka in the other and a tin container of greenstuff for vitamins on our knees. The group commander called for silence and made a solemn toast to our success. We drank to that. At Kursk in the evening the trees were in bud.

Throughout the next day Gena was wearing a white peaked cap at a rakish angle and a shirt that had been ripped from the shoulder right down the front in some nocturnal drunken horseplay. Not as well built as most of the others, he was led by his constant desire to please and make an impression to accept every challenge to a wrestle. And he drank even more than the others, for the same reason. We were now travelling through the land of the Cossacks. By afternoon the trees had fresh leaves.

Most of the group spent their time on the train sewing plastic foam and shin and knee guards into fabric to be tied round their legs. Some had football shin guards which they were sewing on to tracksuit bottoms. This work was always done on the train and not earlier at home, as few ever had time to do it earlier, having to work overtime to earn time off for the trip, and anyway it was no fun doing it at home alone. Necessity being the mother of tradition, doing the needlework on the train had become a custom.

Our group was strictly organised, with a firm commander and an officious 'accountant'. The latter, a babyfaced young man, one of the Sashas, came round with handscales to account for and weigh all our provisions and equipment so as to get the total weight and distribute it evenly. It worked out that all the men except me were to carry 25 kilos on top of their personal belongings, the girls 7 kilos extra and me 14 kilos. It meant each man except me would carry about 45 kilos – nearly one hundredweight. Tents, inflatable floats, paddle blades and food all had to be carried on backs. My load was going to be mainly potatoes. My contribution to the common good had been dozens of tins of stewed meat bought with sterling at a Beryozka hard currency shop (tinned meat was unavailable in ordinary shops). One of the others had also provided some Chinese tinned meat, procured at the Peking restaurant. Other groups on the train, in spite of recent official warnings on food poisoning, had fresh stewed meat that would be far from fresh by the time they came to eat it. Gena said the technique of canning meat was complicated and had not yet been mastered in the Soviet Union. Whatever the subject, Gena had something interesting to say on it, based on solid knowledge. He was intelligent, well-educated and widely read. Once he even corrected me on something I had said wrong about England.

When we woke up the next morning we saw in the distance the Caucasian Mountains. The further south we went the more prosperous and neat the villages became. The trees, now, were close to bearing fruit.

We pulled into Tbilisi, squirmed out of the train with our gigantic rucksacks, clambered aboard a booked coach and headed for Belokany in Azerbaijan. We passed blocks of flats with May Day bunting covering their fronts and then we were out in the country, green hills everywhere and always the road climbing. The mountains became wilder, the air cooler. Now we were going along the side of a hill with a valley below. The road at this point passed through many villages and was called Stalin Street. The driver tried to drown out our Russian songs with Georgian radio music. At a toilet stop I bought at a roadside kiosk a pink-tinted picture of Generalissimo Stalin, who had a pencil in one hand and a pipe in the other while he worked out his war plans over a map on which Moscow and Stalingrad were highlighted with big red stars. The *kioskyor* put it into an envelope for me so it would not get dirty.

We had been travelling for three hours and it was late at night when, empty wine bottles rolling about the floor of the coach and crashing against each other, we reached the Georgia/ Azerbaijan border. The barrier was down. A grey-uniformed *militsia* man and two young men were waiting at the barrier. Orange light was coming from the open door of a hut on our left. The millyman looked up at us through the coach windows, and then thoroughly checked the driver's documents. He handed them back to the driver, who put them on the dashboard and drove on a short way, over a bridge across a stream, and then stopped at a second barrier. This border between two Soviet republics was like a frontier between two countries, with two barriers and a no-man's-land in between. On the Azerbaijan side the driver's documents were again checked thoroughly by an armed guard. One of the young men at the Georgian barrier had got on the coach and he agreed that indeed, 'it is like a border between West Germany and the Soviet Union'. We learnt later that the checkpoint was in fact part of the battle against the illegal transportation of citrus fruits to other republics, where they could be, and were, sold at enormous profit.

We rolled on into Azerbaijan. The young man, seemingly a

simple hitch-hiker, took charge of the whole coach, talking familiarly to everyone in strongly accented but good Russian, and directing the driver. We needed somewhere to camp on the far side of Belokany as a good setting-off place for a 20-kilometre hike to the river in the morning. The young man, as we neared the town, told the driver where to go while engaging everyone in conversation. He was dark and good-looking and very confident: a typical young man of the region. Because he was near the front of the coach and kept addressing everyone in it, he sat sideways on his seat, his legs in the aisle. As he was sitting across the aisle from Anya, he talked to her a bit more often than to anyone else. Zhenya was sitting next to Anya, by the window.

'Are you all Russian?' the stranger abruptly asked, so abrupt and *à propos* of nothing that nobody except me heard the question, and the conversation flowed over it. I was immediately on my guard. I was sure Moscow had informed the local authorities of the Englishman travelling wild in their country, but I knew all about over-zealous or bored local officials and messages that do not get passed on or that get garbled. And anyway I was in a paranoid mood, a common condition of foreigners in the Soviet Union.

Zhenya too had a psychological problem. His jealousy finally overwhelming him, he muttered something to Anya. The dark stranger said to him, 'You don't think I'm trying to chat up your woman, do you?'

Zhenya in fact had two psychological problems. The second now revealed itself. He was a coward. Chickening out, he said feebly, 'No.'

'If you do, we can get off the bus and discuss it.'

'No, no, you don't understand.'

'You mustn't think we're all sex-starved here. How old are you?'

'Thirty-one.'

'Well, I'm twenty-two and I'm more intelligent than you, cleverer, and if I wanted your woman I could probably have her. Is she your wife or just your girl?'

Zhenya hesitated before replying, 'My wife.'

'Show me your passport then.'

If Zhenya had been in a normal state of mind he could have thought up any number of suitable answers, such as 'Get knotted' or 'Mind your own business' but he was cowed, defeated. He waved his hand aimlessly and sat back in his seat and looked out of the window, as though the blackness outside was full of interesting sights.

When we reached Belokany the dark stranger directed the driver to some hotel that we refused even to consider. We could not afford to stay at hotels and we wanted to camp. I wondered if this was another attempt by the stranger to discover if the Englishman he was seeking was in this group. If we stayed at a hotel everyone would have to register and hand in their passports. The commander said firmly, 'We are not staying here. Take us to a place where we can camp.' But the driver, having stopped, refused to go an inch further. 'I was booked to bring you to Belokany and I've brought you to Belokany,' he said, wanting a tip. Suitably tipped, he took us, directed by the dark stranger, to a stony place across the bed of a stream. 'There's nowhere else to camp,' said the dark stranger. Anya, knowing that foreigners received preferential treatment even as they were being spied upon, felt a suitable place would be found if he knew his elusive Englishman was among them: so she told him. And indeed he then took us all the way back to the other side of Belokany to a suitable site; a grassy place just off the road, down a slight incline. We piled out of the coach. For a while I thought the dark stranger intended to spend the night with us but he and the coach eventually sped off dustily into the Azerbaijanian night. For a short while on the journey I had put my picture of Stalin on an empty seat. Now when I looked inside the envelope the picture had gone. The picture cost only one rouble 50 kopecks and copies were available at any kiosk. Why should anyone take it?

When you arrive in the night at an unknown place not seen in daylight you can feel strange and vulnerable. I had not the faintest idea what was across the road fifty yards away. The sound of a stream nearby was the only focal point until we got a fire going. I was tired and felt weird and lost in a peculiar part of the world. The night, what with the dark stranger and the missing picture, was eerie.

The two on duty collected twigs and branches and built up a wood-pile and hung two rectangular pots over it, one containing water, the other *kasha*, cooked grain. The rest of us pitched our tents. Lara and I were sharing a tent made for two with Anya and Zhenya. After putting it up we lounged around outside it waiting for the supper to cook. The others were playing cards by the fire. Gena was messing about, making them laugh. I cannot convey his humour because half of it relied on exuberance and loudness and most of the other half was untranslatable punning and playing on words.

Out of the darkness emerged a local boy, an adolescent. He went straight up to the others and started talking to them. At first I thought he was from a nearby café and was touting for custom, as he kept pointing to somewhere up the road and I could not imagine what else it could be. Lara and Anya laughed at this reaction from another culture. In the Soviet Union no one except black marketeers touts for custom. I knew this, of course. My reaction just showed how confused I was. Then the boy and the commander left the main group and stood talking some distance away in what seemed to me a conspiratorial manner. Lara said the commander was simply trying to arrange some transport for tomorrow, but said herself, 'Why do they have to be so conspiratorial about everything?' The boy was dressed in a black rollneck pullover and baggy trousers and had a very short crewcut. I disliked his confidence. Adolescents should be diffident, I felt, even in that outlandish part of the world.

He was still hanging around when the pot was banged for supper. I could not eat anything because of trouble with my stomach. Wine bottles were being passed round but I could not enjoy that either. When we were properly settled in at our first riverside camp, either tomorrow or the day after, we intended to have a May Day feast, and I hoped my stomach was relieved by then. I thought maybe a walk would help. Lara went with me in the direction of the stream, away from the road. Passing through what seemed to be an orchard, past some rocks and what seemed to be a small statue, we came to a high wall with a gap in it. We went through the gap and were on the dry rocky bed of the mountain stream.

On the way back a figure approached us out of the darkness.

It was the boy. He accompanied us back to the camp, talking airily. He told us that the whole ground we were on used to be the river bed and was now being turned into a park and that the *militsia* had visited the camp while we were taking our walk.

After a few minutes back at the camp I felt the beneficial effects of the walk and wandered off into the trees and rocks. As I squatted among the rocks, enjoying my first such squat for three days, a male figure emerged from out of the darkness and approached me. I hurriedly stood up and pulled up my jeans.

'Hello,' the man said. 'What are you doing?'

'Having a shit,' I said. 'Is it forbidden?'

'It's allowed.'

He looked round the rocks behind me. 'Who else is here?' he said. 'Someone else is here. Who was with you? Why did you go for a walk when the *militsia* came? You're not Russian? What nationality are you?'

I was walking away while he was firing his questions but at the last question I turned aback, doing up the top button of my jeans. I was angry. 'English,' I said. 'I'm English. I have permission to be here. Here's my correspondent's identity card.' I thrust the card at him angrily. He said it was not necessary for me to show him my identity card.

I walked back to the camp, where the boy was talking to Lara and company.

'They won't even let you have a shit in peace,' I said. 'The place is crawling with inquisitive geezers.'

'Not in front of the boy,' said Lara in English.

'I said it for his benefit,' I said. 'I want him to know I know.'

'You don't think he's one of them, do you? Don't be silly.'

'Of course he's one of them. He was following us when we went for a walk.'

'I don't think he is. He's been telling us he's never been to school because where he comes from there are no schools. If he was what you think, he would never tell us a thing like that with a foreigner around.'

I was not convinced. The boy continued with the supposed story of his life. He told us there were over thirty languages in his home region and he spoke them all, in spite of no schooling. I presumed he meant dialects, or he was lying. 'Some wild people live in these mountains,' he said in passable Russian. 'Some never come down to civilisation. When I lived in the mountains I had no shirt or coat and had to kill animals for food. Some people up there still eat raw meat, never having learnt how to cook it. I was stunned when I first came here three years ago with my parents. Now I'm a van driver and have been to Tashkent, Odessa and Leningrad. Not Moscow though.

'Recently I was jailed because of the custom that if insulting words are exchanged with another man I should kill him or be killed by him. I was with my sister and he was making himself a nuisance over her. We were both drunk. I had a dagger and I went for him. The *militsia* broke it up and my father paid a lot of money to get me out. Nowadays money is everything here. That is all everyone thinks about – money, money, money.'

It was now well past midnight. Two men had been standing in the road above us all the while. One whistled, and I was sure it was a signal to the boy, for he left soon after. The two men remained. My tiredness had gone now and indeed I felt like another walk. I suggested we take a stroll along the road, partly because I wanted to see what was there and partly because I wanted to see what the men would do. Zhenya went with me and Lara. We climbed the incline and when we reached the top the two men were standing there waiting for us. 'You cannot go,' one said in very bad Russian. He said something else but I could not understand him and caught only the word '*militsia*'. Lara and I wanted to continue with our stroll anyway, as they did not have a law to stand on, but Zhenya was now very scared and said we should go back. In deference to his fear, we returned to the camp. Lara said to him, 'Why shouldn't we go for a walk?'

'Because we've now got guards,' said Zhenya.

'But this is not a prison camp and we are not criminals.'

But Zhenya had a career to think of, and our metaphysical concern over the right of the individual to take a walk along a public highway was of no interest to him.

So we went to bed instead. Zhenya and Anya, both a bit drunk, started to argue. Anya wanted to go and talk to the two men, to find out exactly the situation. Zhenya said, 'You're only along for the ride. You mustn't keep interfering.'

Anya said, 'I have opinions and I'm entitled to express them.'

They developed their respective points of view for a while and then were silent. Zhenya had warned us it would be very cold and to put on a lot of clothes. I had on two pullovers, two pairs of trousers and a pair of woollen socks over my ordinary socks, and was in a sleeping bag. We were packed like curled-up sardines. The slightest movement disturbed the next person. Lara gave me a goodnight kick. I was just going to sleep when there was an unearthly yell from the middle of the camp: 'Eh-h-h-h!' And again, 'Eh-h-h-h!' I lay there expecting at any moment the flaps of our tent to be pulled apart and a wild-eyed mountain tribesman to peer in, dagger in teeth. A few yells later, the Thing departed. I have never in my life felt so confused and out of my element, although – surprisingly – I slept perfectly.

In the morning, green mountains loomed ahead of us and a nut-brown native sat among us. Clouds had gathered on the mountains. The native, who really was very darkly tanned, was sitting unashamedly right in the middle of the camp, smoking, watching us. He did not speak Russian. He may have been one of the men on the road last night. Cows mooed on the road now, shepherded by a cowman with a stave.

Lara said there was nothing sinister about last night, the two men were simply drunk, and one later wandered into the camp in that condition. But I had the feeling that the police force of two Soviet republics were keeping an eye on me. My paranoid mood had deepened.

Lara agreed it was possible that the strange dark young man on the coach had gone straight to a phone and told the local security men of me, and that led to the fuss.

'It's a nutty country anyway,' I said.

'It is a bit,' she said.

Now we could see our surroundings clearly. The nearby trees were all young, freshly planted. The statue was an unfinished and as yet unnamed bust of a bearded man.

We went to wash in the fast-flowing stream that was once a sluggish river. As we left the camp the nut-brown native got to his feet, walked to the edge of the camp with us and yelled twice. It could only have been a signal. On our side of the stream were the young trees, on the other side green mountains: the only person we could see was a shepherd with a flock of sheep among the trees. Lara believed the surveillance had nothing to do with me. The *militsia* had asked how many girls were in the group, and she believed we were indeed among some wild people who would go crazy at the sight of white Russian girls and if we did have a *cordon sanitaire* around us it was for our own protection. When we returned to the camp the nut-brown native had gone. He returned after breakfast, carrying a battered kettle, a glass and a bottle. Making himself at home, he dispensed tea from the kettle and local *cha-cha* vodka from the bottle. He insisted everyone had some *cha-cha*. He drank most of it himself and within ten minutes was drunk. He lay down on the grass, propped on one elbow. Two adolescent boys joined him, stretching out alongside him. We would be leaving soon, when the commander returned from trying to arrange some transport. I cleared up and Lara went to the stream to wash our utensils.

When the commander returned he told us the *militsia* had informed him an avalanche had blocked our road to the river and had forbidden us to try to get through. 'We'll have to go back to Tbilisi,' he said. The group quickly decided what they would do. Last year they had gone down a river in Georgia, the Rioni. They would go there again. It was not as exciting as the Avarskoye Koisu but that could not be helped. In fact only the commander was genuinely disappointed. A born leader, he needed somewhere to lead. The others were relieved. They knew the Rioni and anyway it was less dangerous. And that 20-kilometre hike carrying 45 kilos would not have been very pleasant either. Suddenly light-hearted, they laughed madly when Gena Tsip put on a performance for them – there were some chickens pecking around the camp, and 'tsip, tsip, tsip' is the sound Russians make when calling chickens. Now they made the sound and of course Gena came flapping up, cackling and stepping like a chicken, exactly as he was meant to.

I had a problem now and a decision to make: I had no permission for the Rioni river. Zhenya said it did not matter, where we were going there were no people, only goats and sheep and cattle. But I did not trust these animals. I considered calling in at the main *militsia* headquarters in Tbilisi and getting them to call Moscow, but tomorrow was May Day and it and the following were public holidays. Few people would be at their desks and those few would be drunk. Another alternative was to go to Sukhumi and spend a fortnight on the Black Sea coast, which Anya was advocating. There were so many foreigners in Sukhumi I would not be noticed. In the end I decided to stay with the others and if questioned about my accent to say I was an Estonian from Tallinn. The English accent is very similar to those of the Baltic republics.

As we walked to the bus station Lara told me that the nut-brown native had followed her with one of the adolescents when she went to wash the utensils in the stream, and sitting beside her and pulling out a tatty wallet, said one word in Russian: '*Dengi*' – 'money'. Thinking he wanted money, she offered him a cigarette instead. He shook his head. She asked the boy to translate. The boy blushed and said at first he did not understand either but then said the man was offering her money 'for work'.

We had to wait a while for the Tbilisi bus, so Anya, Zhenya, Lara and I went and had a look at the town. Belokany, the northernmost town of Azerbaijan, was what Jack Kerouac would have called a crossroads town. We took a bus to the crossroads and back and that was it, except that right at the end of the return bus journey Zhenya nearly got himself knifed.

The bus was crowded and we were standing near the back door, waiting to get off at the next stop. When we moved to get off, a swarthy young man had his foot pressed lightly on Anya's. She gave him a dirty look, and that would have been the end of it except that Zhenya saw the look.

'What's wrong!' he said very aggressively.

The swarthy young man said, 'You want to know what's wrong?' and got off the bus with us. On the pavement, with all the passengers watching, he said, 'Come round the corner and I'll show you what's wrong.'

Poor Zhenya chickened out again. He really should not have started these things if he was not prepared to finish them. He said something in a conciliatory tone but the swarthy young man took his arm and said, 'No, really, come round the corner for a minute.'

Zhenya, defeated again, said pitifully, 'I just don't think you should have trod on her foot, that's all.'

'Fine. Come round the corner.'

Zhenya demurred. The bus was waiting for the swarthy young man and he turned to get back on it. As he did so he said something to Zhenya that sounds silly and funny in English but is a terrible thing to say to a man in Russian. The young man said to Zhenya, 'I'll turn your womb inside out.'

The bus went. I wondered how Zhenya was going to live with himself for the next few days.

The journey to Tbilisi was uneventful; even the border was open now and we drove straight through. Peasants got on and off carrying live poultry. Passengers paid the driver as they alighted and he issued no tickets. This is the 'system' throughout the transcaucasian republics, the local top officials conniving with it for their rake-off. By the time everyone from the bus driver upwards has raked off their percentage the state bus company must be left with far less than fifty per cent of what it should get of passengers' fares if tickets had been bought properly. I had seen this 'system' before and read about it in *Pravda*. Any illegal money-making operation 'on the side' is in the Soviet Union called 'on the left'. Nearly all Caucasian bus drivers drove 'on the left'.

At Tbilisi we had to wait till the evening for our train and arrived at the town of Samtredia at three in the morning, cold and tired. We 'slept' upright on hard wooden waiting-room chairs. Big freight-wagons slammed around outside and Gena sang over and over again a song like 'Ol' Macdonald had a Farm', consisting mainly of noises. Trains thundered and flashed past the windows, signals fell with a clang, whistles screamed, the whole building seemed to shake whenever a train passed, and there was permanent cacophony from the shunting. At dawn a cleaning woman came splashing around, necessitating the removal of our feet from the floor. Lara and I went for a stroll. A platform for local dignitaries stood in front of the town hall, ready for the May Day parade to file past. Old women were sweeping the streets, which were already roped off. Back at the station, we watched the buses coming into town bringing in the peasants to the parade. I was hoping we could stay and watch the parade but the commander was anxious to get to the river so when a bus to Kutaisi came we got on it. We reached Kutaisi after an hour's drive.

We had not waited in the bus station square at Kutaisi for longer than twenty minutes in the hot sun when a state bus pulled up and the driver offered his services 'on the left'. The commander agreed to a 'fare' of ten roubles each. I had read about this variant of driving 'on the left' in *Pravda* as well: drivers using a state bus like a private mini-cab service. The paper reported one case of a driver whose scheduled route was to Baku airport, and who, when he heard that the flight to Yerevan was delayed, took his passengers all the way there, a two-day journey of 1,600 kilometres, the 'fare' being the same as the cost of the plane ticket.

Our leader told the driver there were fifteen of us, not eighteen, thereby hoping to save thirty roubles. We had done this with all transport, starting with the train from Moscow.

We piled into the bus. The driver went off to eat. While we were waiting two officials from the local branch of the nation-wide *Tourist* organisation got on and I got off and went for a walk so they would not see me.

The Russian word *tourism* means travelling through nature and encompasses such sports as mountain walking as well as shooting the rapids. In 1959 shooting the rapids was banned because of the number of fatal accidents but, as the commander said, 'You can close a stadium but you can't stop a river from flowing' and *touristi* went anyway and, because of the lack of control, the number of accidents soared. Five years later a young enthusiast named Yuri Sturmer went to the authorities and insisted on its again being legalised. Now the sport is highly organised under the control of the trade unions. The unions finance some trips. Ours was self-financed. When a group starts out on a trip it sends a telegram to its home organisation and to the local organisation. If it has not arrived at the scheduled finishing point on time a search is made at the expense of the home organisation. To prove that the thing has been done someone in the group always takes a cine-camera and films the rafts or kayaks on the difficult sections.

The officials sat and chatted for a while with the others while I was making myself scarce. According to the officials there were seventeen groups on the Rioni that season.

The driver returned, the officials wished the group good luck and left, I got back on and we set off, going up all the time, even before we had left the town. We saw the river swirling and seething below us, brown and dirty, with houses perched on its steep stone banks.

We left the town behind. Now tea bushes grew on the slopes around us. The road continued to mount and now we were surrounded by green mountains, bright in the sun. The road was white and dusty. The disturbed dust rose and hung in the air behind us. After we had been travelling a long time we stopped at a lone café. A big portrait of Stalin was on the wall facing the door and would have made a marvellous photo, especially if the fat, sullen, sweaty-chested proprietor would stand under it, but Zhenya advised against both taking a picture and talking to the proprietor. Then we continued the journey, the white dusty road winding back and forth on itself, climbing all the time. At a place called Ambrolauri the driver was ordered to stop by a tall millyman. The driver meekly jumped from the bus, and we watched in stupefaction as he was marched up the dusty road to the *militsia* post. Most believed he had been nabbed for driving on the left. I was scared that the long arm of the Soviet law was reaching up the Rioni valley for an errant Englishman. Several of the group stood around in the road. They were the first to see the driver returning. They shouted the news to us. He had only been gone a few minutes. He said casually as he climbed back into the bus, 'He's an acquaintance of mine,' and we continued.

This region was Colchis, kingdom of Medea's father, where Jason and the Argonauts sought the Golden Fleece, which still figures on the municipal crest of Kutaisi. The Rioni used to be called the Phasis, and is reputedly the ancestral home of the bird *phasianus colchicus*, or pheasant. The river almost cuts Georgia in half, rising near the Georgia/Russian Federation border in the main range of the Caucasus and emptying into the Black Sea.

We were now following the valley of the swiftly flowing river. The valley narrowed and the road climbed to the town of Oni. Sheer rock rose for thousands of feet on the other side of the river. Suddenly I saw my first raft. It was upside down, stranded on a sandbank in the middle of the river below. A lone figure, conspicuous in an orange lifejacket, stood on the sandbank. We told the driver to stop and jumped out and stood at the side of the road while the commander and some of the others ran down the slope to see if he needed help, but before they reached the river he had righted the raft and continued on his journey downstream. It was unheard of for someone to shoot the rapids alone. The group assumed his colleagues were nearby.

At the beginning of the journey someone had said, 'There's the Rioni on the right,' and ever since Gena, who was sitting next to Zhenya, had been keeping up a mock guided tour, shouting, 'The Rioni on our right, Zhenya on my left!' Whenever we passed a difficult section of the river those on the far side left their seats and leant over to look out of the windows and discuss it. A few members of the group had not been on the trip here the previous year. All rivers and sections of rivers were graded from 1 to 6, 6 being the most dangerous. Only the most highly qualified and experienced were allowed to attempt Grade 6 rivers. The Rioni was graded 3 with elements of 4 and 5 and one Grade 6 'super rapid' at Utsera, which we were now approaching. At Utsera the river narrowed to pour through a canyon, the walls of which rose vertically out of the hurtling water. The commander explained that those perpendicular cliffs meant that if there was an accident and someone got hurt there was nowhere to land for rest and treatment. Just past the rapid there was a sandbank, the only haven. We could start from Utsera but we went a dozen kilometres further upstream to 'warm up'. The dozen kilometres would take one hour to navigate, and the preparations and reconnaissance of the three kilometres of the approach to Utsera and the rapid itself would take a whole day. The actual rapid would take seven minutes.

We went the extra dozen kilometres and stopped at a good camping site on the riverbank. Three of the group ran away behind the bus up a wooded slope on the other side of the road but the driver saw them and we had to pay the full money for eighteen people. He had earned in one day what would have taken him a month to earn if he had kept to his scheduled route. His bus still displayed its number and route destinations and it looked slightly bizarre to see a municipal bus that was supposed to be calling at Rustaveli Street, Piroshvili Prospect and the town hall turning round and descending a dusty mountain road 132 kilometres from the town.

There was the sound of rushing water. The water curled on itself, forming funnels and whirlpools. We made a fire, chopped logs for seats and put up the tents. Some went to the village for wine. Gena said, 'It's a sacrilege not to drink oceans of it here.' He said the remembrance of the amount of wine they drank last year still made him feel ill. It had been decided to have our May Day feast a couple of days late, after the rafts had been made, to make it also a celebration of setting off at last. They were eager to start, impatient. Babyface Sasha, sitting on a log doing his sums, a mass of tiny figures on graph paper, reckoned up what we had spent. It had been planned that the entire trip would cost each person forty roubles: we had each spent seventy roubles already just on getting there. When the others returned with the wine we sat and had supper and drank it. It was very dark red, the colour of strong tea, with bits of something floating in it, bought at the house of a man who spoke not a word of Russian. To me it tasted sharp and I did not drink much. I slept badly, being unable to get warm.

In the morning I saw we had camped in a beautiful, perfect place. Green fir-treed mountains surrounded us, with snow-capped ones looming behind them. Every single driver hooted us as he passed, throwing up dust on the road. There were six tents, the best being the commander's, a smart blue and orange Polish affair. The commander took the whole business very seriously. He had told me himself these trips were the most important thing in his life and someone else had told me his wife was close to divorcing him because of his preoccupation with the sport. In the coming autumn the group, under his leadership, planned to attempt the most dangerous river of all, the Obikhingo, which flows from Peak Communism in the Pamirs, the highest mountain in the Soviet Union. Preparations and training for Grade 6 rivers like the Obikhingo last a year. Grade Sixers are almost full-timers. 'I enjoy it more and more,' he had said to me. 'I can't live without it. It's like a disease. Grade 3 rivers like the Rioni are not interesting anymore. We've all been doing this for ten years and it's no more exciting than going to the pictures.'

We began making the rafts immediately after breakfast. The main body went up the wooded slope on the other side of the road with axes in hand to chop down and shape logs. The rest of us blew up the floats, which were sausage-shaped balloons about twelve feet long. I sat on the ground and made myself giddy. I blew and blew until my head ached and my fingertips tingled. When I was finished I needed the magic of 100 grams of vodka. At supper that evening the crew including Babyface Sasha and Gena announced they wanted to leave for Utsera the following day. Their raft was ready and they did not want to wait for the other two rafts to be finished. After some discussion the commander reluctantly agreed they could go and we would all meet up in a couple of days at a spot past Utsera. One of his objections was that their raft had been put together too quickly to have been done well. Another was that they would miss the feast.

When I woke up the next morning, after another bad night, they had already left the camp to reconnoitre the rapid. They came back in the late afternoon and said they were ready to leave immediately after a quick meal – at least, four of the six said they were ready. One said that if they left now they would reach Utsera at dusk, when it would be too dangerous, and he refused point blank to go. Gena was reluctant but allowed himself to be persuaded to go, his judgement, as ever, overcome by his desire to please and make an impression. So after a quick meal the five of them set off, dressed in crash helmets, lifejackets and shin and knee guards. There was almost an accident as soon as they pushed off. The current drove the raft straight back to the bank into some overhanging branches. They all had to duck fast to avoid scratched faces and being swept off the raft. The photographer took his cine-camera and got a cattle truck to take him to Utsera by road.

The others finished their rafts, lashing together the thin logs and then lashing the rafts to the floats. Wooden handles were tied to the blades of the paddles for one raft while two long rudders were shaped for the other. Then we all helped to prepare the feast. We had soup, my Beryozka stewed meat, smoked sausage, salad and even sweets for a dessert, plus the obligatory ocean of wine, plus a bottle of vodka each. Gena was supposed to have been the wine distributor but now someone else was detailed to the task. Lara and I went for some mineral water from a spring that gushed out of an iron pipe to trickle down to the river, reddening the stones and rocks on the way. After filling our pots we drank some of the effervescent, sulphurous water from cupped hands. While I was waiting for Lara to finish drinking I sat on a rock and disturbed a colony of green-tailed lizards, which scattered like ants. A puddle of ordinary water was speckled with tadpoles. Lara told me they are called 'bigheads' in Russian.

It was dark when we got back to the camp, with a thin slice of moon in the sky. The feast was almost ready, the tin utensils neatly laid out on a big transparent plastic sheet that was held down at the sides by stones. Shaped logs for seats were spaced round three sides, with the blazing fire on the fourth. We were waiting for the photographer to return when a cattle truck stopped on the road and he jumped from the cabin. He ran to the camp. 'Perevernulis!' he shouted. 'They overturned!' The commander ran to his tent to get a torch and the first-aid kit and he and Zhenya and some of the others ran to the cattle truck. As they joined the photographer I heard him tell them Gena was hurt. The cattle truck turned and went back down the road. Lara and Anya and I were concerned at first but were told that rafts capsize all the time. But we could not have our feast with half the group gone, and Gena hurt. We sat round the plastic sheet for a long time until someone said quietly, 'We might as well eat.' Some of us did eat, in silence, but others, including Anya and Lara, could not. The fire was kept up for a while but then was allowed to die down. Small orange sparks flew into the darkness and the charred pieces of smouldering wood slipped quietly apart. The food could be heated up the following day. Lara and I went to bed. I had been so cold the last two nights I was scared of falling ill. I had on my two pullovers, tracksuit bottom, woollen socks and a woollen bobble hat and was still cold. I got up and put on trousers over the tracksuit bottom and rearranged the stuff I was lying on around the sides of the tent. I still could not sleep and was lying there worrying about becoming ill when Zhenya entered the tent by torchlight. Anya was with him. I looked at my watch. It was 2.30.

'Well?' I said.

'Pogib,' said Zhenya. 'He's dead.'

In the morning everyone had bloodshot eyes. Two of the four that were with Gena had injuries; one had a bandaged hand and was limping while Babyface Sasha, also limping, had a scratched face. They told us what happened: they had successfully navigated the most difficult spot and had congratulated each other and relaxed a bit when the raft capsized on a relatively safe stretch of water. Three were thrown clear but two were trapped, apparently by the thongs that rafters hold and sometimes tie round the wrists as a precaution against being jerked off balance. One of the trapped men could cling to the raft and keep himself above water but the other, Gena, was trapped underneath the raft. He was dragged along the stony river bed for one hundred yards, sandwiched between the bed and the raft. When the others had struggled to the raft and released him he had a horrific bruise on his chest and was unconscious. They managed to steer the raft onto the sandbank. They laid him on the raft. Then they released the other trapped man. They could not stay on the sandbank as it was already dusk and Gena needed medical attention. They righted their battered raft and pushed off again. One of the floats came loose in some more turbulence and the raft listed heavily. As the commander had feared, the raft was not well made. While they were engaged in fixing this in the semi-darkness the unconscious Gena slipped off the raft and was swept away. The photographer had come running back to us as they reached the sandbank. He had stopped filming after the difficult section had been passed and had not filmed the capsizing.

Babyface Sasha was downing vodka steadily throughout the narrative. Obviously feeling a need both to talk and to drink, he repeated his narrative to others at the same time as finishing the bottle. I returned to my tent. There was nothing to do now except wait. Zhenya went into the village to see about transport back down to Kutaisi while the commander went to Oni to inform the *militsia* and order a coffin. The *militsia* told him the body had been found by a local man a long way downstream. There was not enough money for all of us to fly back to Moscow with the body so the commander was going alone with it. He would have to see Gena's widow. The commander, a strong man needing and seeking responsibility and difficulties, had devoted his life to this sport. Now he would be stripped of all his sports degrees, forbidden to lead a group for about five years, would not be allowed to go to the Pamirs in the autumn, and even his career could be affected. A *militsia* inspector, furious, had even threatened him with criminal proceedings. The inspector had come from Kutaisi to investigate the accident. Writing down depositions in his notebook, he suddenly looked up at the commander and exclaimed, 'You'll go to jail for this! How could such a thing happen?' Taken to Utsera, he took one look at the rapid, turned away without a word and never mentioned criminal proceedings again.

Zhenya arranged for a cattle truck to take us part of the way. It came in the afternoon with a Stalin calendar on the dashboard. We climbed on the back, the two injured men shunning our outstretched helping hands. They had great dififculty climbing up onto a tyre and then over the side of the lorry but they felt guilty for Gena's death, were ashamed of their injuries and ignored our offers of help. As soon as we moved out of the camp a sow and five piglets moved in, snuffling around the two abandoned, nearly-finished rafts.

The lorry roared off; I lurched, someone grabbed me, and I sat down. We had to keep slowing down to go round cattle on the road. We went past Utsera, with its cliffs and sandbank. Only Zhenya was standing and only he saw the place. He said, 'Utsera' but no one said anything or got up to look. The driver refused payment when he dropped us off. We thanked him and waited for another lift. It soon came and we continued the journey back down the beautiful Rioni valley, the green mountains shining in the sun.

Chapter Seventeen
SWEET AND SAUR

On September 10, when I saw fluttering on lamp posts along Leninsky Prospect red flags with a five-pointed star and Arabic script inside a wreath of wheat ears, I only vaguely wondered which obscure country was being represented in talks at the Kremlin that day, and when I read on TASS later that the president of Afghanistan, Nur Muhammad Taraki, had had talks with President Brezhnev, at which he had been assured of continued all-round Soviet support, it barely registered. The *Morning Star* did not have the space to report every Kremlin visit and even when important world figures arrived in Moscow for talks the paper usually used agency tapes, recognising that I would not have the sort of easy access to embassy contacts available to the team at Reuters. So I took no interest in the Taraki visit. Nor did I exactly jump with professional excitement when four days later Taraki was overthrown in a violent coup: nor when three weeks after that TASS quoted Kabul Radio as saying Taraki had succumbed to a severe and prolonged illness – though I, along with everyone else, did strongly suspect lead poisoning as the illness. Afghanistan became a matter of professional concern for me only on December 27, when Soviet troops went into action in Kabul against the government of Taraki's successor, Hafizullah Amin, and it was announced that Amin had been deposed and executed and replaced by one Babrak Karmal. On the last day of the 1970s, the decade of *détente*, politicians of six capitalist countries met in London to discuss Afghanistan. The rise in international tension that has accompanied the 1980s began on the very

176

first day. On New Year's Day, 1980, the West German government formally proposed at a NATO meeting in Brussels that the
West consider a concerted boycott of the Moscow Olympics as
part of its response to the Afghan crisis.

I had barely risen from the torpor following new year
celebrations when I was asked if I would care to go to
Afghanistan. The Soviet and Afghan authorities were arranging
a visit for Moscow-based Communist correspondents. I was
naturally very excited. Government and Soviet troops were now
engaged in harsh conflict with rebels opposed to the Saur (which
means April) revolution. I had visions of sending battle-front
dispatches, ignoring bursts of crossfire from the hills, maybe
sustaining a small painless wound. This was indeed a long way
from football reports from the Upton Park press box on
Saturday afternoons! I would write the word 'shots' in a report
once again – that would be the only thing in common between
the two types of reporting. Afghanistan was the best place in all
the world for a foreign correspondent to be during that new
year. It was an important time in history and if I could convey
just a little of what was going on my tarnished reputation would
be refurbished. I felt the glamour of the occasion, of informing
friends I would not be seeing them for a week or two because I
was 'going to Afghanistan'. Their reactions pleased me. Lara,
though glad for me, was worried about my safety, which
heightened the pleasurable feeling of embarking on a great
adventure. Life could bring nothing sweeter.

The trip turned sour, though. It soon became clear that we
had been flown to Kabul as a counter-balance to the 'unfriendly'
correspondents at a big Babrak Karmal press conference on the
first day and that no one had given a minute's thought as to
what we should do afterwards. So what did we do? Believe it or
not, we watched telly. A war was going on outside, a conflict
that the whole world was following with bated breath, and we
watched telly. We could not understand a word, of course, but I
got the distinct impression we were not missing much. The only
programmes seemed to be news, native dancing and bearded
mullahs droning over enormous holy books. We drank tea,
gazed at the life-sized cardboard Air France hostess in the hotel
lobby who was stiffly '*A votre service*' and splashed out on beer

we did not really need or want, the way one does when one is bored. Mealtimes were a big event, looked forward to and lingered over, as though we were unemployed or institutional-ised. I could not have imagined it possible to be at the scene of an event that was changing world history and for it to be so boring. Kabul at that moment was the most important town on earth. It was surrounded by artillery, beyond which roamed hordes of ferocious rebel tribesmen. If we had taken a car a few miles along any of the roads up into the hills there was a real danger of our being ambushed. As it was, the only danger I faced was from the attentions of a burly waiter who fancied me. When I ordered a beer he asked me so suggestively if there was anything else I wanted it made my colleagues snigger.

Our hosts had neither time nor inclination to arrange visits or interviews for us so at the end of the trip we had as many unanswered questions as we had started out with. The biggest question of all regarding Afghanistan was whether or not there really were plans in Washington for a direct assault on the country from Pakistan. As early as March 29, 1979, an article in *Pravda* had accused the US and China of conspiring to over-throw Afghanistan's new government. At this stage the con-spiracy was confined to the supplying of arms, money and subversive material to various reactionary Afghani groups, of which, said *Pravda*, the CIA regarded 'the Moslem Brothers' organisation as the most 'promising'. In the ensuing year, could this aid have escalated as it did in Vietnam, with the Pentagon supplying military advisers and more and more weapons until it reached a point where it could be said to be directly involved? Three days after the Karmal coup, *Pravda* was saying, 'The forces of internal counter-revolution and foreign reaction hoped that the Saur revolution would be unable to parry the blows that would be dealt it. They came to believe this so much that they were naming the days and months when they would make a triumphant entry into Kabul' – in other words, as soon as the mountain roads and passes became open in the spring. Western commentators did not take this suggestion seriously. In an article in the *New Statesman* on January 4, 1980, Fred Halliday dismissed it in passing: 'The Russian claim that Afghanistan was subjected to a direct aggression by foreign powers is, of course, a fiction.' *Of course?* As far as the Russians were concerned, there was no 'of course' about it. When a group of British Communists in Moscow suggested to a Soviet official that the Soviet action had been hasty, he angrily replied, 'So we should have waited until *after* the counter-revolutionaries had attacked? That would have made it all right?' I was told by other Soviet officials of the reactionaries' 'great plans' for the spring, while a top political commentator said, 'Afghanistan would have been a second Chile. On the doorstep of the Soviet Union. We couldn't allow that. We don't agree with the export of revolution but we will not agree either to the export of counter-revolution.' There was no doubt the Russians believed that within a year the Americans would at the very least have had a network of spy bases in Afghanistan to make up for the loss of their bases in Iran. In spite of whatever mistakes the Soviet leaders may be deemed to have made, in spite of any supposed miscalculations and over-reactions, this was a central fact. Rightly or wrongly, the country felt threatened. And I would certainly not dismiss the threat as being, 'of course, a fiction'.

One serious and typical mistake was made by the Soviet media. After the Saur revolution of 1978 Afghanistan was as much in the public eye in the Soviet Union as, say, Angola or Ethiopia, i.e. it got a lot of coverage. The attempts of the Afghan government to redistribute land, to liberate women, to eradicate hunger and illiteracy, were reported with enthusiasm, unlike in Britain, where they were not reported at all. Much was said in the Soviet press at this time about both generous Soviet aid to Afghanistan and the threat from the territories of Pakistan and China. The Soviet media did not reveal, however, the problems within the Afghan leadership. Afghanistan had had a left-wing revolution: that was all the Soviet people knew or needed to know. From now on things could only get better. The Soviet Union was supporting Amin, after he took power. Overnight – literally, on the night of December 27/28 – Moscow changed its line. Suddenly, the Soviet papers were slamming Amin as an 'agent of imperialism' who had butchered his comrade Taraki and drowned the country in blood.

It seems that the Soviet Union simply could not stop the feuding between the two rival groups of Afghan revolutionaries, and that this split seriously undermined what could have been very successful policies. I saw no objective reason why these difficulties should not have been publicised. In spite of all the diplomatic considerations, I believed the Soviet people could have been given at least a hint of the background to the troubles, especially as there had recently been a lot of talk of Soviet propaganda failing to satisfy their 'growing educational and cultural level and demands'.

But would openness really have changed anything? When the most open country in the world connived in the destruction of Chilean socialism, the job still got done. The presidential palace was still bombed, the Chilean president was still shot dead, thousands of socialists and trade unionists were still imprisoned, tortured and killed. No, the Soviet Union's traditional circumspect manner of giving news and information was a side issue.

In the new and scary world situation that developed throughout 1980 I began to understand how older British Communists who had grown up in the cold war period could argue that when great issues of war and peace were at stake responsible Communists should not write about domestic Soviet shortcomings. Now I too felt it was inappropriate, even juvenile, to write about Moscow queues, when foreign cowboy politicians were itching to press buttons so there would be no Moscow to queue in. Now I understood how hardliners were made. When the Soviet media criticised those fraternal parties such as the British that had expressed concern over the legality or otherwise of the Soviet intervention, I recalled Lara's comment: 'We've got enough problems without worrying about the delicate feelings of liberal foreign Communists.' There was such a polarisation taking place that it was a case of starkly deciding, in the last analysis, whose side you were on. This ideological polarisation could lead people to assume automatically that anyone adopting any position agreed with all its associated attitudes and views, which was not necessarily so. My position was clear. Wellington said the difference between him and Napoleon was that Napoleon was always looking for battle whereas he, Wellington, was always trying to avert it. This seemed to me the essential difference between the Soviet Union and the United States and this determined my position. I did not automatically assume, as did so many in the confrontation between East and West, that I had through sheer good fortune been born on the side of the angels. I believed the Russians had valid grounds for feeling threatened. I did not believe that they were paranoid, or that they had plans to conquer the world. I agreed with E.P. Thompson when he wrote:

> 'The basic postures of the Soviet Union seem to me, still, to be those of siege and aggressive defence . . . The United States seems to me to be more dangerous and provocative in its general military and diplomatic strategies, which press around the Soviet Union with menacing bases.'

Russians share with Jews a racial remembrance of the holocaust of the second world war. I recalled the young TASS mechanic who installed my teletype machine after six months' wait, when I said jokingly, 'A world war could have broken out and I wouldn't have known' and he replied with feeling, 'Don't say it.' And Raisa Iosifovna on Victory Day in 1980 made a solemn toast to peace with such heartfelt sincerity it brought a lump to my throat: 'Here's to the victory over the fascists. May fascism never come again. May there always be peace.' And we clinked glasses, threw back our vodka and were silent for a while. In homes and restaurants throughout the country that same toast was being made with the same moving solemnity. I cannot say it was being made with more than usual feeling that year, for the toast to peace had always been a heartfelt one, but certainly over all, like an unseen formless cloud, there floated and swirled the poison of apprehension.

And this hardening of positions, this weakening of *détente*, had to happen in the very year I would be taking Lara to England. It would have been bad enough at any time, taking her away from all that she knew and loved to a place she already had misgivings about, and now was the worst of times. Rabid curs of war would be unmuzzled, adherents to hostility unleashed. There would be much snapping and snarling. Lara, deeply patriotic, was not going to take kindly to such raving enmity.

Chapter Eighteen
DOMOI

Up until the months preceding our departure for London Lara was happy. She had her translating and teaching work, her family and her friends and the flat was the biggest she had ever lived in. The two main rooms formed an L, with the passage also L-shaped, and doors connecting all, so it was possible to chase round the flat in circles. I used to give Pick piggyback rides round and round and we used to play hide-and-seek, hiding in the wardrobe, behind the settee or in the kitchen or bathroom. Whenever it was my turn to hide I had to shout 'Cuckoo!' to give him a clue. He would laugh with delight at finding me and toddle off to hide himself. When we were playing together like this Lara was filled with a deep content.

Outside as well was one vast playground for Pick. There were swings and a sandpit and a big grassy hollow with slopes just perfect for sledding down in winter. We bought a sledge and took Pick there nearly every day. Other children, even older ones, always had an adult sitting behind them on the sledge for safety, but although I too did so occasionally it was purely for my own pleasure, and usually Pick went down on his own, thrilled as he slid down the smooth slopes on the gathering speed of his sledge. The other parents were horrified, claiming that if he fell off he could hurt himself, but he often *did* fall off, and was never hurt. And when other children slipped or tripped the parents or the grandmother would immediately be all over them with solicitous concern, while when Pick fell we just said casually, 'You all right?' As a consequence, all the other children cried every time they fell over, even when they were not hurt, while Pick never cried. The slopes were packed at weekends so they resembled a Breughel landscape, hundreds of small black figures on a white background. The range of things used to slide on was amazing – standard plain metal sledges with a painted wooden slatted seat such as Pick had; flash Finnish plastic affairs with handbrakes and steerable runners; simple large plastic discs like dustbin lids; skates, of course, and skis; and rough sheets of tin. Sometimes you had to wait your turn at the top, and there was also at such times the danger of a collision at the bottom if someone did not get out of the way quickly enough. It was my duty to haul the sledge back up to the top each time, which was a slithery business.

This sledding with Pick was the only exercise I got, and due to inadequate exercise and surfeit of alcohol I was putting on a lot of weight. As Lara also was getting very little exercise, we resolved to go jogging. A friend gave us an English book, *The Complete Jogger*, by Bruce Tulloh, which recommended that beginners start by brisk walking. We never got beyond the brisk walking. But the nightly excursions were useful anyway, for we discovered them to be one of the few opportunities we had for talking together, with no interruptions or distractions. The Pick and work commitments that prevented us from talking also prevented us from getting out on our 'constitutionals' until around midnight or even later. But we took full advantage of them, striding down deserted Leninsky Prospect to the white birch trees of Gorky Park and along the embankment at the bottom of the Lenin Hills, often forgetting the prime reason for being out and lapsing into a stroll, until we realised it and then, feeling guilty, actually breaking into a trot for a short distance.

We went to bed ridiculously late every night, not having to worry about tending Pick in the morning, for Raisa Iosifovna did it, dressing him and cooking his *kasha* and feeding him. Often by the time Lara and I got up she and Pick would be snuggled up on the settee with a story book.

Raisa Iosifovna was a marvellous woman. Her generosity and sweetness of character as well as her toughness and independent mind showed clearly on her face. Loving Pick dearly, she never once lost her temper with him. She was always busy, from habit and because she was living with us in order to help. Washing, cooking, sewing, shopping . . . the only time she allowed herself a bit of relaxation was late in the evening when, with Pick safely asleep, she would kick off her slippers, put her legs up on the settee, switch on the table lamp and either go through the six daily newspapers and several magazines I subscribed to, or watch television. She would often fall asleep before the night's programmes ended. Lara meanwhile would be in the kitchen with her translating, occasionally coming to me with a question: 'Terrichka, how do you say so-and-so?' As far as Lara was concerned, it was a full, busy, happy life. Then she fell ill.

Lara had always had a cavalier confidence in her strong physique, regarding it as an asset that put her on an equal footing with the macho Russian men. She had played football with tough boys, carried heavy rucksacks, gone swimming in May and braved her first Moscow winter in a thin quarter-length cotton jacket. She fulfilled the 'man's role' in her all-women family and had a reputation for stoicism among her friends, who seriously believed that Lara, like the proverbial bolshevik, would never be seen crying. I, of course, knew better. But that winter, something in her snapped. To this day we do not know what was wrong exactly, though the ailment was obviously psychosomatic: the thought of going to live in England was literally making her ill.

Towards the end of the winter she developed a cough. It got worse and worse until on March 27 she saw a doctor, who said she had inflammation of the lung and was not to go out for ten days. That very night she had a terrible fit of coughing and at the end of ten days it was no better: nor did it get better right up to the day we left Russia. We tried everything: nightly massage, various forms of heat treatment, Altai berries, caviar, a concoction of vodka and honey, propolis and, as a last resort, the daily ingestion of ten drops of diluted thousand-year-old birdshit.

This birdshit is called *mumiyo*. Found only in the very oldest ranges of the Tien Shan mountains, it is held to have great revitalising properties, more efficacious even than ginseng or deers' antlers. Its curative powers are reckoned to be so all-embracing as to aid even the mending of broken bones. Patients are supposed to rest for an hour after taking it and then eat. 'It's very strong,' said Lara. 'I feel as though I were drunk.' Prescribed at a state clinic but obtained through friends, one tiny lump cost us 25 roubles. Brown and sticky and wrapped in cellophane, it looked exactly like a toffee. Lara and all her family believed firmly in the healing properties of folk and herbal medicine, a belief shared by most of their compatriots.

But even birdshit did not help. Lara grew unreasonable and irritable and impossible to please. Precisely because she was so fed up I bought her the two volumes of a new big Russian-English dictionary, beautiful books with gold lettering on green covers, costing 33 roubles 40 kopecks for the two, and she ungraciously said she did not need them. Then I bought her a cake, which she said she did not want. Finally we had a big bust-up over nothing and I went for a walk alone at midnight. She was tearfully contrite the next day. Then she was told at the clinic that she was no better and would have to stay indoors for another ten days. Tormented by all this, she had no enthusiasm for the preparation for our departure. Only Pick was excited by it: '*Ya khochu v Angliyu,*' he would say. 'I want to go to England. *Skoro mi poyedem v Angliyu?* Are we soon going to England?'

And Raisa Iosifovna would answer sadly, '*Skoro, skoro.* Soon, soon.'

'*Gdye Angliya?*' he asked. 'Where's England? Point to it with your finger.'

'It's a long way away, Dannichka.'

Raisa Iosifovna was not looking forward to our departure. She believed she might never see Lara again. She recalled her remark to Nadia's mother Natalya Ivanovna when Nadia left for America with Ben: 'My daughter will never leave me. I have every sympathy for you.'

Anya was often with us, and she also had bronchial trouble. With my aversion to problems of any kind, I have always had a violent dislike of illness. Now there was an atmosphere of sickness and dejection, the flat full of the smells and paraphernalia of illness and the two sisters coughing and hawking and spitting and sighing and having long hypochondriacal discussions.

And in the middle of it all, Lara had somehow to get her exit visa. Although she had been to England before she still had to fill

in the same detailed forms as previously and present all the same
documents and OVIR made all the same trouble and erected all
the same obstacles. Lara had to borrow a Cyrillic typewriter
again, then collect two forms from our local ZHEK, where the
lady passport officer moaned, 'You'll ruin us, we do not have
many forms' but gave two anyway, which OVIR would then not
accept as they were endorsed with a wrongly-shaped stamp,
rectangular instead of round or triangular. Little difficulties such
as this sorted out, Lara handed in her domestic passport and
received her external one. Before departing for good from
Moscow in the autumn we spent a fortnight's holiday in
London, going by train. Neither of us particularly wanted to
spend a fortnight in London when we would be living there
within four months, and the only reason we went was because
by going to England Lara was allowed to change roubles into
pounds, which we could then bank. We needed every pound we
could get.

At Harwich, because of Pick and an immigration official
expressing special interest in Lara, we were last through the
customs, where we were stopped and our luggage searched. This
meant we missed the connecting train to London, entailing a
two-hour wait for the next one. Ken was supposed to be meeting
us at Liverpool Street station. I phoned to tell him of the delay
but he had already left home for the station. We believed it was
possible for the station to have a ship's passenger list so they
could check that all passengers were off the ship for the train
connection but the ticket inspector insisted otherwise: 'Couldn't
be done, mate.' Lara fumed: 'This wouldn't happen in Russia.'

We sat in the station buffet, sipping coffee at 33p a cup,
watching people who, not having to queue for essentials, queued
instead to play with the brightly flashing Nudges Unlimited
pinball machine (the Hi-lights machine next to it being temporarily out of order); and, two hours later, observed from our train
as it pulled away from the station a vast array of brand new
shining Ford cars, cars parked nose to bumper and side by side
as far as the eye could see. Pick was excited by all he saw. Lara
was from her previous trip already slightly nauseated by the
West's affluence.

Ken met us at Liverpool Street, having assumed we had

missed the first train and waiting for us, and drove us to my parents' place. On the second day of our holiday, I was upstairs in the bedroom when Lara came up very agitated and said firmly that we were leaving. My father had been annoyed by Pick and had roughly grabbed hold of him and shaken him. This, I agreed, was intolerable. I phoned a married couple I knew and within an hour we were packed and had left my parents' house. My father was perturbed at our swift reaction and I knew pitiful apologies would later follow, as indeed they did. 'I'm not a bad man,' he said. 'You just got me on a bad day.' My friends had three baby girls (two being twins) and Lara and I spent an uncomfortable, cramped week sleeping on a divan, all of us being woken up several times each night by one of the four children. The incompatibility of my father and Pick also meant we now had nowhere to live when we came to London in the autumn.

Bob Evans, knowing of my disenchantment with the *Morning Star* (Sam and I were now barely on telexing terms), had written a letter of introduction to the Reuters news editor, Ian MacDowall, whom I now phoned for an interview.

I went to Reuters' head office at the bottom of Fleet Street confident that a letter of introduction from such a highly regarded company man as Bob would be enough to get me a job. Mr MacDowall handed me a subbing test, in which a series of news flashes about a siege at the Ruritanian embassy had to be written up into a narrative. The bits and pieces included references to actual events, such as the American embassy staff being held hostage in Tehran and the siege at the Iranian embassy in London. I had been told that eighty per cent of applicants secretly regarded as a waste of time the endless churning out of news that is the Reuters reporter's job, and that the employers wanted people interested in the minutiae of world affairs as well as broad knowledge. The Ruritania flashes spelt famous politicians' names wrong and contained other traps. Basically, an intro had to be chosen and the story put together smoothly and condensed into so many words, with the deliberate mistakes corrected. And, as I realised after, sources had always to be given. My journalistic career had been spent entirely at the *Morning Star*, where to save space sources were often omitted – a cardinal journalistic sin. Doing the test was so similar to what I had been doing every day at work for the last ten years I automatically wrote that the event took place 'yesterday', as one would for a daily paper – and omitted some minor sources. I then did some shopping. When I returned to where we were staying there was a phone message from Mr MacDowall informing me I had failed the test.

For the last few weeks I had been complacently picturing a future that consisted of living at home with my parents and working at Reuters, a picture that promised physical and financial comfort. Now the picture was shattered. Now nothing lay ahead except what I fought for myself. And I had no stomach for the fight. It seemed daunting. A job at Reuters would have been the breakthrough into mainstream journalism, a natural progression. Not getting it was a severe setback. I would now have to return to work in Rust House, which was the last thing I had wanted or expected. In expectation of finding work else-where I had let my relations with the *Morning Star* editors deteriorate to such a low level they barely existed. I had foolishly burnt my bridges before reaching the other side. The editor had even informed me that from October I had six months to find another job.

We returned to Moscow on June 4 for our final four months in the Soviet Union, months to be dominated by the Moscow Olympics. I would have to cover them of course, and Lara also had a job for their duration, as personal secretary to Bob at the Reuters office in the press centre.

On the very next day we discussed seriously for the first time the wisdom of our going to live in England. 'We're secure here and have nothing there,' Lara said. But it was too late. She had her external passport and the *Morning Star* was expecting me back.

Lara began her temporary job for Reuters on June 10: on the 27th I received my accreditation at the press centre and the following day, my birthday, attended the official opening of the centre: on July 6 Lara was wheezing again, and two days later returned from her job having difficulty in breathing. She went straight to bed while I called an ambulance. She was not taken to hospital but next day had a slight temperature. I spent a long time in the evening preparing various medicines. Two days later we went to the theatre to see a play starring Lara's favourite actress, Inna Churikova, and had to stand at the back for the first half (two hours) because we arrived late and our booked tickets had been sold. After the performance we waited a long time in pouring rain for a taxi, with Lara coughing and saying, 'My heart hurts.'

The Games opened in a three-hour spectacle on Saturday, July 19, the rain clouds that had covered Moscow for three weeks dispersing as though at a signal from the USSR Research Institute for Hydrometeorological Information, which had promised fine weather. Lara got a press enclosure seat through Reuters, and we watched the spectacle together.

I enjoyed covering the Olympics. Stan Levenson came, so I was working with him once more, which was pleasant after the aggravation with Sam Russell. Each evening we would phone or telex our stories and then retire for a relaxed meal, Lara sometimes joining us. I was working properly again and so could enjoy my leisure properly again. The only worry was Lara's health. Although Bob was pleased with her work, she was wheezing and coughing throughout and there was always the fear it would get worse and she would be unable to work. We kept up the massage and heat treatment, though a difficulty arose when the plastic handle of a blue-ray lamp fell to pieces in my hand. Two bits of plastic dropped off and the handle came away from the lamp. We spent half an hour rejoining them with adhesive tape. Afterwards my hands as well as Lara's nose received heat treatment. I said mildly, 'Why does nothing here work properly?'

'Oh, all right!' she angrily exclaimed.

After the Games were over the rains came back. It really was as though some god on Mount Olympus had thrown a switch. And possibly because of the weather Lara fell badly ill again. We could depart for London at any time now but she was too ill so instead we arranged for her to spend three weeks in a sanatorium in the south, near Yalta. In order to be admitted she had to have tests at a clinic, where she had to present her passport. When she showed her external passport, having exchanged it for her domestic one, the staff were nonplussed and did not want to admit her, as the external passport was not a valid document inside the country. They relented however and she had her tests, at which she was deemed ill enough to be admitted to a sanatorium, and she left for Yalta on August 16.

While she was away nine big wooden cases for the transportation of our things were delivered and stored in the living room so that it resembled a warehouse.

Autumn came. Women looked much more elegant in their autumn coats than in their flowery summer cotton dresses. Olympic advertisements were replaced in the streets by 26th Party Congress slogans. The latest Moscow joke went the rounds: President Brezhnev was having a haircut during the Olympics, and the barber asked him what could be expected in the country after the Games. Brezhnev did not reply. A few minutes later the barber asked again. Again no answer. The barber clipped some more, and then asked again. Brezhnev remained silent, but his bodyguard said to the barber, 'Don't ask him again. You can see he's not going to answer. Why do you keep asking that question?' And the barber replied, 'I don't care whether he answers or not but each time I ask him, his hair stands on end and it's easier to cut.'

Lara returned on September 11, bronzed though still not completely recovered. But our departure could not be delayed any longer. Never have I witnessed such scenes of pandemonium as preceded our removal from Moscow. The flat was full of big wooden boxes, and there was wrapping and banging for days on end as all our earthly goods were done up in old *Pravdas* and *Izvestias*, laid carefully in the boxes, and the boxes hammered shut. The noise was terrific – and the dust brought back Lara's cough. Lyalya packed our crockery in one evening like an artist producing a work of art, and then, her bit done, retired from the fray. Anya, Sasha, Raisa Iosifovna, Zhenya, Lara, Pick and I all had our own priorities: all was noise and confusion. Several days would pass with no packing done at all. On September 18 an American friend studying at the university came to say goodbye and we sat drinking till one in the morning, when Lara insisted she and I accompany our friend to the university. It was freezing cold and I was concerned about the wisdom of this walk for Lara but she insisted and the next day was coughing badly. I was furious, and Lara reacted by saying she had an 'acceptable suggestion' – she would remain in Moscow till she was better. We made up, but she was as ill as ever. At the end of the day that we finished packing, she coughed violently till four in the morning from the dust. Raisa Iosifovna seriously suggested she did not go to England. But arrangements were too far advanced to be cancelled. Farewell parties were now being held, one of which was held round Lara's bed, as she was too weak to get up. The day before we left, I took Pick for one last walk, him pulling a lorry on a ribbon. A pretty girl in a white kerchief was gathering leaves by the armful and dumping them in an orange box on wheels. She had on thick gloves, a lumpy quilted coat and a shirt over tracksuit bottoms, but was of the age and type that could still look attractive even in that get-up. She smiled at Pick. '*Privyet, malinky*,' she said. 'Hello, little one.' Pick, used to strange females' salutations, regally ignored her. A *babushka* asked him his name and he gave his usual answer to this common question: 'I don't want to say anything.'

'I didn't catch it. Vasya?' the *babushka* said.

Her grand-daughter playing nearby was putting leaves in her toy lorry. A young mother, her baby asleep in a pram, sat on the low branch of a tree, leaning against the trunk, her face lifted to the watery sun. Two shapely university students, linking arms, as Russian girls do, walked by in mini-skirts. The trees were yellow, golden and red. Moscow is beautiful in the autumn.

My Olympiad was over. A lot of water had frozen under the bridge. I was leaving with a sick wife, a son who did not speak English, nowhere to live and hardly any money. *Nichivo*. Never mind. I was going home, where there were cafés and pubs and fish and chip shops, where snow and ice were rare enough to cause headlines and where the only queues were for buses and pinball machines.

We left on Thursday, October 16, from the new airport, sharing the VIP lounge with a black man in a spot of bother on account of having overweight luggage and no money to pay for it. Raisa Iosifovna did not drive out to the airport with us: we said goodbye to her in the flat. She looked piteously forlorn standing alone in the middle of the bare living room, which, stripped of all our personal things, was now little more than a hotel room. When I kissed her goodbye she was crying. 'Look after Lara, Terrichka,' she said. 'She's very ill.' In the departure lounge I felt Anya's tears on my cheek as I kissed her goodbye. 'Write to me every week, even if it's only a postcard,' she sobbed, and said pointedly '*Poka*' – 'For the time being' – instead of the more final '*Do svidaniya*'.

As we departed up the ramp to the plane she called, 'We shall miss you!'

I turned and waved. The hostess wanted us to hurry up, as being VIPs we were the last passengers to go on board and the plane was waiting for us.

'*Idi, idi,*' Anya called. 'Go on, go on.'

The hostess smiled. '*Domoi?*' she said. 'Going home?'

'*Da,*' I said. '*Domoi.*'

Our flight to London was not a happy one. I was dejected by the contrast between my confident journey out to Moscow four years before and my ignominious retreat. What I had envisaged as an important chapter of my existence now seemed a footnote. Four years before I had expected to be married by now but I had also expected some sort of development in my career. Apart from the journalistic limitations of working at the *Morning Star*, one could barely keep a family on its wages. The Moscow job had been my big chance to break out, and I had muffed it. Early on I had considered writing a book but the idea had foundered for want of direction, sunk in a morass of themes, none of which had the slightest originality. It had seemed to me that the only experts on the Soviet Union were those who had lived there for over twenty years and those who had been on short trips. My four years had raised questions rather than provided answers. Nothing I could write could convey the texture of life there. Only a great novel could do that and I was not any sort of novelist, let alone a great one. On the flight to London I felt as though I were flying from one planet to another. Mere words were inadequate to describe the difference between the two alien worlds. I had already had some experience of the endeavour. In trying to describe to English people one well-known aspect of Soviet life, I had no other recourse but to use the word 'bureaucracy'. The English replied, 'We have bureaucracy here.'

And I could not convey to them the difference, could not explain that really I was talking about a different phenomenon for which there was no word. So I had given up trying to write a book. All that I could say had been said with varying degrees of inadequacy and ignorance hundreds of times before. My articles had also foundered for want of direction. Four years before I had been a golden boy flying to an exciting, glamorous assignment. I was returning unrespected and full of worry about the future. I felt it could be said of me, as Heine said of Musset, 'There's a young man with a promising past.' In Moscow I had become middle-aged. There is all the difference in the world between being in your early thirties and approaching forty. Then you were young, now you are not. Then I was lithe, now I was plump; then I was sober, now I drank; then I had dreams, now I had forebodings.

Lara too was full of apprehension. A single piece of hope was that one doctor had said that if it was an allergy she was suffering from there was a good chance that with the complete change whatever caused it would no longer bother her. Her last desperate course of treatment had been the intensive use of *banki*, little glass jars that were warmed up with matches and affixed to her back. As they cooled, they sucked up the flesh, a very painful treatment that was supposed to ease the bronchial tubes.

She felt sick for much of the four hours in the plane and coping with boisterous Pick in the confines of the cramped passengers' cabin was very trying, even though he was in a good mood. Ken met us at Heathrow and we drove direct from the airport, with VIP tags on our luggage, past hundreds of beautiful rose gardens, to Greenwich Council's unit for homeless families.

Chapter Nineteen
HALFWAY HOUSE

It was a brick building that had once been homes for firemen, next door to a garage that in those days had been a fire station. Lara and I walked, and Pick toddled, into a small waiting room. A rickety chipped formica table, a scruffy sofa and two cast-off armchairs stood on cracked old linoleum. The building was disturbingly quiet. The offices were along a corridor cut off by a closed door with a notice reading No Entry. As there was no bell, I did not see how it was possible to let anyone know we were there. Luckily, a woman emerged. 'Someone will come to see you,' she said. An official came after a while, suitably officious. Elderly but upright, he was dressed soberly in dark suit and tie. He wore also, however, an incongruous straggly moustache, the long loose ends of which he was chewing. His job being homeless families, he had hardened his heart. Compassion there was not. 'Come and give me some details,' he told me, and, as Lara stood up, 'Not you. Just your husband.' I followed him into another room in which there was only a table and two hard chairs. We sat at the table and he produced a form from his sober suit. In order to ask me my name and age he had to let go of his moustache. While he contorted his mouth to regain it, I told him I had lived in Greenwich all my life before going to work abroad and had now come to him direct from the airport. He was not impressed. Questioning further between contortions, he ascertained, purely for business purposes, not because he was interested, that I had been in Moscow.

'Why didn't you stay in Moscow?' he asked.

'It's not the most pleasant town in the world in which to live,' I said.

'I've been abroad,' he said. 'I think London's the best town in the world to live in. We have no vacant flats at the moment.'

Correct and proper and lacking the hostility of an equivalent Soviet official, his reserved manner made it plain nevertheless that he was there to do a job, not engage in idle chit-chat with unfortunate supplicants. This was fair enough. But I found disconcerting his lack of curiosity. He acted as though couples from Russia dropped on his doorstep every day of the week, as though he was *bored* with finding homes for couples from Russia. Did he not realise that we had breakfasted that very morning in the Land of the Soviets? Was he not the teeniest bit interested in what I had been doing? Apparently he was not. Was he so lacking in romance and imagination? Apparently he was. Bob Evans had wanted to do a Reuters story on my marriage to Lara, for, as he said, a British-Soviet wedding was still uncommon enough to be an interesting event. But not to old Emiliano Zapata here. He addressed me as though I were just another lumpen prole, of the kind he was accustomed to dealing with. Munching away on his loose ends, he took my parents' phone number: he would call if anything turned up.

We had no choice but to go to my parents' house. We could not lumber my friends again, not for an indefinite period. After dropping off our luggage we went to Woolwich and bought a camp bed for Pick, Lara being impressed that you could simply go to a shop and buy something like that the very day you needed it. We put it and Pick in the back upstairs room, which was a spare room with a sink and a spin drier. My mother did her washing in that room. It was a bad night. Pick kept waking up, wet the bed twice and woke up for good at five o'clock because it was eight, Moscow time. We spent most of the following day at my friend Pete's, followed by another bad night, with Pick again wetting the bed and this time waking up at six. My father asked if we could spend a couple of nights at Pete's to give him a break. He did not have it in him to suffer the small sacrifice of a few nights of broken sleep in order to help a close relative through a difficult time. Pete was ill however, so we could not stay there. At Lewisham shopping centre that

Saturday Pick ran off and got lost. He could not explain anything to anyone because he did not speak the language. When we found him he had poohed himself. I had imagined that shopping at least would be enjoyable after Moscow. My parents went to the local working men's club in the evening, and after putting Pick to bed Lara and I listened to music on my father's small 'music centre' in the front room. Lara had a look at my mother's nick-nacks and cried when she saw a ceramic tea pot shaped like a country cottage that had been a wedding present. 'My mother's never had a single beautiful thing,' she said. 'It's unfair.'

On Monday we received a phone call from a Mr Lee of the homeless families unit: a flat had become vacant in one of their properties. The property was a dilapidated Victorian house due for demolition. The flat was on the first floor. It was filthy but otherwise did not seem too bad. The floorboards were bare except for a dusty carpet in one room, and the walls were flaking. But there was some furniture, including an old iron double bedstead and a grease-caked electric cooker. Ken and I set about cleaning the flat. We had just begun when a bearded youth entered and said, 'Hey man, this is my flat.' He was Australian. He and his English wife and baby girl had been the previous tenants. They had gone to Wales in their dormobile for a few weeks and Lee had assumed they had vacated the place. The Aussie said he had left some money with a friend to pay the rent. I had a signed and dated tenancy agreement and the keys and so was not perturbed. At first he wanted to be nasty about it, as though it was my fault and we were not in the same leaky boat. But I remained calm, and his wife was reasonable, and we were soon discussing the problem properly. Basically it was his problem. He resolved this problem by pretending he did not really want to return. Backing up this line, he told me horror stories about the place. There were rats, apparently. And neighbours. The neighbours one got in this type of abode had to be obscene to be believed.

The furniture belonged to him. As he had nowhere to take it he graciously agreed we could use it, including the bed. He would sell us the electric cooker for £20. I agreed as it was so convenient to have a cooker already fitted. He left, we finished the cleaning, rolled up and stored away the carpet that was beyond dusting, borrowed a calor gas heater from my parents' neighbour and bought an oil-filled radiator, and moved in. By way of celebration that evening we had a feast of fish and chips and vodka. We had bought a loaf of brown bread, Lara being appalled at the price of 41p, and a packet of salt, which fell unnoticed out of the shopping bag so that when we needed it for our fish and chips it was gone. We would have welcomed neighbours at that point no matter how obscene, to borrow salt from, but there were none. It seemed we were the only tenants. I do not know why we could not have moved in on the day we arrived from Moscow. We drank our best Russian vodka out of teacups, which, along with the unsalted fish and chips, gave me indigestion. During this feast we discovered just how cold and draughty the flat was. It was also dark, for the electricity had been disconnected. A London Electricity Board man was supposed to come and reconnect it in the morning. I waited for him. At midday I found a yellow LEB card downstairs by the front entrance, on which he had untruthfully written he had called but no one had been at home. As our heating and cooking as well as light depended on it, I dashed to a phone box. An LEB emergency electrician came in the evening to reconnect us.

Draughts of freezing air poured into the flat from between the bare floorboards, past the loose-fitting window frames and wainscot and through a wide gap under the front door. The radiator heated the room it was in by about one degree. The calor gas heater was also fighting a losing battle and the smell of its fumes was so bad we decided not to use it. Rising damp had reached as far as it could go and was on its way back down again. A hand placed on a wall came away glistening wet. Pick began coughing on the very first night. A health visitor routinely called, a charming young lady who listened sympathetically to our troubles, then said she could do nothing. We could not see what her function was. She was not a doctor and had no power to advise a doctor or get us moved.

One day we were visited by a group of hippies. They informed us they were friends of the Aussie. They resided in Wales normally. It seemed there was a dispute over the carpet. They reckoned it was theirs. I told them they could take it. One of them, on asking where Lara came from and being told, said he was of Ukrainian descent and could speak a few words of Ukrainian. He proved it by doing so. Then he informed us he had two spare keys to our flat. This piece of news we found disturbing.

'You might as well give them to me,' I said.

'No, I think I'll hang on to them,' he said, with a slimy grin.

When they left I made another dash to the phone box to call another emergency number, this time of the council's housing office. Two men came within a few hours to fit a new lock.

I resumed work at the *Morning Star*, on the foreign desk, covering for Sam, who was convalescing after an operation. Lara phoned me to say the electricity had been cut off. I told the LEB I was a new tenant with a young child and that heating and cooking depended on electricity and that I had paid £45 deposit. No one cared. So I phoned the LEB publicity officer, a right smoothie who assured me we would be reconnected before the day was out. We were not. We spent that night, and Lara spent the following day, with no heating, cooking facilities or light. We were switched back on at six the following evening.

While on holiday in London in the summer Lara had registered with the Central Bureau for Educational Visits and Exchanges and been offered a part-time job as a foreign language assistant teacher at Robert Clack comprehensive school in Dagenham, one of the very few comprehensive schools in Britain to have Russian on the curriculum. Arriving too late for the start of the academic year on September 2 we wondered if she had lost the job. We also wondered if it was worth taking anyway, Dagenham being so far. But the job was still open and the annual salary of £2,300 for twelve hours a week would come in handy, so she took it. In order to be at Dagenham in time she had to get up at five-forty. The journey entailed taking a 21 bus to New Cross (easier said than done), catching an underground train and then taking another bus. On the first day she asked the conductor to put her off at the station and he said, 'Certainly, love,' and then forgot, so she went past it. This was not the first time this had happened to her on buses. 'It's "love" this and "love" that and then they forget all about you,' she said.

We managed to find a nursery for Pick. It was in Sidcup Road,

the other side of Eltham, too far to walk. A bus went from door
to door but unfortunately it was the infamous 21 service. This
and the expense prompted us to buy a second-hand bike each.
On the back of mine I fitted a child's seat, and took Pick to the
nursery in this manner. Lara's getting to work by London
Transport also entailed inordinate trouble and expense, so she
took to cycling most of the way.

One day I was sitting in the kitchen when I heard paper
rustling in the pantry. I suspected rats immediately but, the
thought being too horrible to contemplate, told myself it was an
empty bag falling from a shelf. When the noise continued I told
myself it was a draught rustling the bag. I could not bring myself
to get up and open the pantry door to have a look, for I had
visions of a cornered rat leaping out at my throat. When we
looked later in the day we found huge lumps gnawed out of a
lump of bread. The next day half a cabbage was eaten.

Pick was coughing incessantly. We would lie awake in the
night listening to it and wake up early in the morning and listen
to it. We registered at our local doctor's, a plump Indian woman
called Mukerjee. Lara could not understand a word she said.
Another complication was that Pick refused to take any medicine. We took him to my old doctor's surgery, where he ran
amok. We saw a Dr Dawes, who had lived in Canada. He said
that whereas in such cold climates as Canada and Russia
coughing was considered the symptom of an illness and taken
seriously, in damp but temperate England children ran about in
winter coughing like mad and no one thought anything of it. It
was true, and I thought it a sensible thing to say, but Lara was
not satisfied. Dr Dawes said, 'He's a normal naughty child, isn't
he?' as Pick jumped up and down on his scales. We agreed he
was. 'Then there's nothing to worry about,' he said. Two days
later we had to call an ambulance at three in the morning. Pick
had brought up his supper, had a very high temperature and was
retching so violently he kept vomiting. As he threw up in the
doorway on the way out to the ambulance one of the ambu-
lancemen said sarcastically to his colleague, 'This is a good
night's work, isn't it.' A baby simply coughing and throwing up
is not strictly an affair for an emergency ambulance. At the
hospital Pick had hysterics and would not let the young bearded

doctor look at his throat or do anything with him. The doctor gave up, adamantly prescribing medicine that we had already told him Pick would not take. He then vanished, bottling out of responsibility. We sat around in the deserted waiting room, me thinking there would be an ambulance to take us home. A nurse informed us otherwise. I called a cab.

Lara was appalled by all this. In Moscow when Pick was ill an ambulance came to our flat with a doctor and a nurse who treated him at home. No one here seemed to care that we were living in a damp, freezing, draughty condemned dilapidated house that was destroying the health of our child. Pick looked terrible. We believed his health was being undermined permanently. All our daily long walks in Moscow, all our previous care, was, as Lara said, sobbing, 'All in vain.' The strain and worry was beginning to show on her face too. Amazingly, however, and fortunately, her bronchitis had gone.

We fixed plastic sheeting over the windows in a vain attempt to keep out the draughts. In the slightest wind they billowed like sails.

Keeping clean was a big problem. The bathroom was in an alcove looking out onto the street. Two of the walls had big windows, which let in freezing draughts. It was the coldest part of the flat. Washing there was like washing in the open air and anyway there was no hot water, so it was impossible to have a bath. I was better off than Lara in this regard as there was a shower at work that I could use. Once we went to a sauna. On most days I went to work unshaven.

Lara was late three days in one week collecting Pick from the nursery because of waiting for 21 buses that did not come. On the third day she phoned me at work in tears. She had waited forty-five minutes for a service that was supposed to be about every twelve minutes, and Pick had had hysterics at the nursery, thinking he'd been left. All this came after her getting up at five-forty in the morning for a two-hour cycle ride to Dagenham, three or four hours teaching, and then the ride back.

On Saturdays we usually went to at least one jumble sale, and often two, doing our shopping afterwards at Lewisham market just before the stalls packed up, for then fresh fruit and vegetables could be got at their cheapest. One Saturday she went alone and, passing a Key Markets trolley in the street, put her heavy shopping in it and pushed it along. She was stopped by police, who were unpleasant and accused her of stealing it.

Meanwhile, we had acquired neighbours. One woman, middle-aged and muddled, had apparently been living in the top flat all the time but was so quiet we did not know she was there. Then a couple moved in immediately above us who were not quiet. Not at all. Elvis Presley was their favourite singer, 'You'll Never Walk Alone' their favourite song. They also enjoyed the Late Night Movie. One night, the movie going on very late indeed, I banged the ceiling with a broom handle. The man came down the next day, a bit drunk, and asked what I had in mind. I explained that his telly and his Elvis were a bit too loud too late at night. He explained he was deaf in one ear, the result of a childhood infection. He would be, of course. In halfway houses you do not get shortsighted neighbours or arthritic neighbours, you invariably get deaf neighbours addicted to Elvis Presley and late night movies. He also had a dog, violating his tenancy agreement. He insisted he needed one to guard his stately home. It took its duties seriously, warning off burglars by barking at all hours of the day and night. Lara said it was amazing how similar the couple was to the same type you would find in Russia. They were naturally on social security. The woman was pregnant until the day the dog jumped on her stomach.

Another couple moved in to the flat next door, he also unemployed, she also pregnant. But they were much younger, not even in their twenties, and he was black and she was white.

We made the acquaintance of the middle-aged woman when she came down to us one morning to ask if we could lend her a pinch of tea as there had been a mix-up at her social security office and she had no money. We invited her in for breakfast and, taking a calculated risk, lent her a fiver. She returned the fiver: but we still regretted befriending her as she was nutty. She had other meals with us and used any excuse to come down for a chat but whenever we passed her in the street she would not look at us. She had a furtive, nutty manner. She had lived in the top flat for two years because childless single people were not given priority. Recently she had been taken to hospital with concussion after part of her kitchen ceiling fell in on her. Several pots and pans had been dented beyond use, she complained. 'I can't stand it any longer,' she said. 'I would rather be in prison.'

Lara had been having a lot of time off work because of Pick's illnesses. She had to take another day off when he woke up at six in hysterics with earache. Because of the boredom for both of them, being stuck in the flat so often with nothing to do, she rented a small black-and-white television set from Radio Rentals, and was promptly infuriated by the film *Silk Stockings*, with its dummy Russian characters who did not even speak with the right accent and its facile assumption that all Russians would jump at the chance to live in the West.

Pick's earache went after a couple of days and that Saturday we had just made our plans for the day when his temperature suddenly shot up: tonsillitis. It being Saturday, I had to call an emergency doctor, who, after making his diagnosis, insisted on prescribing medicine that we assured him Pick would not take.

'It tastes nice,' he said. 'Of bananas.'

'We know all about these flavours,' I said. 'They don't fool him. We've been through all this.'

'Try,' he said, backing out of the door. 'It's pleasant.'

He could not wait to get away. He almost ran out of the door, urging us over his shoulder to persevere with his banana medicine. Not a single person we met seemed to have any understanding of, or compassion for, our predicament. It seemed it was too far beyond their experience and they had not enough interest to try and imagine it. I saw indifference or contempt on every face. One of the problems about being down and out is that everyone assumes it must somehow be your own fault. You get the feeling the whole world is against you. The milkman refused to deliver milk to us because no one in that house ever paid his bill. Shop staff were unbelievably rude. Everyone felt beautifully superior.

We had a weekend of undiluted misery, unable to get the flat warm and Pick ill with tonsillitis and refusing to take the medicine. On the Monday he had to go to hospital by ambulance for a long-lasting antibiotic injection in his thigh. I had to arrange this at Dr Mukerjee's surgery, which made me late for work. I was late again the following day simply because Lara was close to utter despair and I could not leave her. The editor called me into his office for a rollocking.

Next day was Christmas Eve. We went shopping at Lewisham. Lara wanted to buy some clothes for herself. She always favoured tight gear, and always tried on clothes at least one size too small. She tried on a pair of jeans but could not zip them up. The salesgirl said, 'They're meant for a teenager.'

'That's why she can't get them on,' I said.

Lara took exception to this. Outside the shop, she said she believed we should separate. 'I'll go back to Russia,' she said. 'It'll be very hard. But I'll manage.'

She later asked me to forgive her for this outburst but we had been getting more and more irritable with each other. She had an exasperating habit of adding 'Uh?' to every statement and question before I'd had time to reply. It was a nervous habit, she explained, revived from childhood.

'It's all falling apart, isn't it,' she said.

I agreed: 'It's not much fun.'

'We should have stayed in Russia.'

She was unbearably lonely and homesick. Andrei Sinyavsky, a satirical writer who emigrated to France after leaving a Soviet labour camp, was once asked which he found harder – his first six months in the camps or his first six months in Paris.

'The first six months in Paris,' he replied. 'When I was in the camps, I was still in Russia.'

And Sinyavsky in Paris had a proper home. We were living out of suitcases, from each of which a VIP tag hung tauntingly.

I was not as comforting as I should have been. I had no words of comfort. As far as I knew the editor meant what he said when he gave me six months to find another job. Four months remained, after which I would be unemployed as well as homeless. With three million unemployed, no qualifications and work experience too varied and unusual to interest any employer, I began to envy the prescience of a boy I'd known who twenty years ago had joined the Port of London Authority because of the secure pension. I became dejected thinking about that missed Reuters job. Stan told me one of the worst subs the *Morning Star* had ever had managed to land a job there. Ian Fleming, through his mother, got to see the Reuters head, who 'liked the look of him and gave him a job.' And I read in dozens of journalists' autobiographies the passing sentence, 'I got a job at Reuters.' It seemed anyone could get a job at Reuters. Anyone but me. I'd had a letter of recommendation from one of their most valued correspondents, and I still failed to get a job there.

I tried elsewhere. I felt my best bet was to return to sports journalism. I had been a highly respected member of a small group of football reporters, all of whom worked for fringe publications. In stadium press rooms up and down the country we had formed a companionable alternative to the travelling circus of the big papers. They had all since progressed. Some had joined the circus. I contacted them, to no avail. With disappointments piling up to make a thick wall of frustration, I lost my integrity. I had always been contemptuous of those who justified a reprehensible job with 'If I didn't do it someone else would' or some other rationalisation. Now I myself would have done anything, would have jumped at the chance to be an unprincipled hack on some scurrilous rag: but no one offered me such a desirable post. I felt shaky (my legs and hands actually shook). Things had gone wrong.

Lara also was not happy in her work. There were two problems apart from its being on the other side of London: one, the teacher she was assistant to was a Czech who hated the Soviet Union, and imparted this hatred to the children along with the Russian language; and two, Lara was horrified at the passivity of her working-class pupils. Of all the shocks she'd had in this country, this was one of the strongest, possibly because least expected. 'They watch television eight hours a day,' she said. 'They want to get any kind of job as soon as possible when they leave school, purely to earn money. There are no dreams in their life, no daring, no original thoughts, not many thoughts at all. I can't get them interested in anything. They accept too easily that nothing concerns them, that they can't do anything or change anything. Anything to do with politics, even the race question, they are indifferent to: it's none of their business. Libraries, theatres, mean nothing to them. They don't even know London. Above all, they have no dreams. The girls all want to be receptionists or secretaries, the boys anything. They've been robbed of their childhood dreams. Talking to them is like talking to their parents. They're already set to join the grey mass of the working class. And not one is the slightest bit interested in learning Russian.'

The job nevertheless kept her sane, for the alternative was idle, hopeless days in the flat, with the sound of the harsh, raucous voices of the other tenants coming in with the wind under the ill-fitting doors to obtrude upon the spirit.

Any marriage has flat, lustreless periods. It is not surprising that this was such a dull, abrasive time for Lara and me. Consider our circumstances – deprived of every comforting possession, in a freezing halfway house with rats and noisy, quarrelsome, rough, degraded neighbours, having an unsettled, permanently sick child on our hands . . . Ideally, we should have been making an effort towards imaginative understanding. But we were too preoccupied with Pick's health and the horror of our situation to grasp the need for this. Strangers when we married, we had never had the chance quietly to get to know each other. Now there was a disturbing lack of communication.

Everything in me seemed to militate against talking. I could never unburden myself effortlessly, and this had always made Lara suffer. Added to this now was superstition, an unwillingness to voice hopes or fears in case it tempted fate. Unemployment, nuclear war, Pick becoming dangerously ill . . . we were so vulnerable, and wanted so much a better life. Always when threatened my instinct was to withdraw. I wished not to hurt either Lara or myself. In my desire not to say anything to cause pain, I said nothing at all, which hurt more than anything I could have said. Lara, alone and isolated, felt the cold in our dilapidated house far more even than during the Freeze of Glory, when she'd had friends and family around her. Knowing all this at the time, I still could not unburden myself. It was as though my heart was walled in.

One night while we were sitting in the kitchen, with the stove rings switched on for warmth, I smelt burning: faintly at first and then, suddenly, strongly. Knowing then what it was, I dashed into the bedroom. In an attempt to warm our bedclothes I had stupidly laid the oil radiator flat in our bed. Two cotton 'blanket envelopes' we had fetched from Russia were scorching, brown and smoking with parts already burnt through. They were the only things in the flat for which we had feared burglars, the only things we would have missed. 'What did we come to England for?' asked Lara. A couple of days later we had a big bust-up. We again discussed the possibility of her returning to Russia. We made up the next day but I do not subscribe to the popular belief that flaming rows are worth it for the fun of making up.

The nervous tension brought back her wheezing and coughing. In an effort to ward off a serious development of the condition she did exercises every morning before going to work, which meant getting up even earlier, and ceased cycling to work, believing the cold air aggravated it. She now had a murderous time getting to and from work, having to use public transport. It cost £4.50 a day. One day she was thirty minutes late at work and the next day was late again in collecting Pick from the nursery because the 21s came in a convoy; the first two were full up and the third driver chose to overtake them at the bus-stop without bothering to pick up passengers. The poxy service left her in tears two days running. It is the custom of 21s to travel in convoys. Once I was waiting at a stop and one appeared from around a corner in the distance and a man said very matter-of-factly, 'Here they come.'

While shopping on the last day of 1980, in a department store while Lara was at a far counter choosing presents for her family, Pick had a tantrum of alarming proportions. It began when he picked up from a shelf a large expensive bar of chocolate. I wrestled it from him and replaced it on the shelf, the wrapper torn. As I dragged him away, a saleswoman said we had to buy it. I said over my shoulder it was already torn. Lara joined us, having heard his screams, I picked him up and we hurried out. The pavement was crowded with shoppers. He kicked and screamed. We carried him to a quieter side street. It was impossible to do anything with him. He had completely lost control. So we left him there on the pavement and walked away out of sight behind a wall to see what he would do. He undressed. Normally, as he well knew, we could not allow this because of his illnesses, but this time we let him get on with it. He took off his overcoat and threw it to the ground. Then his shoes. This was all he could manage, so he redoubled the strength of his screams. I have never seen anything like it. He calmed down finally, after a very long time, though for some time after that he could only breathe in sobs.

Thus ended 1980 and our third month in England.

Chapter Twenty
ON THE FERRIER

Kidbrooke was once the proposed site of the Grand National Cemetery. Covering 150 acres, it was to have prevented 'the Danger and Inconvenience of burying the Dead within the Metropolis', with an inner area reserved for the very wealthy and 'great and distinguished persons whose wisdom, bravery, genius and talent have conspicuously contributed to the glory of the country'. This plan being abandoned, there was built instead many years later a dumping ground of the living, persons at the other end of the social scale. It was named the Ferrier estate, and it was here that Lara and I were offered a maisonette.

The Ferrier estate was by a park that had been the home ground of my football team. Then, there had been nothing behind the park but a boggy wasteland. That end of the park adjoining the marsh was always susceptible to flooding, with consequent postponed matches. Now the bog had been drained and the huge sprawling grey housing estate built on it. As we had known it was possible we would be allocated a place on this estate, we had already had a look around. If I had not lived in Moscow I would have been unreservedly critical of it, regarding it as a hideous blot on the landscape, a concrete tumour. Everything on it was made of prefabricated light grey concrete slabs. As it was, I thought the architects had made a valiant effort. There were tower blocks but they did not form the bulk of the estate and were broken up by low buildings and even terraced houses with little back yards. There were grass squares and young trees. It had been hailed as a model council estate of the 1970s. But Lara did not like it, and it must be said it was not the sort of place anyone would choose to live in if they had an alternative. The award-winning architects who designed it certainly had no intention of living there. The trouble was, we would not be given a choice. Homeless families, having jumped the housing queue, have to take what they are offered, because once they have been offered a place they can no longer be considered homeless. (Normally council tenants wishing to move are given up to three refusals.) Although only ten years old, the estate was already defaced by vandalism. The architects in their idealism had designed glass outer doors for the public staircases: only the wooden frames remained, which you stepped through without opening.

Draughts through the empty door frames blew about the litter, of which there was much – discarded wrappers of ice lollies and crisps, cigarette packets, fag ends. The concrete staircase was filthy, with graffiti and substances smeared on the walls. Our front door had been forced at some point: gouges and a dent and crack disfigured the wood near the lock. A second lock, added privately by previous tenants, had been removed by them when they left, leaving a hole. Inside, the maisonette was magnificent. It was big by any standards and by Russian standards it was huge. The kitchen, especially, seemed palatial. At the top of the maisonette was a patio overlooking a grass square and the park. There were plenty of storage cupboards; and there was central heating. On the day we moved in Lara said for the first and only time, 'I'm glad we came to England.' We celebrated with Russkaya vodka. We knew we would take the comfort for granted after a while but for the moment she was content. We set about the joyful tasks of moving to a new home: I ordered two pints of milk a day from the Express milkman, eager to show Lara the unique British service of the daily milk delivery; bought wrapping paper to line the kitchen drawers; collected my old solid MFI desk from my parents'; joined the local library; transferred my bank account; and bought some house plants. There was a disconnected phone, and we had it reconnected. With perfect timing, our things arrived from Moscow a few days after we had moved in. If they had arrived earlier I do not know where we could have put them. Sea water had leaked into one of the boxes and spoilt one or two things but apart from that everything was in order. Nothing was broken. We settled in, luxuriating in the warmth. At work, I returned to my old job on the sports desk.

Summer came, windows were thrown open and the breezes on the Ferrier carried family altercations and such witty rejoinders as, 'Bollocks, you wanker.' Adolescents thundered along the tiled walkways on roller skates, stopping only to scribble a quick graffito or two on a urine-etched breezeblock. Sirens of the emergency services, moaning through a cacophonous world, became as much a part of our daily life as the services of the postman and the milkman.

For next-door neighbours we had on our left a couple whose joy it was to go to the pub every Saturday night and come home to what the police called a 'domestic'. The place on our right was filled by a young couple with a boy younger than Pick. I never saw the man, for two weeks after moving in he moved out. The girl, a peroxide blonde with blank eyes and enormous bristols, entertained a series of gentlemen friends, including the window cleaner. Unable to work because of the baby, she made ends meet by nicking things from our patio. All the patios had small connecting doors as a fire safety measure. A mop vanished, then a jumper from the clothesline, then some pot plants, then a rug, then a stylish hold-all intended for Sasha; then we blocked her passage by placing heavy objects against the connecting door. Both the RACS and Express milkmen had stopped delivering milk to her because she did not pay the bill, and she compensated by nicking ours. Every sentence she uttered contained a swear word, even those addressed to the child. 'Fucking' replaced every adjective and was often placed at the beginning of a sentence for emphasis, e.g. 'Fucking stop it.' She would say things to her boy like, 'Piss off my foot.' One night when she was entertaining one of her friends we heard murmurings and giggles and then, 'Ah-h-gh! Cunt! You wake that fucking kid up!' She need not have worried. She had woken up the whole estate but the effing kid slept on. She told us once, 'I'm learning the baby to walk.' Later she would learn him to talk. Poor little sod.

The estate was dominated by adolescents – their graffiti, yells and music. Branded with American Christian names like Darren, Kelly, Shane and Scott, they roamed and lounged aimlessly, chewing gum, smoking fags and listening to pop music on big transistor radios that they always carried with them. Most were of average intelligence: they were not thick, nor lumpen. But their high spirits lacked charm, their vitality was without grace. They faced either a dead-end job or deadening unemployment and they knew it. I felt sorry for them but they were boorish and noisy and I would have much preferred to be sorry for them from a distance.

There was a hard core of nutters, a separate gang, skinheads in combat jackets and prominent bovver boots. We rarely saw them but it was their graffiti that were the most vilely racist and pornographic, they who systematically broke windows for fun (eighteen in one weekend) and it was probably they who dreamed up a dangerous new twist in vandalism – setting fire to parked cars. Four cars were destroyed in a fortnight, one of them in an underground car park. The vandals poured petrol through the car window and set it alight. If a petrol tank had ignited the car would have been like a bomb. Another fire game was to push burning newspapers through letter boxes (though the police believed younger children were responsible for this).

The extent of crime can be gauged from the fact that in one week the RACS milkman was beaten over the head with a stick and robbed of £200 in takings by two men in balaclava helmets with eye slits; armed robbers escaped with £11,000 from a raid on the estate's rent office, grabbing the money from Group 4 security men; and in one day there were three burglaries. Once there was a knock at our door; going to answer it, I could see through the frosted glass it was a full-grown male, and I saw him run away when he saw there was someone in. The statistics and the atmosphere discouraged dawdling when walking home through the estate at night. You felt twitchy if someone was walking close behind you and relief at finding the front door still locked.

Lara had not envisaged this sort of life when we left Russia.

'It's like a ghetto, really, isn't it,' she said.

'In football,' I said, 'a team that has been promoted usually needs a settling-in season before it can think of finishing high up in its new division.'

'I'm not sure we've been promoted,' she said.

I sang the title line of the pop song, 'I never promised you a rose garden.'

'But you did!'

When the year's contract with Robert Clack school ended she did not renew it, choosing to study for an interpreters' course instead. To pass the test for this she needed to brush up her second foreign language, French. She listened every day to the French radio, and I fetched Le Monde from the office for her to read. With the test for the course looming, I thought it a good idea for her to have a long weekend package holiday in Paris. She did not relish the idea but I persuaded her and went ahead and booked it. On the morning of her departure, I said, 'I'm nearly as excited as you are about it.'

'You're probably more excited than me,' she replied.

But she loved Paris. 'It's like a much more civilised Georgia,' she said on her return. She had walked for hours, delighted with the boulevards and cafés. Many men accosted her, of course, and because she had gone to speak French she spoke to some of them. Only one turned unpleasant when it became clear she was prepared only to talk to him: all the others she found urbane and charming. She was grateful to me for insisting she go. The short visit was not sufficient for her to improve her French enough to pass the test however and she was not surprised when she failed it. 'To pass it next year,' she said, 'I'm going to have to spend several months in France.' Although I had misgivings about this, it was out of the question for her to stagnate as a housewife on the Ferrier. So we asked around about possible jobs in France. A friend came up with the idea of grape picking. As the season was well advanced, we moved fast. I went to the French embassy for details of the regions and bought a map of France. She was too late for the south. Rheims seemed to be the place to start out for grape picking in September, so the following day before going to work I called at the French railways office in Piccadilly for a Rheims timetable, having trouble with the French girl because she could not understand what I wanted. I had to write Rheims on a piece of paper. Few English-speaking foreigners could ever understand my accent.

At just after four, the time Pick should have been collected by,

I received a phone call at work from Mrs Treacher, the head of the nursery. Lara was still not there. 'I told her the next time she was late that would be it,' Mrs Treacher said. 'Well, this is it.'

Finding Mrs Treacher's nursery had been our one bit of good luck since coming to England. She had converted the ground floor of her terraced house. The rooms were small and cosy, the staff warm and patient. Pick loved going there. As he had not known any English at first the staff bought a Russian phrasebook. Nearly every day he proudly fetched home something he had made or drawn. The staff seemed to have an inexhaustible fund of ideas.

The desperate search for another nursery that was open all day, with Lara due to leave for France in a week, confirmed that Mrs Treacher's really was outstanding. Others were too big and the staff not as dedicated. We found a Montessori centre in Blackheath in the end which, being nearer and staying open till five-thirty, was more convenient, but the fee was £24 a week and its size intimidating after the cosiness of Mrs Treacher's.

I'd hurriedly arranged to have my holiday at this time as there was so much to do. Pick and I saw Lara off from platform 6 at Charing Cross. He was upset when the train pulled away, and four days later he went for the first time to his new nursery. I could have done without that sort of timing. He would not let me leave him. I stayed till lunchtime, after which I took him home. We called at the library on the way, where he insisted on making a noise. I carried him outside, where he had a tantrum. I resented my holiday being spent like this. I had visions of Pick never settling in at the Montessori. What then? Even Spock had no answer to that. He was fine the next day, and I played with him in the evening with his Fisher-Price village and his farm and zoo animals, but the day after that he cried when I left him and they said he was grizzly all day. He cried when I left him for the remainder of the week. On the Friday we visited my parents and my father said in front of him, 'Is he missing Lara?'

'You're stupid sometimes,' I said.

'Well, is he?'

Pick proceeded to have a tantrum. My father said, 'Bring him back when he's nine' and 'Can't you see a child psychiatrist?'

My financial situation was impossible. The rent had been

increased to £34 a week. With food costing £25 and the nursery £24, essential regular outgoings exceeded my income by £2. I had no option but to cheat on rail fares. I simply used a day return ticket over and over again. On the outward journey, I flashed the pink piece of paper at the collector as I breezed through the barrier. I did the same on the return journey, and at Kidbrooke station paid the fare from Blackheath, one station up the line – 20p. The local ticket collector was glad to pocket this daily 20p for beer money, while I saved several pounds a week. I would use a ticket till it became frayed and obviously old. A day return handled with care could last for weeks. One morning a collector rebuked me for using a cheap day return in the rush hour. He held the ticket and looked at it all the while he was rebuking me and finally clipped it and handed it back without noticing it was over a month old.

Most mornings I had been taking Pick to the Montessori on the back of my bicycle, on the pavement of the busy Eltham Road. On the A-Z map the estate's ring road almost touched at one point a small side street leading directly to Blackheath. The map did not show if there was a connecting pathway or not. If there was, that way would be much more direct and quicker than the Eltham Road route. I went and had a look. There was: and going through it, leaving the Ferrier estate for Blackheath by this short pathway, was like Alice stepping through the looking glass, into a place where everything was different. There were secluded cul-de-sacs, detached houses, flower gardens, neat lawns and trimmed privets. The people strolling about dressed differently and spoke a different dialect. The coarseness of the Ferrierites was only fully realised when you made that short step into Wonderland. Lara reckoned there was a council estate type, characterised by lack of self-respect. Young women on the Ferrier would yell out for all to hear the most foul language. I, and the whole square, once heard one young lady scream at another, 'Go and fucking wank yourself, you old bag!' On the estate there was always some noise. It might be only children playing but it could equally be a 'domestic', DIY banging, an ice cream van's Harry Lime Theme on tubular bells, motor bikes, dogs barking, Radio One or adolescents with their music or at their horseplay. In Wonderland all was tranquil. Trees rustled, birds sang, people conversed in soft tones. And roses grew in beautiful gardens.

When I resumed work, provision had to be made for Pick to be collected from the nursery and looked after till I returned. I came to an arrangement with Pete. He would do the honours in midweek when I required it and I would look after his two boys when he went to work as a sports sub at the *Sunday Mirror* on Saturdays. On the first Saturday, Pick fell asleep at midday, making us late. Pete was frantic. 'Where've you *been*!' he said, hurrying to the station. It rained the whole time, so the three boys, aged three, four and seven, could not go out. Pick and the four-year-old, named Terry after me, kept fighting. I did not have a minute's respite from three-thirty till eight-thirty, when Pete's two went to bed. Pick stayed awake and we went home on my bike when Pete returned at eleven-thirty.

Pick got up at seven the next morning in spite of the late night, announcing himself cheerily as usual with 'Here I am!' as he entered my bedroom. I dragged myself out of bed to dress him. He played in the square outside all day, then fell asleep just as I had prepared a meal of lambs' liver, chips and tomatoes. I ate his as well as my own portion. Putting him to bed, I popped out to the off-licence for a bottle of whisky but there was a queue and I returned without. I had only been gone a few minutes. Pick was standing at the open front door, naked and crying. Titselina from next door was with him. Her jeans, she said, had blown over to our patio and she had called to get them back. Her knocking had woken up Pick. Now he was hungry and I had nothing for him to eat except some tinned Irish stew which he did not want. I read to him as usual when he went to bed later in the evening. When he fell asleep the phone rang and woke him up again. It was a wrong number. I had to read to him again. I had gone to the offy to buy a drink because I thought the evening would be boring.

Pete said it was too difficult having his Terry with Pick, so we would have to cancel our arrangement. He looked after Pick once more to give me time to make alternative arrangements. After I arrived to take him home Pick poohed himself. I showered him at home and put him to bed and during the night he wet the bed and vomited. I did not have enough bowls for all the dirty clothes and sheets. The following night he was again sick. He rolled in it while asleep so that next morning it was all over his face and body and matted in his hair. I cleaned him up and the bed; took him to the nursery; took the washing to the launderette; dashed to work; hurried back afterwards to collect him from another friends' house, Dave and Joan's.

That Saturday I got drunk, as it was the first anniversary of my return from Moscow and I felt like a little celebration by way of relaxation. After putting Pick to bed I hurried to the offy and bought a half-bottle of whisky and two tins of Special Brew and drank it all while watching the film *Blum in Love* on television. Then I vomited it all back up. When Pick came cheerily into my bedroom at six-thirty the next morning I did not see how it was possible for me to survive the day. If he had been in a stroppy mood that would have been the end of both of us. But he was marvellous. I pleaded with him to play on his own and let me sleep and he did, bless him. He let me sleep till nine. And then when I got up, still feeling delicate, he was very good, no trouble. I had to go to work that day. I was very late, for I had to take him round to Dave and Joan's and when the time came to leave our flat he was outside, nowhere to be found. I spent thirty minutes looking for him before he turned up. Stan had been phoning the office for over an hour by the time I arrived, was very angry and had been preparing to come in himself. Apologising, I explained the situation.

'You'll destroy yourself,' he said.

If that sort of life had gone on for much longer Stan could have been right but I had only to hang on for another week. Pick and I had one more week of domestic vexations and minor crises: then Lara returned.

Ruddy-cheeked and healthy, she was very pleased with herself. Everything had gone according to plan. Arriving in Rheims in the early afternoon of a Friday, she had got a room for one night only at the *Centre de Séjour* for £3. She left her heavy bags there and went straightaway to look for a job, going at first to the wrong employment agency. The right one was the other side of Rheims. She walked there. Officials there laughed at her French and her disconcerted look when they told her there was no work but she could go on Sunday to the station, where some jobs might just possibly be allocated. She thought they were taking the micky, especially when they said any time on Sunday would do. She asked painfully in her French, 'What's the earliest reasonable hour?' Ten a.m., they said. '*Merci*,' she said, bewildered. Then she wandered about Rheims, tired and hungry, scared to buy any food, of spending money she was not going to be able to earn. She watched television at the hostel in the evening, thinking that at least she would have picked up some French from that before she returned to London on Sunday. When the television room was closed she joined the company sitting around a table in the hall. The company consisted of two Cockneys, an Irishman and a Scot – all there for grape picking and all having spent a week sitting in the hostel. Now they all had jobs, starting on Monday. None of them spoke any French. The doors were locked at eleven. At midnight a gang of German priests came in through the window. One of them changed a 10-franc note for Lara so she could phone me. She spent two worried nights at the hostel and at eleven on Sunday morning was at the station, where she filled in a form and sat by the employment agent. Alongside sat several dozen other expectant *vendangeurs*. Two hours later she and the others were on their way to the best grape farm in France. They were met by the charming couple who owned it, who were roasting a huge duck over a charcoal fire for them. The food remained magnificent throughout their stay. The working day began at seven-thirty and ended at five-thirty, with two breaks. Her back ached but not as much as she had feared. She enjoyed it all enormously. All her workmates were French, so she could practise her language. The village was beautiful. Everything reminded her of Russia. 'They kiss one another all the time, they care, they help and laugh and joke and never leave you alone except when you want to be alone,' she wrote.

When the work was over there she moved on to Alsace, hitch-hiking there with an American girl called Michelle. Alsace was crawling with hundreds of prospective *vendangeurs*, dragging their belongings behind them. It seemed there was no work, no lodging and no hope. Some had been sleeping for several nights on the floor at the railway station. The station was closed between one-thirty and six and they had to spend that time outside. Lara and Michelle spent the night in the car of their last lift, the driver having got a grape-picking job in advance and the lodging that went with it. It was not the most refreshing night's sleep they had ever had but it rained heavily during the night and they were very happy to have a roof over their heads. The following morning they hitch-hiked to a village where they were told there were no jobs, went to another vineyard's office and in a few minutes were in a mini-bus clothed in rubber boots, coats, trousers and hats and armed with buckets and secateurs, travelling in pouring rain to a vineyard. They lunched outside in the pouring rain and arrived at their vineyard of work in the evening. The farm provided no lodging and no food apart from lunch. They were paid the lowest possible wage, £1.80 an hour, less £1 a day for the lunch. Lara, however, met a woman called Chantal who had just moved to the area from Paris with her six-year-old daughter and six-foot-tall lover, and Chantal invited her to stay with them in their beautiful old house in the mountains, where they drank fresh milk and ate home-made bread. The couple were also *vendangeurs* for the moment, before they found permanent jobs in the area. Lara stayed there a month.

She returned with the idea of winter sports. Her French had benefited from the grape-picking sojourn but not enough, she felt, to have made the effort worthwhile. She needed to go to France again. The next seasonal work was at cafés and hotels in the mountains for winter sports. She had been told she should be at an employment agency in Grenoble before the end of November. This gave us three weeks. We proceeded with preparations for her to return to France. We bought leg warmers, a fur jacket, knee boots and a rucksack and, at the travel counter in my old firm of Chiesmans, the train ticket. 'I'm now enjoying the only big advantage the West has to offer – freedom to travel,' she said. Friends were aghast. 'What about Pick?' they said. Influenced by them, she had qualms: which she dismissed. 'In Russia if something has to be done you do it,' she said. 'If you have to go and work in Vladivostok for a year you leave the baby with someone.' So off she went again, and, through the Grenoble agency, got a job in Switzerland, up an alp. She worked as a café waitress at a village called Evolène, in place of a girl from Grenoble who had fallen ill.

As for me, I had an easier time than during the first separation. Joan's fourteen-year-old daughter Lorraine agreed to collect Pick, take him to our place and stay with him till I arrived home, usually about nine o'clock, for £3 a night. This arrangement worked well. She would cook spaghetti for an evening meal, after which he would watch television for a while with her before going to bed between seven and eight. He was always in bed asleep when I arrived home. On the few occasions Lorraine could not do it Joan stood in.

Christmas Day we spent at my parents', along with Ken and his wife Sheila and their three children, Susan, Cheryl and Timmy. After dinner and a drink my father wanted a kip alone in the front room and when Timmy and Pick went in there to play with their new toys he told them to 'fuck off', smacking Pick's hand for good measure. Pick was grievously upset and I had to take him out for a long walk.

I saw the New Year in with a bottle of wine at home, having phoned Lara at ten, which was midnight in Switzerland.

Although I at least had a routine this time, and a regular baby-sitter, life was still hectic, with a lot of dashing to and from endless duties. Pick still fell ill occasionally and still had tantrums, and trains were being disrupted by one of the snowiest and iciest winters for many years. All this meant I was tense and nervous all the time. I began to have dizzy spells. I wondered at the time if it was because of my poor diet (I lived on sausages and fried eggs) but now I know it was through nervous tension. One morning I had a very bad funny turn getting out of bed. I felt sick and dizzy. I had to attend to Pick's little needs and wants with the room spinning.

By the time the girl from Grenoble was better Lara had got herself another job in the village, at a hotel. She came home for just one week. She was pleased at how content Pick was and congratulated me. But this week of family reunion did Pick no good. It seemed it would have been better for him if, with only a week possible, she had not come at all. After her departure at the end of the week, he began refusing to go with Lorraine from the nursery. With me, he would go to bed in a foul mood, asking for trouble, and would start up again immediately on waking in the morning. He would throw things and refuse to eat his meals.

Before, I was pleased with myself at how well we got on together. I felt we were mates. Now he had turned into a raging monster and I felt I had lost control. I had no authority. I would reprimand and scold, persuade and order, without the least effect. I took him for a routine birthday check-up and the doctor, after testing his reactions and eyes and intelligence and saying he was a delightful child, said that children cannot be disciplined till they are about seven, that children of Pick's age have to be persuaded or distracted. I had felt this instinctively but these methods most of the time no longer worked. Pick would not be persuaded or distracted. If discipline was not to work either, I did not know what to do. We would lose our tempers with each other. I would shake him and yell at him and throw him on the bed and actually hit him in anger. He would ferociously hit me back. In the street, he would lag behind saying, 'Where are you, Dad? I can't see you!' for the benefit of passers-by. It was bizarre. I was right in front of him. And he would say plaintively for no reason in the street, so that passers-by could hear, 'Please don't hit me again, Dad!' I could never enjoy his company any more, for I could never relax. I had to be ultra careful about everything I said and did. He could at any moment, for no reason, go into a tantrum. Sometimes, by remaining calm, I could nip it in the bud, but I was finding it increasingly difficult to remain calm. I would lose my temper, a corner of me feeling as I did so that it was a mistake, a luxury I could not afford, and could only make things worse. He never co-operated, not in a single thing, from getting dressed in the morning ('I don't want that shirt!') to going to bed at night. I resented this endless struggle. He was a beautiful child, sturdy, jolly and high-spirited, and he was behaving like a demon. At the nursery they told me he wanted cuddles all the time. And then, the day before his fourth birthday, he said for the first time, in a heartfelt way, with real tears, 'Daddy, when's Mummy coming back? She's been gone a long time, hasn't she.' My heart turned to jelly. I phoned Lara that evening to tell her and to suggest I take my holiday early and we join her for three weeks.

I could not leave for a fortnight because of work commitments and because Pick's name had to be added to my passport. I resolved to stay calm in that fortnight. But then as I was bathing him he, (a) threw in the water the only two clean towels I had left, (b) pulled the plug and let out most of the water, and (c) when I was bending over to wash him, viciously pulled my hair. This was all too much. Furious, I punched him on the thigh. A splashy tantrum followed, a wicked, enervating confrontation. The next day he played up twice with Lorraine, first when she collected him and then when she said he could not have a scone. Refusing to go to bed, he fell asleep on the stairs. He developed a rash on the back of his knees. Once when I collected him at the nursery and would not let him have an apple until we were outside, he had such a tantrum I had to carry him out screaming and kicking. On the Saturday while I was having a lie-in he pulled photographs off the living-room wall, along with pieces of new wallpaper, and then pulled a new seven-foot bookcase on top of himself, having first removed all the books to make the feat possible. The day after that he flooded the kitchen. As soon as I knew our day of departure I informed Lara by phone. Pick spoke to her as well. 'Mummy,' he said, 'I want you to come home.'

'So,' she wrote, 'you're coming Saturday week. C'est formidable! It's such a joy! I didn't like Pick's voice on the phone – it was hesitant, self-conscious, as though he didn't trust me any more. And maybe with good reason – horrible thought. But now, every time I think that you're coming and the day's getting nearer and nearer – I get a delicious excited feeling. I see everything around me with different eyes, looking forward to sharing it all with you.'

Lara always needed to share things, whether it was a peeled orange, an evening at the theatre – or Alpine scenery. Solitary pleasure was for her a meaningless term. Pleasure was always wasted on her unless it could be shared. Although in general she enjoyed her time in Switzerland, and found it interesting, satisfying and rewarding, she did work incredibly long hours and so was often tired – and then sometimes her Judaic melancholy would surface and she would be spiritually bereft, consumed by devastating loneliness. She was terribly far from Russia, in the Val d'Herens, hemmed in by towering Alpine peaks. Even when she was feeling good, out skiing or walking on her day off or in her break, her exultation at the sight of the

Alpine scenery was always tinged with irremediable regret that she had no one to share it with. What was she doing there, hundreds of miles away from anyone she loved, among strangers? She was certain she had no right to see that magnificent view all by herself. So she looked forward very much to our coming.

Pick was also very excited. He kept getting me to repeat the travelling involved: 'First a train, then another train, then a ship, then another train, then an underground train [changing at Paris] and then another train, on which we'll sleep all night, and when we get off in the morning, Mummy will be there.' While I was packing, he was either adding unnecessary things or removing things I'd packed. Prior to departure we had a brief mutual tantrum. On the credit side, he did a fine pooh; and on the journey was marvellous. I am one of those people who, when going on a long journey, like to arrive at the departure point about two hours early. I was true to form this time; there was a mitigating circumstance for my silliness, however, an underground strike, which meant I could not judge how long it would take to get from Charing Cross to Victoria. In the event, a taxi was soon available and did not take long to get there.

The ferry was forty-five minutes late, which left it a bit tight for the connection in Paris. Pick was entranced by the gulls, the 'wobbly water' and our see-saw motion. He sat outside for an hour, then slept inside for two. I was very pleased he had a good kip, for I was worried by the changing of stations at Paris in the late evening if he was tired. A fool on board said it took five minutes by metro to get from the Gare du Nord to the Gare du Lyons. It took half an hour, a mad panicky dash under south-east Paris. In our sleeper, though the top bunk was free, Pick insisted I lie with him the whole night. I was on the outside edge. He slept fitfully. I slept not at all. In the morning the train made its way up the wide Rhône valley, past silver streams falling perpendicularly down the snow-covered mountains and a succession of cone-like hills crowned by small castles. We pulled into Sion. I had been there twice before, first on the way to work in Leukerbad and then passing through on my way to Trieste, but both occasions were so long ago I remembered nothing of the place.

Lara was waiting for us on the flat continental platform. Pick stopped in a sulk because I walked too fast to her and we had a cuddle without him. But then we all had a cuddle together. She was tanned. She had on the fur coat we had bought specially and my reindeer fur clodhoppers. We had a coffee in the station café. Pick played up when she wanted to change his trousers, typically refusing to co-operate. 'You've let him go,' she said. 'He's impossible.' This I felt was unfair. He was a disturbed child because his mother kept pissing off for weeks at a time. I had had a murderous few weeks, and all she could do was voice dissatisfaction. And then, in the bus going up the mountains to Evolène, she asked what clothes I had brought to wear during my stay and disapproved strongly of my choice. She wanted Pick and me to look nice to impress the Evolènards. Our reunions were often like this, an anti-climax: so anxiously awaited, they usually caused as much friction as joy. We missed each other badly when apart and mangled each other's nerves on meeting.

Hotel Eden, where she worked, was full of customers of 'the third age', over fifty. Lara was very busy, working from five in the morning till eleven at night or even later, with just one break (apart from hurried meals) between two and four. In the mornings she tidied up the rooms, at midday helped in the dining room and kitchen and in the evenings served in the bistro. Pick and I were billeted in her small room on the top floor. It was tantalising for Pick to have his mummy so near and yet be unable to see her most of the time. He would stand at the top of the stairs and yell, 'Mum, mum!' Roger the patron was bothered by the noise, worried that it disturbed his guests. Pick had to be kept occupied and amused and out of the hotel. On our first full morning I planned for us to go to my old workplace of Leukerbad, which was also in the Valais, across the Rhône. We missed the early bus down to Sion and there was not another till twelve-thirty, which would be too late. We spent a dreary morning at the slushy roadside on the edge of the village trying to hitch a lift, a morning full of mini-disasters such as Pick crashing full-length in the mud. The whole morning we stood there, cold and bored, Pick inadequately clothed and shod and in a bad mood and no cars stopping. I felt then the closest I had ever felt to complete despair. I felt like simply walking away. We had gone to Evolène in desperation for a relief from tension, and there was none: on the contrary, it was worse, we were in public and had not even home comforts. Standing at that bleak roadside, with Pick pulling at my arms and wanting this and wanting that, I felt like turning everything in. I wanted release.

When we returned to the hotel for our lunch Lara informed me that Roger's wife Marion, seeing how cramped and miserable we were, had arranged for us to stay in their vacant flat across the road. It was a spacious, quiet flat on the top floor of a large wooden house. It had two rooms, one of which had an alcove that was nearly filled by a double bed and could be curtained off by thick maroon curtains. The windows looked out onto a Christmas card scene, in which the snow was here and there illuminated by yellow lamps. Evolène typified the Switzerland that visitors love. At the head of the valley 'Tooth Mountain' spewed clouds from its sharp, jagged point. Opposite us, beyond the green-shuttered Pension Bellevue, loomed the snow-covered Alpine meadows and the ski slopes. Huts and cowbarns stood dotted among the firs, slightly elevated on stone stilts to keep out rodents. Two ski lifts led up into the hills. Matchstick figures glided down. Buildings in the village were roofed with big irregular slates. A blanket of snow many folds deep covered the northern half of the sloping roofs, with the southern half clear. Outside was snow and cold – blizzards would rage. We had an enchanting snug little nest. Staying there made all the difference. Pick could run about and there was space to play. Marion was a wonderful woman, with enthusiastic glittering eyes. As Roger was the cook, she ran the hotel on her own. It being near the end of the busy winter season she was exhausted, actually stumbling and fumbling with tiredness. The night before our arrival she had fallen and fractured her arm. She still attended to all her duties, with her arm in a black sling. She decided that when the current group of over-fifties left in a few days Lara could have a week's leave.

On the sloping paths Pick discovered a delightful sport when he went out for walks with me. This was tobogganing down upon the seat of his trousers. I took a poor view of this, and this was to remain a bone of contention for the remainder of our stay. The idea of doing what I told him never occurred to Pick.

Each morning when we got up I would go to the baker's shop and buy croissants. We would have them with butter, home-made blackcurrant jam, cheese and coffee. The milk and cheese were local but not the butter. We left the milk outside on the balcony every night. In the morning it would be frozen solid. It reminded Lara of milk being sold in lumps in the Ufa market in her childhood, and it reminded me of Norilsk. I would consume half a dozen croissants. 'No French person has more than two at a time,' Lara said.

During her week's leave we visited other villages in the valley and went up several times on a long ski lift, seated and freezing, to the steepest slopes. The operator would let go of the seat and with a jerk it was pulled forward and upward. Up and up it went, over a winding path and a gorge, past some huts, up to where there were no birds or trees, only snow and a view of sweeping glaciers and pristine peaks. Once we saw chamois. Lara, who enjoyed skiing, carried Pick on her back in wide, slow, graceful zig-zags. Our faces got sunburnt and yet as we trudged back down to the valley at dusk our hands would be swollen with cold. After putting Pick to bed, confident he would sleep soundly after all that mountain air, we toured the cafés, *à la* Evolènards. Evolène's one road was lined with cafés. Every evening the Evolènards went on a café crawl. (Spouses went their separate ways, acknowledging with a nod of the head a chance meeting). Lara knew everyone and each passing meeting required a reciprocal '*bonjour*' or '*bonsoir*'. In the Café de la Paix, Café d'Evolène and Café Central we drank rum tea, Valais beer and the Fendant de Sion white wine favoured by James Joyce when he lived in Zurich. The Evolènards were a typical mountain village people: everyone was related to everyone else and they spoke among themselves an exclusive patois. Lara, though her French was now fluent, could not understand a word of it. 'They are savages who wear jeans and drive cars,' she said. Few had heard of even such internationally famous people as Hemingway.

After three weeks Pick and I descended to the flat-land for our return to London, Pick crying bitterly on being informed that Lara was not accompanying us. On the train to Paris a Scottish woman with two young children and a 'Wogs begin at Calais' mentality said, 'It'll be nice tae get back tae civilisation.' She was lucky. We were going back tae the Ferrier.

Lara returned a week later. Roger and Marion were so pleased with her work they wanted her to go back for the summer season. With meals and lodging free, she would bring home in the autumn £1,000. This was a Godfather-type offer, irrefusable. Pick could go and stay with her family in Obninsk. His fare came to almost exactly what it would cost to keep him at the Montessori nursery in that period.

Lara would take him to Russia before returning to Switzerland. Meanwhile, she was glad to be home, able to cook her own meals and have a cup of tea at the exact moment she felt like one. With the test for the interpreters' course imminent, I read out passages from newspapers for her to translate. As the sports desk received the *Daily Mail* I fetched copies home and she translated from those. We would usually laugh at first at the pretentious *Mail* but ended up sickened. The day of the test arrived. Lara said several times she was convinced she would fail. 'I can't feel success,' she said. I saw her off with the appropriate Russian good luck ritual, throwing a potful of water in her wake in the corridor (a cup not being big enough to please the gods of fortune). 'Don't sweep the floor in my absence,' Lara called over her shoulder. Taking the test, at first she could not concentrate. In the general knowledge section, asked to name three living British or American authors, she named Tom Stoppard plus A.A. Milne (died 1956) and C.P. Snow (died 1980). And then, asked to match names with concepts, she put Leonard Bernstein next to Founder of Zionism instead of West Side Story. She passed however. The examiners congratulated her on her French. But as she was the only student for the class interpreting into Russian, it was not worth their while having such a class that year: so for her there would be no course. Maybe next year, they said, if there were then enough students.

Lara was not as downhearted as might have been expected from this setback. In fact at first she was not downhearted at all: she was instead pleased that the test was over and that she had proved herself in French. 'An additional language never did anyone any harm,' she said. But she hated having no career and as the realisation dawned on her that possibly there would be no course for her next year either she became more and more dejected. She hated having no money; she hated being alone most evenings; she hated the indignity of living on a filthy, litter-strewn, graffiti-marked estate; she hated the shallowness and insincerity of the English. She hated everything about her life. There seemed no way out and her feelings of frustration and despair culminated in a crisis in our marriage.

Chapter Twenty-one
'ORRIBLE HAGGRAVATIONS

Lara's flattering first impressions of me had not lasted. Her later impressions were more accurate. She saw me as a very self-centred person, weakly charming, a bit callous, obsessed by the problems caused by my deficiencies, unfit to cope with the meanness of daily living and the undignified scramble for position. My nature, which other people might regard as admirably easy-going or even as enviably artistic, Lara saw as pitifully passive. My serenity, it is true, bordered on ennui, and one could quite easily conclude that I was simply a lazy bastard. I would have days on end of paralysed inaction, not because I was having profound thoughts on the futility of effort ('all is vanity,' etc) but because all I wanted to do was lie down. If we were not to spend the rest of our lives stuck on a disadvantaged council estate, some big effort on my part was required and Lara could not imagine me making it. Tranquil, mute and immobile, I did not know enough people, I did not mix enough: I did not have 'contacts'. This is always a bad thing for a journalist but it is worst of all when he wants to change papers. Lara, like any Jewish matriarch, required her man to sally forth to do battle with the world and yet for her to remain the stronger. I could not express an opinion without her sharply disagreeing and following up with some home truths. We always spoke in English now, which was a shame, because harsh disagreements and home truths can more easily be expressed in Russian as that language is so larded with diminutives. Adjectives and adverbs as well as nouns can be softened. If used to the full, the effect is to give a tinge of 'I still love you' to the most bitter discussions. But I got the home truths unlarded, in hard unpalatable lumps. The art of saying strong things gently is anyway difficult in an alien language. Nuances could have been expressed if Lara was speaking her native tongue, instead of her coming straight out with statements shorn of all ifs and buts, of careful qualifications.

We had other language problems. Lara disapproved not only of the views I expressed but of the accent with which I expressed them. She urged that I take elocution lessons. 'Every time you drop an aitch,' she said, 'it makes me shudder. Can you imagine that?'

In an effort to please her, I did try to pronounce my aitches. I managed to get the number right but could rarely place them in the correct position. Like a caricature of a sergeant-major on the parade ground I would come out with sounds such as ''orrible haccident.' (When she had asked me if I could imagine her feelings, I had replied, 'It's 'ard to himagine.') Pick was already dropping his aitches too. Lara did not want him to grow up in a class-ridden England with a maiming accent. My speech became positively incoherent when I was tired, fed up or uninterested, for at those times I lapsed into a mumble that even English people had difficulty in understanding. And many of our talks became dislocated through me misunderstanding something she had said. She might say of an acquaintance, 'He makes a show,' and I would go off at a tangent, assuming that the acquaintance made a show in dress or deportment, when Lara had meant he made a show of friendship. These misunderstandings had to be cleared up, our steps retraced to the starting point, before the discussion could be continued. Conversations became as arduous as talks between two people with a speech impediment.

There is no doubt that living in England affected Lara adversely. In Evolène she had been bubbling. Back in England, she immediately, from the very first day, felt a dampening of the spirit, so that the most trivial actions or words assumed either a portentous significance or a blank nullity. England to her resembled an overcrowded playpen, supplied with an abundance of toys and comics dignified with grander names, where even the much-vaunted political freedoms were part of a game in which anything could be changed as long as nothing was altered.

The childish condemnation of all things Soviet she took as a personal insult. A furious solidarity with her country raged within her.

'Everything in England is fine on the surface,' she said. 'Everyone's polite and well-mannered. But underneath it you can sense indifference and boredom and uncertainty. Smiling is the big thing. It's effortless and meaningless, the same as the way they say "Thank you" when refused a favour and "Sorry" when bumped into. They're hardly aware of doing it, it's a mere muscle contraction, like swallowing. Should you try to follow them up on their smiles you'll draw a blank. I've tried many times. Even at parties people's faces smoothly express nothing. You ask a question, the face lights up, a parcel of highly articulate information is delivered and, before the lump of grateful admiration in your throat is dissolved, the face is turned away. It's always the same procedure, like in an instant photos booth – blank, flash, blank. You can almost hear the click of the shutter.

'In my more gracious moods I put this lack of communication down to shyness. Yet British shyness, if that's what it is, appears to be a curiously independent and self-assertive little phenomenon. So well protected is it by the thick armour of assurance and superiority that it makes you wonder how on earth it manages to survive, cut off from its natural feeding ground of social blunder. It makes you wonder if within its secure walls it has not quietly degenerated into a smug void. You even feel you wouldn't mind swopping your own awkward, self-conscious, fragile confidence for this socially immaculate character deficiency. And here's the trap! I'm turning into a perfect English lady and from now on it'll be all smiles and no communication. Bugger that! Thank Christ I'm going to Russia soon, before the transformation is complete.'

Lara did not blame anyone for anything. She simply could not understand people here. She could find no connecting link between them and herself. She accepted there were two sides to everything, appreciating very much for example one side of the traditional British respect for privacy and the minding of one's own business. 'If I wore my favourite big hat in Moscow (let alone in Ufa) I'd be treated like an elephant escaped from a zoo,' she said. 'Here if I get an occasional stare I'm almost certain it's a foreigner. And your mother has never said a word to me about anything I do, and it's true that interfering in-laws cause many divorces in Russia. Fine! But in every other way too, your mum might just as well not be there, for Pick, for me or even for you. I think the problems your country is having with youngsters are largely due to this supernatural reserve. In Russia a child once outside the home is everybody's charge. You'll often see a whole bus discussing a youth who had failed to give up his seat to an elderly woman or one with a baby. It does get on your nerves but it helps, too. Here it's nobody's business. I don't know how I'm going to bring up Pick when it's entirely and exclusively my responsibility. I'm scared of the enormity of the task. My individual experience, my personal understanding of life, my capacity for providing continuous guidance, are just not big enough. It's not much fun bringing a child up here, either: whether he's lovely or loathsome, a prodigy or a moron, whether you're a good mother or not – nobody gives a damn.'

Having looked forward in Russia to a never-ending feast of intellectual nourishment, she was indeed impressed by the variety of flourishing schools of thought in the West but unfortunately had reached a stage, predicted by her father, where she felt she had allowed the written word to inhibit her spontaneous reactions too much. Now she wanted to think more for herself. She did need however the kind of feedback provided by verbal communication. 'Russian social nights are ideal for that,' she said, 'before everyone gets pissed. Hitch-hiking across France and Switzerland too was like a second university for me in that regard. In England it somehow never happens without me having to really work for it. Since I am a Russian in the West, most attempted conversations tend to turn political. And again I can't believe my ears. The idea of a free press looked so fabulous from a distance: close up it seems to have stopped people thinking. Where I expected to find an open-minded and questioning community I see instead a population of politely bored individuals, highly regimented (unemployed youths, housewifes and civil servants all know their places equally well) and deeply satisfied to have all this freely available information channelled into their separate private cells. And the nauseating self-righteousness with which the professionals in the media and the specially invited experts denounce Britain's so-called enemies! Would you believe it, dear readers and TV watchers, those naughty Russians have invented diplomatic lying, arms exporting and interference in other countries' affairs! Russia is only interesting as an enemy. "How many Soviet warheads in Europe," etc. Well, I don't know, sorry. But I do know Russians would not get as excited as the British did over the Falklands war, over an obscure cause on strange soil thousands of miles away. "Two bald men fighting over a comb," they called it there. In Russia, patriotism seems to have its roots deep down in the soil. Scratch any Russian and you'll find a cynic, certainly, but scratch a bit deeper and you'll find a patriot. Everyone there is a patriot. Here, it's only the scum who are patriotic.

'Russians who care to form an opinion of their own learn to read between the lines and more often than not end up with a view of world affairs more independent and objective than what I generally see here. Of course we have problems, mountains of them. But do the British really want to know about our problems? A nice well brought up English girl said to me once, with a dreamy smile, "Wouldn't it be fine if the Americans could just quietly drop a few neutron bombs on the Soviet Union? We wouldn't have to be scared of anything any more then, would we?" She was an actress but she never asked me a thing about the Soviet theatre. Maybe she thought we didn't have one. In any case she didn't care.'

Lara was feeling now what I had felt at first in Moscow: a surfeit of new situations and experiences, all of which had to be appraised and interpreted while cut off from all the old familiar guidelines. New expatriates are exhausted at the end of each day from the strain of being unable to take anything for granted. The most mundane things are new and different. Lara was in a condition of unceasing discontent. The present could barely be faced without the support of memories of the past, memories that for the most part could not be shared, even with me, being too personal and rooted too deeply in an alien culture. Nostalgia and regret consumed her. She looked back not in anger but in anguish, convinced she had not given enough of herself to her old friends, for whom she now felt a deep need.

Exile produced another problem: she desperately wanted Pick

to keep up his Russian, and always spoke to him in Russian to that end; but now he replied in English and spoke Russian with Cockney glottal stops. His mother language, to Lara's very great distress, was becoming patchy and faulty. If this continued, the songs and stories and jokes she had been brought up on and which meant so much to her would be lost to him.

In Russia, even though when I met her she had been making only a precarious living and was unregistered, she felt she belonged. In England, she had no identity other than as 'Mrs Bushell' – my wife. She was friendless.

'I'd lived on my own since I was seventeen,' she said, 'and, in what I now recognise as adolescent arrogance, had felt entirely self-sufficient. Little did I know, silly fool, to what extent my confidence depended on my family's unconditional, all-forgiving love, always there for me to lean back on. How vital the offers of friendship pressed upon me continuously – some of them only reluctantly accepted, others not at all. Now, having shed all that and free to exercise my proud individualism to the full, I'm wandering about like a lost soul, looking wistfully into people's eyes, seeking in vain to see myself reflected in them.'

Lara had always had a fluid temperament, a nervous variability, with abrupt fluctuations of mood, surges of cheerfulness and selfless interest followed by plummets into dejection. Now she sank into gloom for unsuspected, inexplicable reasons, and her calm, joyful moments became few. Before, some trifle like a bird singing would set her up for the day. Now, some equally ephemeral downer pushed her into such depths of misery she could not be reached. At least, I could not reach her. She developed a nihilistic philosophy in which nothing mattered, while at the same time getting worked up over the least thing. Her face was often set in a frown of nervous irritability or in a pout of sulkiness. There were many differences between us. We shared few interests. Lara liked a good chat: I was never given much to talking. She loved music: I could not stand it. Books were important to both of us: but we read different authors. As we were both moulded by what we had read, she reckoned this was one explanation for the lack of understanding between us. The only serious authors we had both read and been influenced by were the American writers – Hemingway, Steinbeck, etc –

and, indeed, these had provided us with material for a couple of interesting discussions. Any other subject seemed invariably to lead to an argument. We were dangerously close to the condition described by Dr Johnson: it was a 'miserable thing when the conversation could only be such as whether the mutton should be boiled or roasted, and probably a dispute about that.' Sexually we were shyer with each other than when we were first married. One Saturday evening, for the first time, we calmly discussed our compatibility and the possibility of separating. We had been to a jumble sale, as was our wont on Saturday afternoons. We had bought books for Pick's future, carefully making our choice: a book on trees, one on birds, an incomplete old set of Dickens' novels. At home, in the kitchen, with Pick seated at the table facing the wall, having his supper and nodding off, Lara initiated a blunt discussion. We agreed we did not enjoy each other's company as much as we should. 'The longer it goes on,' she said, 'the more certain I am you don't love me. You don't *need* me. We agreed in Moscow we would work at our marriage. You said you would be more outward-going, more forthcoming, once back home. You're not. We only talk when I force you to. I realise now you can't change, nor should you. I'm the one who has to change, to stop forcing you. And find companionship elsewhere. I prefer active relationships, and active suffering if necessary. You're honest and kind but we have nothing in common.'

Pick's bowed back looked so helpless and vulnerable. He was leaning slightly to one side. He was dropping off to sleep at the table over his supper. And we were talking about separating. Lara turned away to the sink, seemingly preoccupied with washing up. She switched the tap off and turned back and her cheeks were smeared with running mascara. The confusion of my feelings choked me. Perplexed, I wished more than anything that I could speak out clearly and with assurance and take the situation in hand. But an incomprehensible shyness sealed my lips. I knew I would bitterly regret it some day if I did not learn to fathom emotions – my own and Lara's. Lara's feelings – feminine and complex, Russian and intense – were, half the time, to me, inscrutable.

'I'll take Pick,' she said, 'and we'll travel the world looking for

someone who'll love us. Maybe you think I'm not lovable.
Maybe you're right. But maybe not. I think I might still find
someone who'll love me.'

When I thought of us debating over, and then buying, all
those jumble sale books for Pick's future . . . how serious we
were over it, how we cared. We wanted him to know all about
birds and trees. It was important that he know. I mused: 'I
would have liked to see him growing up. I hope he doesn't miss
me too much. I hope he's not unhappy. I hope we haven't
messed him up too badly.' And then I thought of what Lara and
I had been through together and our plans for the future and the
times she had been enjoying herself – and I felt a stirring in the
chest, which in anyone else would have welled up as tears.

We did not separate. Such things are easier said than done,
especially when there is nowhere else to go. Lara could not
simply walk out and go home to mum, not when mum was
1,600 miles away. This complication did not help: it added to
her frustration. We carried on, day by day, some days better
than others. Marion phoned unexpectedly from Evolène to
confirm that Lara would be going. Lara, after a couple of
seconds' surprise, slipped effortlessly into flowing French.
Hanging up, she said happily to me, 'I think I'll be a good
interpreter. After all, I've made a success of everything I've done.
And life will be better then.'

So, off she flew to Russia for a week: depositing Pick with her
family, she returned to London for two days; then away she
went again, revelling in this Western mobility, to the Swiss Alps,
hitch-hiking via Paris – leaving me to reflect and ruminate and
to repeat to myself lines of a Vysotsky song about his actress
wife Marina Vladi, who lived most of the time in France:

> '*Kuda mne do neyo,*
> *Ona uzhe v Parizhe,*
> *Mi snova govorim na raznikh yazikakh.*'

> 'How can I keep up with her,
> She's already in Paris,
> Once again we speak different languages.'

My marriage too was complicated by separations and the speaking of different languages. My marriage, in fact, was highly unusual – and, as a journalist, I knew a good story when I saw one.

I stood now at a fearful point. No sense would be made of my life if I did not do something decisive at once. I'd had various hopes, none realised. Disappointments, though, simplify one's course. As Carlyle said, 'Your possibilities become diminished, your choice is rendered easier.' I had no choice now but to fulfil my childhood ambition to write a book. Freed for the summer of familial duties, now was the ideal time to start. But what conclusions would be drawn? Was I to discover that I had nothing but my talent, that success was to be based on a claim to failure? Ignoring this imponderable, I began anyway, having, as I say, no choice. The work of course deeply satisfied me. Pieces of luck, no matter how big or unexpected, never really mean much. They might afford momentary diversion, ease or excite-ment but in the final analysis the only things we cherish are those that meet in some way an original want; a desire that grew early, of its own accord, undirected – such as my desire to write a book.

I typed steadily for two hours every morning before going to work and by the time Lara returned several chapters were finished. She read them and proclaimed them good. Herman Melville's wife wrote in the Occupation column of his death certificate 'Writer' even though *Moby Dick* was long forgotten and Melville had been a customs inspector for the last twenty years, writing very little. Lara had the same sort of faith. She had always considered me a writer.

When she went back to collect Pick, she stayed in Russia for three months, bringing him just in time to start school. I had not seen him for eleven months. On seeing me at Harwich he said softly 'Papa' with no affectation and clung to my neck for a long time. He had forgotten all his English. Before, his Russian had been baby talk. Now it was pure Russian, correct in syntax, grammar and intonation and far better than mine. He was looking forward to starting school but in the playground going in on the first day, at the sight of the, to him, vast building, he said '*Ya boyus, ya ne poidu*' – 'I'm scared, I'm not going' – and turned back and we had to coax him in. For several weeks it was difficult because he did not understand what was being said, but he gradually learnt English, even though for months to come he spoke it brokenly, saying things like, 'How much years are you?' 'What o'clock it is?' and 'I think anyone didn't live there' and, when with Lara and me, combining the two languages in one sentence, i.e. '*Ya khochu* to eat,' 'Let's go *domoi*' and '*Davai poidyom* to the fair.'

It is a good school and he loves going there. He is learning to read at a phenomenal rate, takes his studies very seriously and is very popular with his classmates. In Russia he had matured and calmed down and now he is a joy to be with. I look forward each day to coming home to him.

Lara and I have regained calmness in each other's company. Our lives have taken on a satisfying stability and a pleasing routine, centred round Pick's school hours. Our alliance is working as well as can be expected, all things considered. She has made some friends of her own. The marriage is sufficiently unconventional to be lent a poetic nimbus.

Lara, on her return from her three months' stay in Russia, was so changed as to be almost another person. She had mellowed. She was so much more relaxed and tolerant that obviously something had affected her profoundly. At first I thought that the reminder of the harsh realities of Soviet life had been salutary, had stopped her comparing England unfavourably with Russia, but the transformation was so complete I wondered about another, deeper, reason and after a while realised what it was. *She had been home*! Lara was like a female Antaeus, needing to touch her mother earth. Her strength derived from contact with her origins. Uprooted, she remained Russian to the core. The months she had spent in England had done nothing to rouse in her the least desire for identification with her husband's country. She could not take its problems seriously. Everything about England seemed to her unreal. Only in Russia was life real and vibrant. She would need to go there every year. This was a big complication. It meant we would never be able to save, for the expense was formidable. Her holidays would always have to be spent there, never anywhere else; and I could not accompany her, for the Obninsk area was closed to foreigners. This was all highly inconvenient. But never mind. *Nichivo*. Ours never had been a marriage of convenience.

Waiting for a 21 bus,
October, 1983.